without passing the burden.

has donated staff time and made arrangements to serve athletes, officials, and reporters during the Games by establishing five special branch offices. We've also raised funds for the U.S. Olympic Team.

We've also assumed the sponsorship of perhaps the finest sports museum in America, the First Interstate Bank Athletic Foundation. This museum houses memorabilia from amateur and professional sports. It will remain a legacy for sports fans to enjoy long after the 1984 Olympics end.

We at First Interstate Bank hope that all Americans will share the pride in proving that free enterprise works.

First Interstate Bank

© 1980 LA Olympic Committee ™   OFFICIAL SPONSOR OF THE 1984 OLYMPICS

Buick is proud to help fuel the Olympic flame.

This year, for the first time in history, the Olympic Games are being funded almost entirely by private enterprise.

Companies both large and small have provided over $100 million toward staging the 1984 Olympic Games. Buick is very proud to be one of them.

As the official car of the 1984 Olympic Games, we're offering a limited-edition Buick, the Century Olympia. To preserve the

OFFICIAL OLYMPIC
SOUVENIR PROGRAM

Games of the XXIIIrd Olympiad Los Angeles 1984

We've passed the torch

This summer, Americans will play host to the first Olympiad financed almost entirely through private enterprise, not taxes.

Tradition would have had the residents of Los Angeles paying for the Games, whether they wanted to or not. Instead, corporate sponsors have volunteered financial support. As an official sponsor of the 1984 Olympic Games in Los Angeles, First Interstate Bank

spirit of the Games, this special automobile comes with unique commemorative touches. Its exterior features gold accent striping, a commemorative hood ornament and front fender and deck lid plaques. Inside, you'll find special tan cloth trim with dark brown accents, and headrests featuring the official U.S. Olympic emblem.

For every Olympia sold between now and July 31, 1984, we will donate $100 to our U.S. Olympic Team. (Buyers must take retail delivery by July 31, 1984.)

We're pleased to be able to help fund the Olympic Games. And quite proud. Proud to have a part in fueling the Olympic flame.

Wouldn't you really rather have a Buick?

STEVE GELMAN
MANAGING EDITOR

JACK NEWCOMBE
ASSOCIATE MANAGING EDITOR

MICHAEL BROCK
DESIGN DIRECTOR

BERRY STAINBACK
ASSISTANT MANAGING EDITOR

MARY MEMORY
SENIOR EDITOR

SUE ELLEN JARES
PICTURE EDITOR

JEFF GOTTLIEB
ASSOCIATE EDITOR

SUSAN SWAN
ASSISTANT EDITOR

LUELLA M.Y. LAU
ART ASSOCIATE

BARBARA W. MURRAY
COPY CHIEF

ROGER M. MOONEY
COPYREADER

J. RICHARD GREEN
ASSISTANT COPYREADER

GEORGE J. AUSTEN
COPY PROCESSING MANAGER

LYNN CRIMANDO
COPY PROCESSING

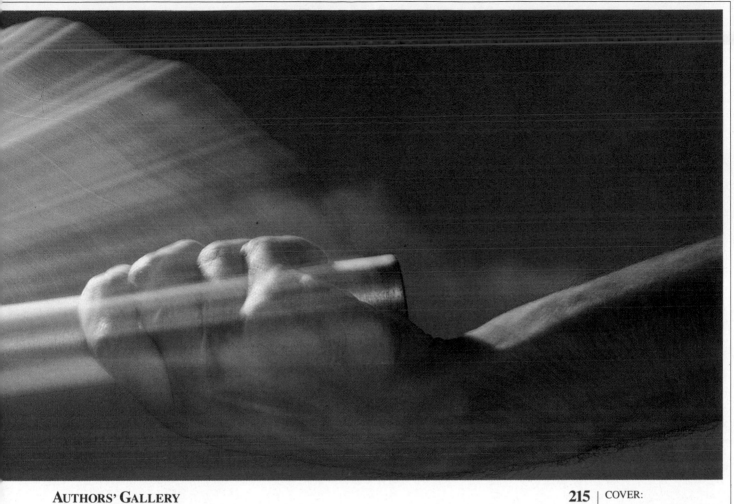

Robert Peak Jr.

COVER:

Above the glow of
the Los Angeles Coliseum,
a torchbearer for the
'84 Games is illuminated
by the five Olympic colors.

Photography by
Robert Peak Jr.

ANGELA M. BIEVER
GENERAL MANAGER

BERNERD F. PLATT
ADVERTISING SALES
DIRECTOR

MITCHEL E. ROTHSCHILD
CIRCULATION MANAGER

WALTER M. KAVNEY
PRODUCTION MANAGER

TRACY T. WINDRUM
OPERATIONS MANAGER

JOHN C. OAKMAN
ASSISTANT
OPERATIONS MANAGER

ALVARO J. SARALEGUI
ASSISTANT TO
GENERAL MANAGER

THE WHITE HOUSE

WASHINGTON

It is with distinct pleasure and pride that I join all Americans in extending warm greetings and welcome to the outstanding athletes, dignitaries, and sports enthusiasts gathered from around the world for the Games of the XXIII Olympiad.

All of us recognize the worthy aspirations of the Olympic movement in seeking to bring together the nations of the world in fulfillment of the historic ideals of peaceful athletic competition, dedication to excellence, and commitment to good sportsmanship. For people around the globe, these Games serve as an inspiring display of international cooperation and a celebration of the finest in the human spirit.

To spectators and participants alike -- we wish you a most happy stay in the United States. And in keeping with the noble and enduring heritage of the Olympic Games, may this XXIII Olympiad plant new seeds of friendship and promote a greater understanding of the world's cultures.

Ronald Reagan

CITY HALL
LOS ANGELES, CALIFORNIA 90012
(213) 485-3311

OFFICE OF THE MAYOR

TOM BRADLEY
MAYOR

Dear Olympic Visitor:

As one of the leaders of the effort to bring the 1984 Olympics to Los Angeles, it is with great personal pleasure that I welcome you to the City of Los Angeles for the Games of the XXIIIrd Olympiad. We are proud to have the Olympics return to our City exactly 52 years after Los Angeles hosted the 1932 Olympic Games.

The Los Angeles Olympic Organizing Committee has done an excellent job of planning the Games and we look forward to the exciting athletic events and cultural activities.

The Los Angeles Memorial Coliseum is the center of activities, but there will be geographical diversity among other Olympic sites. Venues range from Lake Casitas in Ventura County in the north, to the Fairbanks Ranch in San Diego County in the south. We also have the pleasure of hosting the athletes at two Olympic Villages in our City, located on the campuses of the University of Southern California (USC), and the University of California at Los Angeles (UCLA).

The private sector has been very supportive of Olympic activities, and the Games have received numerous corporate financial commitments. Facilities such as the Olympic Velodrome at California State University at Dominguez Hills, the Olympic Swim Stadium at USC, and eight new running tracks throughout the City, are examples of facilities donated by the private sector which will permanently enhance our community. This is in addition to other economic benefits to the community estimated to be in excess of $3.3 billion. We are deeply grateful to all of the corporate citizens who have made this historic partnership possible.

On behalf of the citizens of Los Angeles, I welcome the competitors and visitors to the Host City for the 1984 Olympic Games. It is our desire and expectation that in the spirit of international friendship, the Games of the XXIIIrd Olympiad will be an exciting and rewarding experience for competitors and visitors alike -- an experience worthy of the Olympic tradition.

Sincerely,

Tom Bradley

TOM BRADLEY
Mayor
City of Los Angeles

"AN EQUAL EMPLOYMENT OPPORTUNITY-AFFIRMATIVE ACTION EMPLOYER"

Budweiser

CITIUS · ALTIUS · FORTIUS

LE PRESIDENT

On behalf of the International Olympic Family, I would like to welcome you to the Games of the XXIIIrd Olympiad in Los Angeles, California.

These Games culminate a long tradition, not only for the people of this city, but the world as a whole, which has cherished the Olympic ideal for millennia. The Olympic Games offer an opportunity for the youth of the world to gather in a spirit of friendship, enjoying each other's company as they learn the importance of values that transcend differences in nationality, culture and geography.

The 1984 Olympic Games are, as always the result of a collaborative effort by a diverse, international assembly of groups. As a result of the dedication of thousands of supporters, these Games will, I believe, fully honour the Olympic tradition. I join you in looking forward to their exciting pageantry and successful conclusion.

Juan Antonio SAMARANCH

We made tracks for the Olympics.

When our Olympic athletes pursue excellence this summer in Los Angeles, they'll be doing it on ARCO's track.

Because ARCO, Atlantic Richfield, wanted our athletes to have the best. That's why we funded the building of the new Olympic track and refurbished the Coliseum.

We also wanted our future Olympic hopefuls and our community to have the best. That's why we built seven new Olympic practice tracks at schools in and around Los Angeles. Tracks that will be around long after the Olympics are over, for the people in the community to use and enjoy.

Putting our energy into the community, is just another way that ARCO is putting its energy into excellence.

Atlantic Richfield Company.

Los Angeles Olympic Organizing Committee

Los Angeles, California 90084 USA
Telex: 6831420

Telephone (213) 305-1984

Welcome to Los Angeles and the 1984 Olympic Games. It is with great pride that we present the Games of the XXIIIrd Olympiad.

The Olympic Games have a rich tradition of excellence in human athletic performance. Equally important, however, is the spirit of international joy that pervades the Games. The fact that people from all over the world gather to celebrate the Olympic festivities is indeed a tribute to mankind.

For the past five years the people of the Los Angeles Olympic Organizing Committee have been preparing to give you one of the greatest spectacles in history. We are honored that you are here to attend these Olympic Games with us and wish you an inspiring and memorable experience.

Sincerely,

Paul Ziffren
Chairman

Peter V. Ueberroth
President

Harry L. Usher
Executive Vice President/
General Manager

Games of the XXIIIrd Olympiad Los Angeles July 28 to August 12, 1984

Budget
rent a car

THIS TRIP, YOU DESERVE A LINCOLN.

AND OUR $39.95 PRICE MAKES IT EASY TO ENJOY.

Go ahead. You deserve it. Travel in style on your business trips in a luxurious Lincoln from Budget for only $39.95 a day. Get all that Lincoln comfort at a price that fits comfortably on your expense account.

Enjoy a smoother ride. The extra trunk space. And all that plush room inside. This trip, make it a Lincoln from Budget.

After all, you deserve it.

For reservations and information, see the Yellow Pages, call your travel consultant or call Budget toll free:

800-527-0700

Rates do not include gas, taxes or optional coverages. Offer available at most major airports except following large hub city airports: JFK and LaGuardia, NY; Newark, NJ. The $39.95 rate is good throughout the U.S. and Canada at participating locations when the car is returned to the renting location. Twenty-four hour advance reservation required.

 Sears | **Car and Truck Rental** | Use your Sears credit card at authorized distribution centers located in most Budget offices. For reservations, call toll-free: 800-527-0770.

Offer also available at selected Sears Rent a Car locations.

You get more than just a car at Budget.

THE SCHEDULE

*A day-by-day
hour-by-hour
listing of
all 1984 events—
illustrated
with the
pageantry of
Olympics past*

15

E V E N T S

ARCHERY — El Dorado Park, Long Beach

BASEBALL — Dodger Stadium (Demonstration Sport)

BASKETBALL — The Forum, Inglewood

BOXING — Los Angeles Sports Arena

CANOEING — Lake Casitas, Ventura County

CYCLING — California State University, Dominguez Hills
Artesia Freeway (Team Time Trial); Mission Viejo
(Individual Road Race)

DIVING — University of Southern California
Olympic Swim Stadium

EQUESTRIAN EVENTS — Santa Anita Park, Arcadia
Fairbanks Ranch, San Diego

FENCING — Long Beach Convention Center

FIELD HOCKEY — East Los Angeles College, Monterey Park

FOOTBALL (SOCCER) — Rose Bowl, Pasadena, California
Harvard University, Cambridge, Massachusetts
U.S. Naval Academy, Annapolis, Maryland
Stanford University, Palo Alto, California

GYMNASTICS — University of California, Los Angeles

JUDO — California State University, Los Angeles

MODERN PENTATHLON — Coto de Caza, Orange County
Heritage Park, Irvine, Orange County

OPENING & CLOSING CEREMONIES — Los Angeles
Memorial Coliseum

ROWING — Lake Casitas, Ventura County

SHOOTING — Prado Recreation Area, San Bernardino County

SWIMMING — University of Southern California
Olympic Swim Stadium

SYNCHRONIZED SWIMMING — University of Southern
California, Olympic Swim Stadium

TEAM HANDBALL — California State University, Fullerton
The Forum, Inglewood

TENNIS — University of California, Los Angeles
(Demonstration Sport)

TRACK AND FIELD — Los Angeles Memorial Coliseum
(ATHLETICS)   Marathon (men and women)
Start, Santa Monica College;
Finish, Los Angeles Memorial Coliseum

VOLLEYBALL — Long Beach Sports Arena

WATER POLO — Pepperdine University, Malibu

WEIGHTLIFTING — Loyola Marymount University, Los Angeles

WRESTLING — Anaheim Convention Center

YACHTING — Olympic Yachting Center, Long Beach

continued

THE
MAP OF
SITES
FOR ALL
EVENTS
IN THE
L.A.
AREA

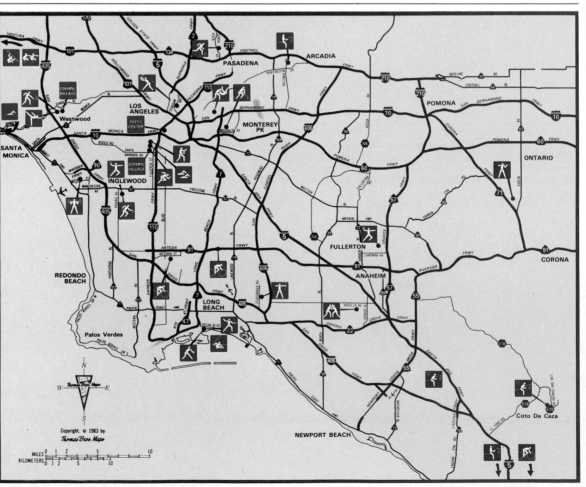

Copyright © 1983 by Thomas Bros. Maps

Star in Motion: © 1980 L.A. Olympic Committee   Pictograms: © 1981 L.A. Olympic Committee

GOLD MEDAL PERFORMER

Sometimes, you only get one chance to take a truly great picture. That's why people who don't have time for complicated cameras, like Olympic gold medalist Frank Shorter, count on the Canon AE-1 PROGRAM. It's a gold medal performer, too.

With the AE-1 PROGRAM, all you do is focus and shoot for great pictures indoors or out, day or night. In any light! When set on "PROGRAM" the

advanced electronics inside provide total automation, so you can concentrate on your subject.

When you want to stop fast moving action, select the shutter-priority mode and choose the shutter speed you need. With the optional Power Winder A2 you can take two pictures

every second, while the Motor Drive MA gives you up to 4fps., so you can follow a runner around the track and get pictures like this.

Flash photography is just as automatic, with the Canon Speedlite 188A.

Eight interchangeable

focusing screens and over fifty Canon FD lenses are also available to help you get just the shot you want, from a wide-angle panorama to a breathtaking telephoto close-up.

So if you want gold medal pictures, ask your Canon dealer about the AE-1 PROGRAM. It's one more reason we're the world's leader in 35mm photography.

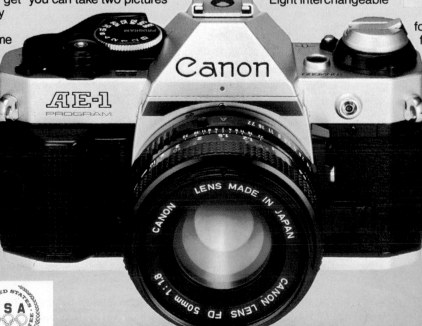

The Official 35mm Camera of the 1984 Olympic Games

Contributor to the U.S. Olympic Team

Canon® AE-1 PROGRAM

Canon USA, Inc., One Canon Plaza, Lake Success, New York 11042 / 140 Industrial Drive, Elmhurst, Illinois 60126 / 6380 Peachtree Industrial Blvd., Norcross, Georgia 30071
123 Paularino Avenue East, Costa Mesa, California 92626 / 2035 Royal Lane, Suite 290, Dallas, Texas 75229 / Bldg. B-2, 1050 Ala Moana Blvd., Honolulu, Hawaii 96814 / Canon Canada, Inc. Ontario
© 1983 Canon U.S.A., Inc.

THE
MODERN
REVIVAL
OF THE
GAMES IN
1896
FILLED
THE NEW
STADIUM IN
ATHENS

Courtesy U.S. Olympic Committee

JULY 28
Saturday

P.M.	EVENT
4:30	Opening Ceremony

JULY 29
Sunday

A.M.	EVENT
8:00	Equestrian – Three-day event—dressage test
8:30	Swimming – Heats—100m freestyle, women
	Heats—100m breaststroke, men
	Heats—400m individual medley, women
	Heats—200m freestyle, men
9:00	Basketball – 2 games—preliminaries, men
	Modern Pentathlon – Riding
	Shooting – Free pistol
	Sport pistol
	Clay target-trap
9:30	Cycling – 79km individual road race, women
	(Held in Mission Viejo, Orange County)
	Gymnastics – Compulsory exercises, men
10:00	Volleyball – 2 matches—preliminaries, men
11:00	Boxing – Preliminary bouts

P.M.	
1:00	Cycling – 190km individual road race, men
	(Held in Mission Viejo, Orange County)
1:45	Field Hockey – 3 games—preliminaries, men
2:00	Weightlifting – Flyweight (up to 52kg), group B

2:30	Basketball – 2 games—preliminaries, men
3:00	Gymnastics – Compulsory exercises, men
4:00	Modern Pentathlon – Riding
4:15	Swimming – Finals—100m freestyle, women
	Finals—100m breaststroke, men
	Finals—400m individual medley, women
	Finals—200m freestyle, men
6:00	Boxing – Preliminary bouts
	Weightlifting – Flyweight (up to 52kg), group A
6:30	Gymnastics – Compulsory exercises, men
	Volleyball – 2 matches—preliminaries, men
7:00	Football (Soccer) – First round match (Rose Bowl, Pasadena, California)
	Opening Ceremonies and first round match (Harvard University, Cambridge, Massachusetts)
	Opening Ceremonies and first round match (U.S. Naval Academy, Annapolis, Maryland)
	Opening Ceremonies and first round match (Stanford University, Palo Alto, California)
8:00	Basketball – 2 games—preliminaries, men

JULY 30
Monday

A.M.	EVENT
7:30	Rowing – Elimination heats, women
8:00	Equestrian – Three-day event—dressage test
	Modern Pentathlon – Fencing
8:30	Swimming – Heats—100m butterfly, men

continued

Show them how it's done.

The U.S. Women's Volleyball Team and Ford Mustang Convertible.

Ford understands the kind of commitment it takes to be the best. And Ford is proud to be one of the sponsors of the U.S. Women's Volleyball team, voted "Team of the Year" by the Women's Sports Foundation.

A world-class carmaker salutes a world-class volleyball team as it takes on the challenge of the '84 Olympics.

OFFICIAL VEHICLE OF THE U.S. VOLLEYBALL ASSOCIATION

Have you driven a Ford... lately?

Heats—200m freestyle, women
Heats—400m individual medley, men
Heats—200m breaststroke, women
Heats—4x200m freestyle relay, men

9:00   Basketball – 1 game—round robin, women
1 game—preliminary, men

Shooting – Small-bore rifle English match
Clay target-trap
Running game target

10:00   Cycling – Individual pursuit—qualification
1km time trial—final

Gymnastics – Compulsory exercises, women

Volleyball – 2 matches—preliminaries, women

11:00   Boxing – Preliminary bouts

P.M.

12:00   Wrestling – Greco-Roman Style—preliminaries—
48, 62, 90kg

1:45   Field Hockey – 3 games—preliminaries, men

2:00   Weightlifting – Bantamweight (up to 56kg),
group B

2:30   Basketball – 1 game—round robin, women
1 game—preliminary, men

4:15   Swimming – Finals—100m butterfly, men
Finals—200m freestyle, women
Finals—400m individual medley, men
Finals—200m breaststroke, women
Finals—4x200m freestyle relay, men

5:30   Gymnastics – Compulsory exercises, women

6:00   Boxing – Preliminary bouts

Weightlifting – Bantamweight (up to 56kg),
group A

Wrestling – Greco-Roman Style—preliminaries—
48, 62, 90kg

6:30   Volleyball – 2 matches—preliminaries, women

7:00   Football (Soccer) – First round match (Rose Bowl,
Pasadena, California)
First round match (Harvard
University, Cambridge,
Massachusetts)
First round match (U.S. Naval
Academy, Annapolis, Maryland)
First round match (Stanford Uni-
versity, Palo Alto, California)

8:00   Basketball – 1 game—round robin, women
1 game—preliminary, men

JULY 31

Tuesday

A.M.   EVENT

7:30   Rowing – Elimination heats, men

8:30   Field Hockey – 2 games—preliminaries, men

Swimming – Heats—400m freestyle, women
Heats—100m freestyle, men
Heats—100m backstroke, women
Heats—200m backstroke, men
Heats—4x100m freestyle relay, women

9:00   Basketball – 1 game—round robin, women
1 game—preliminary, men

Shooting – Clay target-trap
Running game target
Air rifle, women

9:30   Gymnastics – Optional exercises, men

10:00   Cycling – Individual pursuit—quarterfinals
Sprint series
Points race—qualification

continued

PARADE
OF PRANCING
BEARS
ENTERTAINED
MOSCOW'S
OLYMPIC
CROWD IN
1980

Jerry Cooke/SPORTS ILLUSTRATED

McDonald's® invites the whole world to drop in for a swim.

Young swimmers and divers from around the world will make a splash in Los Angeles in 1984. They'll compete in the Olympic Games.

As teams, they will represent many different countries. Yet, as individuals, there's something they all share. Motivation. Energy. Confidence. Because they've all listened to a tiny voice inside that says, "You can do it."

McDonald's independent franchisees all across the country, all over the world, built McDonald's Olympic Swim Stadium as a tribute to them.

It's also a symbol of our dedication to kids everywhere who listen to that tiny voice inside. And follow that voice.

Because McDonald's believes that kind of commitment to excellence doesn't just make better athletes. It makes better kids.

Not just better athletes, better kids.™

©1984 McDonald's Corporation

Proud Sponsor of the 1984 Olympics

IBM PC Software: the value of choosing

Shoes.

If they don't fit, they're not worth wearing.

Software programs.

If they don't fit, they're not worth using.

That's why it's altogether fitting that IBM Personal Computer Software offers you a choice.

Size up the selection.

You'll find many types of programs in the IBM software library. They'll help keep you on your toes in the office, at home or in school.

There are, in fact, seven different categories of IBM programs called "families." A family of software for business, productivity, education, entertainment, lifestyle, communications or programming.

Of course, every program in every family is tested and approved by IBM. And IBM Personal Computer Software is made to be compatible with IBM Personal Computer hardware.

programs that fit.

Putting your best foot forward.

Although every person isn't on equal footing when it comes to using personal computer software, there's something for almost everyone in the IBM software library.

For example, you may be on a shoestring budget and want a big selection of programs with small price tags.

You may be introducing students to computing and want programs that are simple to use and simple to learn.

You may run a business requiring sophisticated inventory and payroll programs. Or you may run a business requiring a single accounting program.

You may write interoffice memos and want a streamlined word processing program. Or you may be a novelist looking for a program with features worth writing home about.

Now you can find IBM Personal Computer Software that fits — to help you accomplish specific tasks and reach individual goals.

Stroll into a store today.

What's the next step?

Visit an authorized IBM Personal Computer dealer or IBM Product Center near you. To find out exactly where, call 800-447-4700. In Alaska or Hawaii, 800-447-0890.

Ask your dealer to demonstrate your choice of programs. Then get comfortable. Sit down at the keyboard and try IBM software on for size.

IBM®
Personal Computer Software

IN PAGEANTRY AT MUNICH, 1972, FOLK DANCERS RINGED THE RUNNING TRACK

11:00	Volleyball – 2 matches—preliminaries, men
	Boxing – Preliminary bouts
	Team Handball – 3 games—preliminaries, men

P.M.

12:00	Wrestling – Greco-Roman Style—preliminaries— 48, 52, 62, 74, 90, over 100kg
1:30	Yachting – First race—all classes
2:00	Modern Pentathlon – Swimming (Held at Heritage Park Aquatics Complex, Irvine)
	Weightlifting – Featherweight (up to 60kg), group B
2:30	Basketball – 1 game—round robin, women 1 game—preliminary, men
	Field Hockey – 1 game—round robin, women 1 game—preliminary, men
3:00	Gymnastics – Optional exercises, men
4:00	Baseball – 2 games—first round
4:15	Swimming – Finals—400m freestyle, women Finals—100m freestyle, men Finals—100m backstroke, women Finals—200m backstroke, men Finals—4x100m freestyle relay, women
6:00	Boxing – Preliminary bouts
	Weightlifting – Featherweight (up to 60kg), group A
	Wrestling – Greco-Roman Style—preliminaries— 48, 52, 62, 74, 90, over 100kg
6:30	Gymnastics – Optional exercises—team finals, men
	Team Handball – 3 games—preliminaries, men
	Volleyball – 2 matches—preliminaries, men
7:00	Football (Soccer) – First round match (Rose Bowl,

	Pasadena, California)
	First round match (Harvard University, Cambridge, Massachusetts)
	First round match (U.S. Naval Academy, Annapolis, Maryland)
	First round match (Stanford University, Palo Alto, California)
8:00	Basketball – 1 game—round robin, women 1 game—preliminary, men

AUGUST 1

Wednesday

A.M.	EVENT
7:30	Rowing – Repechage, men & women
8:00	Field Hockey – 1 game—preliminary, men 1 game—round robin, women
8:30	Water Polo – 2 games—preliminaries
9:00	Basketball – 2 games—preliminaries, men
	Fencing – Foil—individual preliminaries, men
	Modern Pentathlon – Shooting
	Shooting – Small-bore rifle, 3 positions, men Rapid-fire pistol
10:00	Cycling – Individual pursuit—semifinals & finals Sprint—quarterfinals Points race—qualification
	Equestrian – Three-day event—endurance test (Held at Fairbanks Ranch Country Club, San Diego)
	Gymnastics – Optional exercises, women

continued

Robinson's and American Express
WELCOME YOU TO SOUTHERN CALIFORNIA

Get ready for a whole new awakening! Because when you come to Southern California, you experience a different way of life. We capture that "good life" throughout our stores. From the latest trends in fashion to extraordinary imported home furnishings to fine estate jewels to native gourmet delicacies…and more. Every little bit of Southern California you want to take home! While you shop, stay updated on Olympic events and scheduling through the *American Express 1984 Olympic Information Centers*

exclusively at Robinson's. Attend in-store demonstrations by Olympic hopefuls and hear former Olympians relate their own personal experiences. Then tour museums and exotic gardens on specially chartered buses, as a follow-up to art seminars in selected stores. We're honored to join American Express in bringing you these memorable events. Come discover the best of Robinson's and you'll discover the best of Southern California. Robinson's welcomes **The American Express® Card, the official Card of the 1984 Olympics.**

Volleyball – 2 matches—preliminaries, women
Weightlifting – Lightweight (up to 67.5kg),
group C

11:00   Boxing – Preliminary bouts

P.M.

12:00   Wrestling – Greco-Roman Style—preliminaries—
52, 57, 68, 74, 82, 100, over 100kg
Finals—48, 62, 90kg

1:30   Water Polo – 2 games—preliminaries
Yachting – Second race

1:45   Field Hockey – 2 games—preliminaries, men
1 game—round robin, women

2:00   Weightlifting – Lightweight (up to 67.5kg),
group B

2:30   Basketball – 2 games—preliminaries, men

4:00   Baseball – 2 games—first round

5:00   Modern Pentathlon – Running

5:30   Gymnastics – Optional exercises—team finals,
women

6:00   Boxing – Preliminary bouts
Weightlifting – Lightweight (up to 67.5kg),
group A
Wrestling – Greco-Roman Style—preliminaries—
52, 57, 68, 74, 82, 100, over 100kg
Finals—48, 62, 90kg

6:30   Team Handball – 3 games—round robin, women
Volleyball – 2 matches—preliminaries, women

7:00   Football (Soccer) – First round match (Rose Bowl,
Pasadena, California)
First round match (Harvard
University, Cambridge,
Massachusetts)
First round match (U.S. Naval

Academy, Annapolis, Maryland)
First round match (Stanford University, Palo Alto, California)

7:30   Water Polo – 2 games—preliminaries

8:00   Basketball – 2 games—preliminaries, men

AUGUST 2

Thursday

A.M.   EVENT

7:30   Rowing – Semifinals, men & women

8:30   Field Hockey – 2 games—preliminaries, men
Swimming – Heats—400m freestyle, men
Heats—100m butterfly, women
Heats—200m breaststroke, men
Heats—100m breaststroke, women
Heats—4x100m freestyle relay, men
Heats—800m freestyle, women
Water Polo – 2 games—preliminaries

9:00   Basketball – 1 game—round robin, women
1 game—preliminary, men
Fencing – Foil—individual preliminaries, men &
women
Shooting – Small-bore rifle, 3 positions, women
Rapid-fire pistol
Clay target-skeet

10:00   Cycling – Sprint—semifinals
Team pursuit—qualification &
quarterfinals
Volleyball – 2 matches—preliminaries, men
Weightlifting – Middleweight (up to 75kg),
group C

11:00   Boxing – Preliminary bouts

continued

THE
U.S. TEAM
AND
SIXTY-EIGHT
OTHER
NATIONS
MARCHED
IN THE
RAIN IN
HELSINKI,
1952

ENGINEERED
FOR TOTAL RESPONSE
PONTIAC 6000

"Total response" may be an engineering "buzz" word to many people, but every *driver* can appreciate what it means when test-driving the 1984 Pontiac 6000.

Total response *is* balanced performance, and it's the very essence of the new Pontiac 6000. In the Pontiac 6000, total response means controlled ride motions *without* harshness, while maintaining minimal lean in hard cornering. It means power rack and pinion steering for excellent road feel and quick response time in everything from parking maneuvers to sweeping mountain bends.

And it means an electronically fuel-injected engine that delivers genuine operating efficiency,* while providing enough punch to skillfully merge onto a freeway.

The totally responsive Pontiac 6000. One of the most distinctive and technically advanced front-wheel-drive cars built in America. Drive one today, and see for yourself what totally responsive *really* means.

*Pontiac 6000 offers an EPA EST MPG of ㉕ and a highway estimate of **39**. Use estimated MPG for comparisons. Your mileage may differ depending on speed, distance, weather. Actual highway mileage lower. Some Pontiacs are equipped with engines produced by other GM divisions, subsidiaries or affiliated companies worldwide. See your Pontiac dealer for details.

PONTIAC ▼ WE BUILD EXCITEMENT

IF HE CA DO IT ONCE, HE CA DO IT 300 TIMES.

When you record a once-in-a-lifetime performance on Maxell HGX High Grade, you can relive it over and over again. And still get better color resolution, sharper images and clearer sound than you can with ordinary video tape..

Because Maxell uses finer, sharper magnetic oxide particles more densely packed on the tape's surface, and a unique binder system that keeps them there play after play.

So why settle for an ordinary video tape, when you can extend your playing life with Maxell.

VHS and Beta videocassettes

OLYMPIC STADIUM IN MONTREAL, 1976, FEATURED A ROOF WITH A SKYVIEW

Team Handball – 3 games—preliminaries, men

P.M.

12:00	Wrestling – Greco-Roman Style—preliminaries—57, 68, 82, 100kg Finals—52, 74, over 100kg
1:30	Water Polo – 2 games—preliminaries Yachting – Third race
2:00	Weightlifting – Middleweight (up to 75kg), group B
2:30	Basketball – 1 game—round robin, women 1 game—preliminary, men Field Hockey – 1 game—round robin, women 1 game—preliminary, men
4:00	Baseball – 2 games—first round
4:15	Swimming – Finals—400m freestyle, men Finals—100m butterfly, women Finals—200m breaststroke, men Finals—100m breaststroke, women Finals—4x100m freestyle relay, men
5:30	Gymnastics – All-around finals, men
6:00	Boxing – Preliminary bouts Weightlifting – Middleweight (up to 75kg), group A Wrestling – Greco-Roman Style—preliminaries—57, 68, 82, 100kg Finals—52, 74, over 100kg
6:30	Team Handball – 3 games—preliminaries, men Volleyball – 2 matches—preliminaries, men
7:00	Football (Soccer) – First round match (Rose Bowl, Pasadena, California) First round match (Harvard University, Cambridge, Massachusetts)

First round match (U.S. Naval Academy, Annapolis, Maryland)
First round match (Stanford University, Palo Alto, California)

7:30	Water Polo – 2 games—preliminaries
8:00	Basketball – 1 game—round robin, women 1 game—preliminary, men Fencing – Foil—individual finals, men

AUGUST 3
Friday

A.M.	EVENT
8:00	Field Hockey – 1 game—round robin, women 1 game—preliminary, men Rowing – Finals (7-12 places), men & women
8:30	Swimming – Heats—200m individual medley, women Heats—200m butterfly, men Heats—100m backstroke, men Heats—4x100m medley relay, women Heats—1,500m freestyle, men Water Polo – 2 games—preliminaries
9:00	Basketball – 1 game—round robin, women 1 game—preliminary, men Fencing – Foil—individual preliminaries, women Sabre—individual preliminaries, men Shooting – Air rifle, men Clay target-skeet
9:30	Track and Field (Athletics) – Heptathlon 100m hurdles, high jump, women

continued

THE WORLD WILL
A TASTE FOR

Enjoy

Coca-Cola

Trade-mark ®

SHOW YOUR COLORS WITH PRIDE. This is your Olympic Cheering Card. Wave it proudly for all the world to see. (To use, tear gently along perforation.)

ALWAYS SHARE
THE BEST.

	Triple jump qualifying, men 400m hurdles first round, men 400m first round, women Shotput qualifying, women 100m first & second rounds, men
10:00	Cycling – Sprint—finals Team pursuit—semifinals & finals Points race—final Volleyball – 2 matches—preliminaries, women
11:00	Boxing – Preliminary bouts
11:30	Equestrian – Three-day event—jumping test

P.M.

12:00	Wrestling – Greco-Roman Style—preliminaries—57, 68, 82, 100kg
1:00	Baseball – 2 games—first round
1:30	Water Polo – 2 games—preliminaries Yachting – Fourth race
1:45	Field Hockey – 2 games—preliminaries, men 1 game—round robin, women
2:30	Basketball – 1 game—round robin, women 1 game—preliminary, men
4:00	Track and Field (Athletics) – 800m first round, women Heptathlon shotput, 200m, women 800m first round, men 20km walk final (start & finish), men Shotput final, women 10,000m first round, men

5:00	Swimming – Finals—200m individual medley, women Finals—200m butterfly, men Finals—800m freestyle, women Finals—100m backstroke, men Finals—4x100m medley relay, women
5:30	Gymnastics – All-around finals, women
6:00	Boxing – Preliminary bouts Wrestling – Greco-Roman Style—Finals—57, 68, 82, 100kg
6:30	Team Handball – 3 games—round robin, women Volleyball – 2 matches – preliminaries, women
7:00	Football (Soccer) – First round match (Rose Bowl, Pasadena, California) First round match (Harvard University, Cambridge, Massachusetts) First round match (U.S. Naval Academy, Annapolis, Maryland) First round match (Stanford University, Palo Alto, California)
7:30	Water Polo – 2 games—preliminaries
8:00	Basketball – 1 game—round robin, women 1 game—preliminary, men Fencing – Foil—individual finals, women

AUGUST 4
Saturday

A.M.	EVENT
8:00	Rowing – Finals (1-6 places), women
8:30	Field Hockey – 2 games—preliminaries, men

continued

THE CITY TOASTMASTER KEPT SPECTATORS INFORMED AT THE LONDON GAMES IN 1908

BBC Hulton Picture Library

The Winner!

Go for the gold with the eighteen karat gold Rolex Day-Date
President. Hailed as the world's first waterproof watch, it is still
the champion of durability and high performance.
Pressure-proof to 330 feet.

TIFFANY & CO.

S A L U T E   T O   E X C E L L E N C E

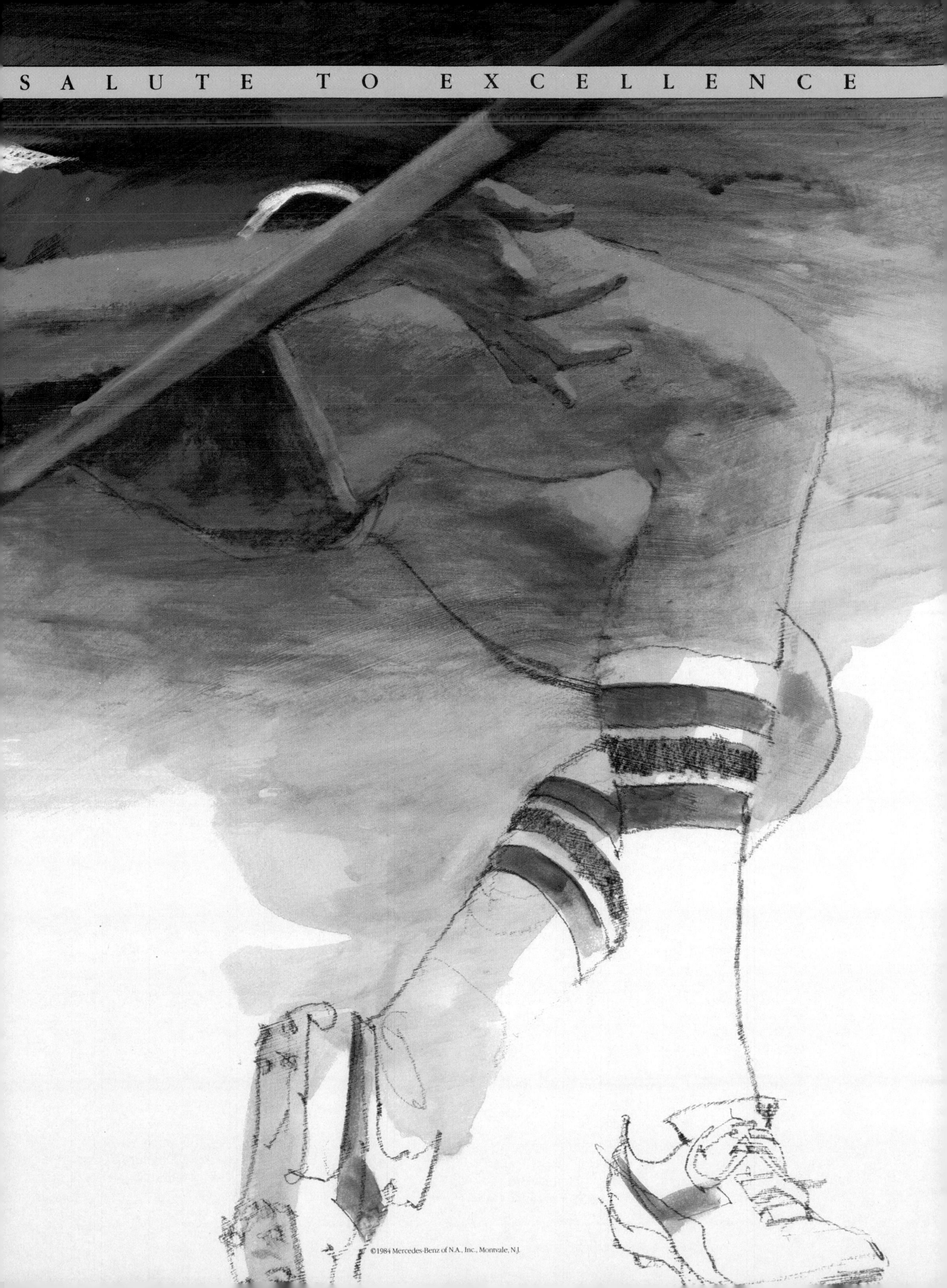

MASSED GYMNASTS PERFORMED AT MUNICH CEREMONIES THAT DREW 122 NATIONS

Sven Simon

	Swimming – Heats—200m individual medley, men
	Heats—200m butterfly, women
	Heats—200m backstroke, women
	Heats—4x100m medley relay, men
9:00	Basketball – 2 games—preliminaries, men
	Fencing – Foil—team preliminaries, men
	Sabre—individual preliminaries, men
	Shooting – Clay target-skeet
9:30	Track and Field (Athletics) – Heptathlon long jump
	400m first round, men
	400m second round, women
	Javelin throw qualifying, men
	100m first round, women
10:00	Baseball – 2 games—first round
	Volleyball – 2 matches—preliminaries, men
	Weightlifting – Light heavyweight (up to 82.5 kg), group C
11:00	Boxing – Preliminary bouts
	Team Handball – 3 games—preliminaries, men

P.M.

2:00	Equestrian – Jumping training competition
	Weightlifting – Light heavyweight (up to 82.5kg), group B
2:30	Basketball – 2 games—preliminaries, men
	Field Hockey – 1 game—preliminary, men
	1 game—round robin, women
4:00	Track and Field (Athletics) – 100m second round, women
	Heptathlon javelin throw, 800m (final event)

	100m semifinal, men
	800m semifinal, women
	800m second round, men
	Triple jump final, men
	400m hurdles semifinal, men
	100m final, men
	Judo – Extra lightweight
5:00	Swimming – Finals—200m individual medley, men
	Finals—200m butterfly, women
	Finals—1,500m freestyle, men
	Finals—200m backstroke, women
	Finals—4x100m medley relay, men
5:30	Gymnastics – Apparatus finals, men
6:00	Boxing – Preliminary bouts
	Weightlifting – Light heavyweight (up to 82.5kg), group A
6:30	Team Handball – 3 games—preliminaries, men
	Volleyball – 2 matches—preliminaries, men
8:00	Basketball – 2 games—preliminaries, men
	Fencing – Sabre—individual finals, men

AUGUST 5

Sunday

A.M.	EVENT
8:00	Track and Field (Athletics) – Marathon, women
	Javelin throw qualifying, women
	400m hurdles first round, women

continued

DRIVE ON THE RADIALS THAT DRIVE ON.

Bridgestone makes a complete line of high quality SuperFiller steel-belted radials that drive on. One is right for you.

All share SuperFiller technology. A unique hard-rubber insert in the bead area, called SuperFiller, allows for a flexible sidewall and even, road-grabbing contact pressure to enhance traction, braking and handling.

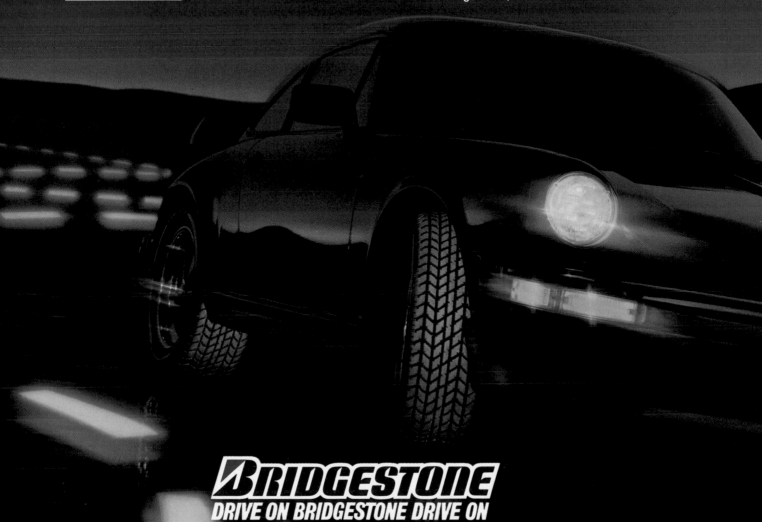

Drive on the Potenza, our VR-rated ultra high-performance radial. An advanced design extra wire insert laminated to the SuperFiller wedge gives added durability and improved responsiveness. The two steel belts, nylon protector layer and nylon cap ply give added strength at high speeds. The straight groove, water-channeling tread pattern and special tread compound work with SuperFiller to enhance traction, wet and dry.

Drive on the Potenza or drive on any of Bridgestone's other quality radials. The complete Bridgestone line includes radials for large and small cars, off-road vehicles and light trucks.

And, when it comes to taking on the elements, the new Bridgestone all-season radials are compounded to drive on in snow, ice, wet and dry surfaces.

See your Bridgestone dealer about these and many other SuperFiller steel-belted radials. Then drive on Bridgestone, drive on.

BRIDGESTONE
DRIVE ON BRIDGESTONE DRIVE ON

"*Stretching for Gold!*"

At photo and video stores now. Television image simulated. Copyright law may restrict certain uses of copyrighted material. Special offer ends August 31,

When the moment means more. Tape it.

L os Angeles, 1984. Where the best in the world like Edwin Moses will be struggling, striving, stretching for glory and gold. How could you trust moments like these to anything other than Kodak tape?

Introducing Kodak video tape
It's the newest way from Kodak to capture—and keep—the sights and sounds of every moment; the colors are beautifully accurate, unmistakably Kodak. But the moments are *all* yours.

Introducing "Moments of Gold"
Get this unique offer from Kodak: an exciting 2-hour tape of medal-winning performances by the century's greatest athletes. Available now at special low prices. For details, see your participating dealer, or write: Kodak Tape Offer, Eastman Kodak Company, Dept. 841 VP, 343 State St., Rochester, N.Y. 14650.

Kodak

HGX
EXTRA HIGH GRADE

Kodak
Video Cassette
T-120

VHS

VHS

And keep it. On Kodak video tape.

	110m hurdles first round, men
	Hammer throw qualifying, men
	Field Hockey – 1 game—preliminary, men
	1 game—round robin, women
	Rowing – Finals (1-6 places), men
9:00	Basketball – 2 games—round robin, women
	Cycling – 100km road race team time trial (Held on Artesia Freeway, Route 91)
	Fencing – Foil—team preliminaries, men & women
10:00	Diving – Springboard preliminaries, women
	Volleyball – 2 matches—semifinals, women
	Weightlifting – Middle heavyweight (up to 90kg), group C
11:00	Boxing – Preliminary bouts

P.M.

1:00	Baseball – 2 games—first round
1:45	Field Hockey – 2 games—preliminaries, men
	1 game—round robin, women
2:00	Weightlifting – Middle heavyweight (up to 90kg), group B
2:30	Basketball – 1 game—semifinal, men
3:00	Diving – Springboard preliminaries, women
	Football (Soccer) – Quarterfinal match (Stanford University, Palo Alto, California)
4:00	Track and Field (Athletics) – 100m semifinal & final, women
	Long jump qualifying, men

	110m hurdles second round, men
	400m second round, men
	400m semifinal, women
	Javelin throw final, men
	800m semifinal, men
	400m hurdles final, men
	Judo – Half lightweight
5:30	Gymnastics – Apparatus finals, women
6:00	Boxing – Preliminary bouts
	Weightlifting – Middle heavyweight (up to 90kg), group A
6:30	Basketball – 1 game—round robin, women
	1 game—semifinal, men
	Team Handball – 3 games—round robin, women
	Volleyball – 2 matches—semifinals, women
7:00	Football (Soccer) – Quarterfinal match (Rose Bowl, Pasadena, California)
8:00	Fencing – Foil—team finals, men

AUGUST 6

Monday

A.M.	EVENT
7:30	Canoeing – 500m heats, men & women
8:30	Field Hockey – 2 games—preliminaries, men
	Water Polo – 2 games—final round
9:00	Tennis – 16 matches
9:30	Track and Field (Athletics) – Pole vault qualifying, men

continued

OLYMPIC TORCH WAS CARRIED THROUGH DELPHI IN 1936. AT RIGHT, BEARERS REACHED IMPERIAL PALACE, TOKYO, 1964

Left: Photoworld/F.P.G.; Al Fenn/LIFE Magazine © Time Inc.

IF YOU CAN'T COME TO THE POST OFFICE FOR OLYMPIC MEMENTOS, THE POST OFFICE WILL COME TO YOU.

At each of these Olympic events throughout the Los Angeles area, you'll find Olympic stamps. Because at each event listed, you'll find a conveniently located Olympic Post Office. 27 in all. And each will have all 24 colorful Olympic stamps, special Olympic postal products, and the usual services like package shipments, money orders, and Express Mail® service.

So if you have trouble locating the 1984 Olympic Games, just look for the nearest Post Office.

Athletic Event	Olympic Location/City
Archery	El Dorado Park, Long Beach
Baseball	Dodger Stadium, Los Angeles
Basketball	The Forum, Inglewood
Boxing	L.A. Sports Arena, Los Angeles
Canoeing	Lake Casitas, Ventura
Cycling	C.S.U. Dominguez Hills, Carson
Equestrian	Santa Anita Park, Arcadia
Fencing	Long Beach Convention Center, Long Beach
Field Hockey	East Los Angeles College, Monterey Park
Gymnastics	Pauley Pavilion, U.C.L.A., Los Angeles
Handball	C.S.U. Fullerton, Fullerton
Judo	C.S.U. Los Angeles, Los Angeles
Modern Pentathlon	Coto de Caza, Trabuco Canyon
Rowing	Lake Casitas, Ventura
Shooting	Prado Park, Chino
Soccer	Rose Bowl, Pasadena
Swimming & Diving	U.S.C., Los Angeles
Tennis	U.C.L.A., Los Angeles
Track & Field	Los Angeles Memorial Coliseum, Los Angeles
Volleyball	Long Beach Sports Arena, Long Beach
Water Polo	Pepperdine University, Malibu
Weightlifting	Loyola Marymount University, Los Angeles
Wrestling	Anaheim Convention Center, Anaheim
Yachting	Downtown Long Beach Marina, Long Beach
Opening & Closing Ceremonies	Los Angeles Memorial Coliseum, Los Angeles
Cultural Events	
"Olympic Philatelic Exhibition"	Pasadena Center, Pasadena

U.S. Postal Service

© 1984 USPS

WE'RE GIVING

People, know-how and state-of-the-art communications.

Motorola's best people and products will play a vital role in making the 1984 Los Angeles Olympics the smoothest run and best coordinated in history. In addition to providing communications equipment for the U.S. team, we'll be installing, operating and maintaining complete radio communications systems for the Games.

It's an immense project, demanding extraordinary performance from our people and equipment. We're happy to accept this challenge, because it gives us an opportunity to show the world how good we are at what we do.

More than 300 Motorolans will be working behind the scenes, providing supervision and technical expertise. They'll help link together all aspects of the Games through tightly-knit radio communications and wide-area radio paging that will cover a 200-mile region. Thousands of Motorola 2-way radios and

pagers will be in use—in the Olympic villages, at competition sites and by personnel enroute. Here's a brief look at some of them.

DYNA T·A·C Cellular Portable Telephone. The world's first and best portable phone. This compact, hand-held unit will enable key personnel to call any phone in the world from their cars, street locations or even from seats in the stands.

MOSTAR Trunked Mobile Radio.
This multi-channel, 2-way radio will be installed in hundreds of vehicles, allowing game officials and security people to hold private, interference-free conversations while on the move.

IT OUR BEST.

That's how Motorola supports the 1984 Olympics.

Official Radio Communications Sponsor for the 1984 Olympic Games

EXPO "Handie-Talkie" FM Radio. Our rugged, pocket-sized 2-way radio will aid coaches and trainers in coordinating practices, and prove useful to spotters and sports commissioners. No larger than a pager, the EXPO performs beautifully in the toughest environments— dust, water and temperature extremes.

OPTRX Display Pager. The versatile OPTRX pager will furnish information to delegation heads, Olympic officers— anyone needing instant data. It offers visual display messages up to 80 characters long, making it ideal for statistics and scores. The OPTRX will be tied into the International Telex Network, allowing pages from overseas

to be received in seconds.

SENSAR Pager. This compact pager will be an invaluable aid to managers of Olympic events and the press. The world's smallest pager, SENSAR offers big features, including message storage.

Go with the best. The same state-of-the-art communications equipment that will be working for the 1984 Olympics can work for you. For more information, write or call us toll-free: Motorola, 1301 E. Algonquin Road, Schaumburg, IL 60196. Phone: **1 (800) 367-2346**, Ext. **84.**

Tomorrow's communications today.

 MOTOROLA
Communications and Electronics Inc.

ESTADIO OLIMPICO WAS OPENED IN MEXICO CITY FOR THE 1968 CEREMONIES AND TRACK AND FIELD EVENTS

Rene Burri/Magnum Photos

	200m first & second rounds, men 3,000m first round, women
10:00	Basketball – 2 games—quarterfinals, men
	Synchronized Swimming – Duet routines preliminary
	Volleyball – 2 matches—preliminaries, men
11:00	Boxing – Preliminary bouts
	Team Handball – 3 games—preliminaries, men

P.M.

1:00	Baseball – 2 games—semifinals
1:30	Water Polo – 2 games—final round
	Yachting – Fifth race
2:00	Weightlifting – First heavyweight (up to 100kg), group B
2:30	Field Hockey – 1 game—preliminary, men 1 game—round robin, women
4:00	Track and Field (Athletics) – 110m hurdles semifinal & final, men Hammer throw final, men 400m hurdles semifinal, women 400m semifinal, men 400m final, women 800m final, women Long jump final, men 800m final, men Javelin throw final, women 3,000m steeplechase, first round, men 10,000m final, men

	Judo – Lightweight
4:30	Diving – Springboard finals, women
5:00	Basketball – 2 games—quarterfinals, men
	Football (Soccer) – Quarterfinal match (Stanford University, Palo Alto, California)
6:00	Boxing – Preliminary bouts
	Weightlifting – First heavyweight (up to 100kg), group A
6:30	Team Handball – 3 games—preliminaries, men
	Volleyball – 2 matches—preliminaries, men
7:00	Football (Soccer) – Quarterfinal match (Rose Bowl, Pasadena, California)
7:30	Water Polo – 2 games—final round

AUGUST 7

Tuesday

A.M.	EVENT
7:30	Canoeing – 1,000m heats and repechage, men 500m heats and repechage, women
8:00	Field Hockey – 1 game—preliminary, men 1 game—round robin, women
8:30	Water Polo – 2 games—final round
9:00	Fencing – Foil—team preliminaries, women Epée—individual preliminaries, men
	Tennis – 16 matches
10:00	Diving – Springboard preliminaries, men
	Equestrian – Team jumping competition
	Volleyball – 2 matches—finals (5-8 places), women
11:00	Boxing – Quarterfinal bouts

continued

We proudly support America's finest athletes.

GMC is the Official Truck of the 1984 Olympics. We wanted to do our part. And we think it's appropriate. A GMC truck, such as our S-15 Jimmy, is a rather athletic sort of vehicle. But not, perhaps, at first glance.

An S-15 Jimmy is compact, stylish and comfortable, with options available much like an elegant car: power steering, automatic transmission and air conditioning, to mention a few.

But a 4x4 Jimmy can also flex some muscle. After all, it *is* a tough, dependable GMC truck. So it can go just about anywhere, on the road or off. GM's Insta-Trac system lets you shift from two- to four-wheel drive without even stopping.

To celebrate its prowess, we've created a special limited edition Jimmy with special trim like the one below. It's sort of a Jimmy in jogging togs.

Buckle up and take a look at one at your nearest GMC dealer. Look in the Yellow Pages.

For a free copy of GMC's 28-page, "How To Live Comfortably With A Truck," please write to: GMC Truck Merchandising Drawer 30093, Dept. O65, Lansing, MI 48909.

Official Truck of the XXIIIrd Olympiad Los Angeles 1984

A truck you can live with.

GM MARK OF EXCELLENCE

Limited Edition Olympic Jimmy

P.M.

12:00	Wrestling – Freestyle—preliminaries—48, 62, 90kg
1:30	Water Polo – 2 games—final round
	Yachting – Sixth race
1:45	Field Hockey – 1 game—round robin, women
	2 games—preliminaries, men
2:00	Weightlifting – Second heavyweight (up to 110kg), group B
4:00	Baseball – 2 games—finals
	Diving – Springboard preliminaries, men
	Judo – Half middleweight
	Volleyball – 1 match—final (3-4 places), women
5:00	Basketball – 2 games—finals (1-4 places), women
6:00	Boxing – Quarterfinal bouts
	Weightlifting – Second heavyweight (up to 110kg), group A
	Wrestling – Freestyle—preliminaries—48, 62, 90kg
6:30	Team Handball – 3 games—round robin, women
7:30	Water Polo – 2 games—final round
8:00	Fencing – Foil—team finals, women
8:30	Volleyball – 1 match—final (1-2 places), women

AUGUST 8
Wednesday

A.M.   EVENT

7:30	Canoeing – 500m semifinals, men & women
9:00	Basketball – 2 games—semifinals, men
	Fencing – Sabre—team preliminaries, men
	Epée—individual preliminaries, men

Tennis – 16 matches
Volleyball – 2 matches—semifinals, men
          1 match—final (9-10 places), men

9:30	Track and Field (Athletics) – Decathlon 100m, long jump, shotput, men
	Discus throw qualifying, men
	200m first & second rounds, women
	1,500m first round, women
10:00	Archery – 70m women, 90m men
	Synchronized Swimming – Duet routines final
11:00	Boxing – Quarterfinal bouts
	Team Handball – 3 games—preliminaries, men

P.M.

12:00	Wrestling – Freestyle—Preliminaries—48, 52, 62, 74, 90, over 100kg
1:30	Yachting – Seventh race
2:00	Equestrian – Team dressage competition
	Weightlifting – Super heavyweight group B
2:30	Archery – 60m women, 70m men
3:00	Basketball – 1 game—semifinals, men
4:00	Track and Field (Athletics) – 200m semifinal & final, men
	Decathlon high jump, 400m, men
	Pole vault final, men
	400m hurdles final, women
	400m final, men

continued

IN
NIGHTTIME
BERLIN A
'CATHEDRAL
OF LIGHTS'
DRAMATIZED
THE 1936
OLYMPIC
SITE

The spirit of individualism and dedication to excellence are the makings of a champion.

As well as the Centurion Executive™ Sportswatch.

In every arena, the striving to perfect one's abilities is cause for admiration.

The ability to perfect thinness with accuracy has been achieved in the Centurion Executive Sportswatch from Concord Collection. (A design feat made possible by an ultra-thin electronic quartz movement.)

Expectedly, it is rugged. Water-resistant. Shock-resistant.

However, the bracelet is a unique interlinking of 18K gold, as flexible as a leather strap. The case is hand-carved, one curve at a time.

The Centurion Executive. It makes the bulky sportswatch passé.

From the Concord Collection, totally hand-crafted in Switzerland.

CONCORD® COLLECTION

all the world

"THE MILK CHOCOLATE MELTS IN YOUR MOUTH—
NOT IN YOUR HAND"®

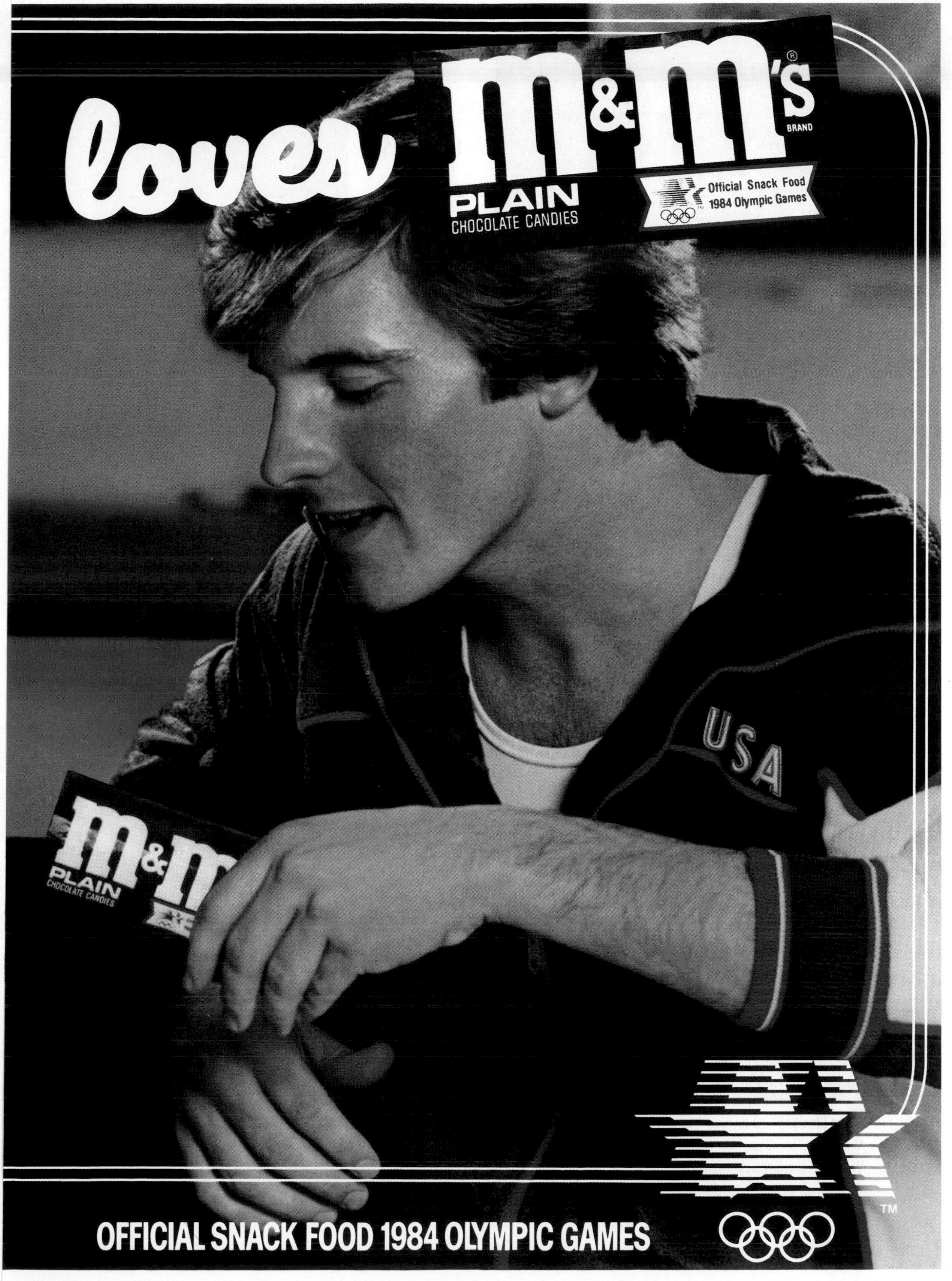

loves
m&m's
BRAND
PLAIN
CHOCOLATE CANDIES
Official Snack Food
1984 Olympic Games
USA
m&m
PLAIN
CHOCOLATE CANDIES
OFFICIAL SNACK FOOD 1984 OLYMPIC GAMES
TM

FUJI FILM CAPTURES THE THE EMOTION OF MEN,

Sports and photography—two important forms of human expression that teach, inspire, and bring the world closer together.

As a company that is strongly committed to improving worldwide communications, Fuji Photo Film is proud of its role as innovator in the entire field of image information, and major supporter of international sports.

THE OLYMPIC GAMES AND BEYOND.

Fuji's track record includes sponsorship of the 1982 World Cup, the 1983 U.S. Pan American Team, the U.S. Swimming Team, the U.S. Amateur Basketball Association, the U.S. Gymnastics Federation, the 1984 U.S. Olympic Team and the 1984 Los Angeles Olympic Games. Fuji will also sponsor the 1986 World Cup.

As a fund raising project, Fuji initiated "Shooting for the Gold." This 2½ year effort will document on Fuji film the dedication, the physical and emotional strain, the triumphs and disappointments of the finest U.S. athletes as they train and compete in the Los Angeles 1984 Olympic Games. Proceeds from a limited edition art book, museum exhibits, and photographic auction will be donated to the U.S. amateur athletic movement.

50 YEARS OF FIRSTS.

Since its founding in 1934, Fuji has been dedicated—through research and development—to satisfying consumer demand for innovative, high quality communications products. Some recent Fuji innovations include:

• New Fujicolor HR 1600, the fastest color print film in the world. It gives excellent picture quality in lower light conditions and in faster action situations than ever before.

• Oscar and Emmy award winning Fujicolor A250, the first color negative motion picture film with exceptionally high sensitivity at this exposure index.

• Fujicolor AX, an advanced high-speed color negative motion picture film with a high sensitivity of E.I. 320 and wide exposure latitude. Fujicolor AX will be used to shoot the official documentary film of the Los Angeles 1984 Olympic Games.

• Fujicolor 400, the world's first high-speed, color negative film.

• Fuji Super HG, the world's first super high grade home video cassette,

DRAMA, THE BEAUTY AND WOMEN AND GAMES.

Photo by Walter Iooss, Jr.

featuring improved levels of picture quality and tape running stability.

• Fujica DL-100, the world's first drop-in loading, fully automatic 35mm camera.

GET THE TRUE PICTURE.

Fuji's advanced technology has also developed Fuji HR film—a high resolution print film that no one else has. (The higher the resolution, the truer the color and sharper the picture.) Fuji HR film is available in 35mm, 110, 126 and disc.

In slide film, Fuji has designed a unique "L-Coupler" technology. It allows Fuji to make a thinner emulsion layer, which results in a sharper image. Fuji-chrome comes in ISO's 50, 100 and 400.

Press photographers from all over the world will rely on Fuji film products and Fuji processing to record the excitement and drama of the greatest sports event in the world. The one that is about to take place.

FUJI *Imaging the Future* FUJI FILM **50** Years · Since 1934

Gymnastics – Rhythmic preliminaries, women

Wrestling – Freestyle—preliminaries—52, 57, 68, 74, 82, 100, over 100kg
Finals—48, 62, 90kg

6:30 Team Handball – 3 games—round robin, women

7:00 Basketball – 1 game—final (3-4 places), men

7:30 Water Polo – 2 games—final round

8:00 Fencing – Sabre—team finals, men

AUGUST 10
Friday

A.M.	EVENT

8:00 Canoeing – 500m finals, men & women

Field Hockey – 1 game—final (11-12 places), men
1 game—round robin, women

8:30 Water Polo – 2 games—final round

9:00 Tennis – 4 matches, semifinals

Yachting – Olympic boardsailing exhibition

9:30 Track and Field (Athletics) – High jump qualifying, men
4x400m relay first round, women
4x400m relay first round, men
Discus throw qualifying, women
4x100m relay first round, women
4x100m relay first round men

10:00 Archery – 70m women, 90m men

Basketball – 2 games—finals (5-8 places), men

Fencing – Epée—team preliminaries, men

11:00 Team Handball – 2 games—finals (9-12 places), men

P.M.

12:00 Wrestling – Freestyle—preliminaries—57, 68, 82, 100kg
Finals—52, 74, over 100kg

1:15 Field Hockey – 2 games—finals (7-10 places), men
1 game—round robin, women

1:30 Water Polo – 2 games—final round

2:00 Equestrian – Individual dressage competition

2:30 Archery – 60m women, 70m men

4:00 Track and Field (Athletics) – High jump final, women
100m hurdles semifinal, women
4x400m relay semifinal, men
4x400m relay semifinal, women
Discus throw final, men
1,500m semifinal, men
100m hurdles final, women
3,000m final, women
3,000m steeplechase final, men

Judo – Heavyweight

4:30 Diving – Platform finals, women

6:00 Gymnastics – Rhythmic preliminaries, women

Wrestling – Freestyle—preliminaries—57, 68, 82, 100kg
Finals—52, 74, over 100kg

6:30 Team Handball – 2 games—finals (5-8 places), men

Volleyball – 2 matches—finals (5-8 places), men

continued

STATE TRUMPETERS AND THE LORD MAYOR OF LONDON CLOSED THE 1948 GAMES

Photoworld/FPG

AMERICA'S ATHLETES HAVE NEVER LOOKED BETTER.

This deceptively simple-looking stick figure is, in fact, a sophisticated computer analysis of an athlete's movements.

An analysis that will help isolate and correct errors in an athlete's form.

Through the application of this technology, Data General is working with the United States Olympic Committee Sports Medicine Group in Colorado Springs to help improve the performance of our Olympic athletes.

And today we're making the same kind of technology available to business and industry.

By working closely with you, just as we do with the United States Olympic Committee, we can increase your company's productivity and improve its performance.

Because in a field that's every bit as competitive as the Olympic Games, you've got to be more than a step ahead of everybody else.

You've got to be a generation ahead.

◖Data General
a Generation ahead.

Data General, 4400 Computer Drive,
M.S. F134, Westboro, MA 01580.

COME ALIVE, COME AND DRIVE **THE FIRST**

If we could give you the keys and an open road…this magnificent machine would capture your soul forever. It's a whole new world of driving where art and technology intersect. It's the Nissan 300 ZX. And it is major motion.

MEMBERS OF MEXICO'S BALLET FOLKLORICO SWIRLED ACROSS TRACK AT 1972 CEREMONY

Sven Simon

7:00	Basketball — 1 game — final (1-2 places), men
	Football (Soccer) — Final match (3-4 places), (Rose Bowl, Pasadena, California)
7:30	Water Polo — 2 games — final round

AUGUST 11

Saturday

A.M.	EVENT
8:00	Canoeing — 1,000m finals, men
	Track and Field (Athletics) — 50km walk final (start & finish), men
	Shotput qualifying, men
	4x100m relay semifinal, women
	4x100m relay semifinal, men
	800m wheelchair final, women
	1500m wheelchair final, men
9:00	Yachting — Olympic boardsailing exhibition
9:15	Field Hockey — 3 games — finals (1-6 places), men
10:00	Archery — 50m women, 50m men
	Diving — Platform preliminaries, men
	Fencing — Epée — team preliminaries, men
	Tennis — 2 matches, finals
11:00	Boxing — Final bouts

P.M.	
12:00	Volleyball — 1 match — final (3-4 places), men
	Wrestling — Freestyle — preliminaries — 57, 68, 82, 100kg
2:00	Team Handball — 2 games — finals (1-4 places), men (Held at The Forum, Inglewood)

2:30	Archery — 30m women, 30m men
3:00	Diving — Platform preliminaries, men
4:00	Track and Field (Athletics) — Discus throw final, women
	4x100m relay final, women
	High jump final, men
	4x100m relay final, men
	4x400 relay final, women
	4x400m relay final, men
	Shotput final, men
	1,500m final, women
	1,500m final, men
	5,000m final, men
	Judo — Open category
6:00	Boxing — Final bouts
	Wrestling — Freestyle — finals — 57, 68, 82, 100kg
6:30	Volleyball — 1 match — final (1-2 places), men
7:00	Football (Soccer) — Final match (1-2 places), (Rose Bowl, Pasadena, California)
	Gymnastics — Rhythmic finals, women
8:00	Fencing — Epée — team finals, men

AUGUST 12

Sunday

A.M.	EVENT
8:00	Equestrian — Individual jumping competition
11:00	Diving — Platform finals, men

P.M.	
5:15	Marathon, men
6:30	Closing Ceremony (Men's marathon finish included)

continued

電話しなさい, 待っていますよ

RUF' DOCH MAL AN. SIE VERMISSEN DICH

TELEFONA, NON DIMENTICARLI

TÉLÉPHONEZ, ILS S'ENNUIENT DE VOUS

CALL, THEY REALLY MISS YOU

RUF' DOCH MAL AN. SIE VERMISSEN DICH

NON DIMENTICARLI

ILS S'ENNUIENT DE VOUS

待っていますよ

No matter how far you may be from home, it's easy to stay close to the people you love. By telephone. It feels so wonderful, and costs so little, to hear the voices of loved ones. And they'll love hearing from you. So give the special people back home something really special. Call.

We Bring The World Closer.

AT&T

When the world gathers for the main event, it carries our name.

SCHEDULE AND TICKET INFORMATION

The Los Angeles Olympic Organizing Committee has operators on duty to answer your questions about the Olympic Games. Call (213) 305-8383 for information on Olympic events and schedules, venue locations, and other Olympic topics.

For questions about tickets, call (213) 741-6789. Customer service representatives can handle problems involving tickets, and will know if tickets are available for specific Olympic events.

Information about the Olympic Arts Festival can be obtained by calling (213) 741-7777.

Telecommunication Device for the Deaf (TDD): (213) 305-7028.

A MERRY HAPPENING OF HOOPS FILLED THE FIELD AT THE MOSCOW GAMES

P. Habans/Sygma

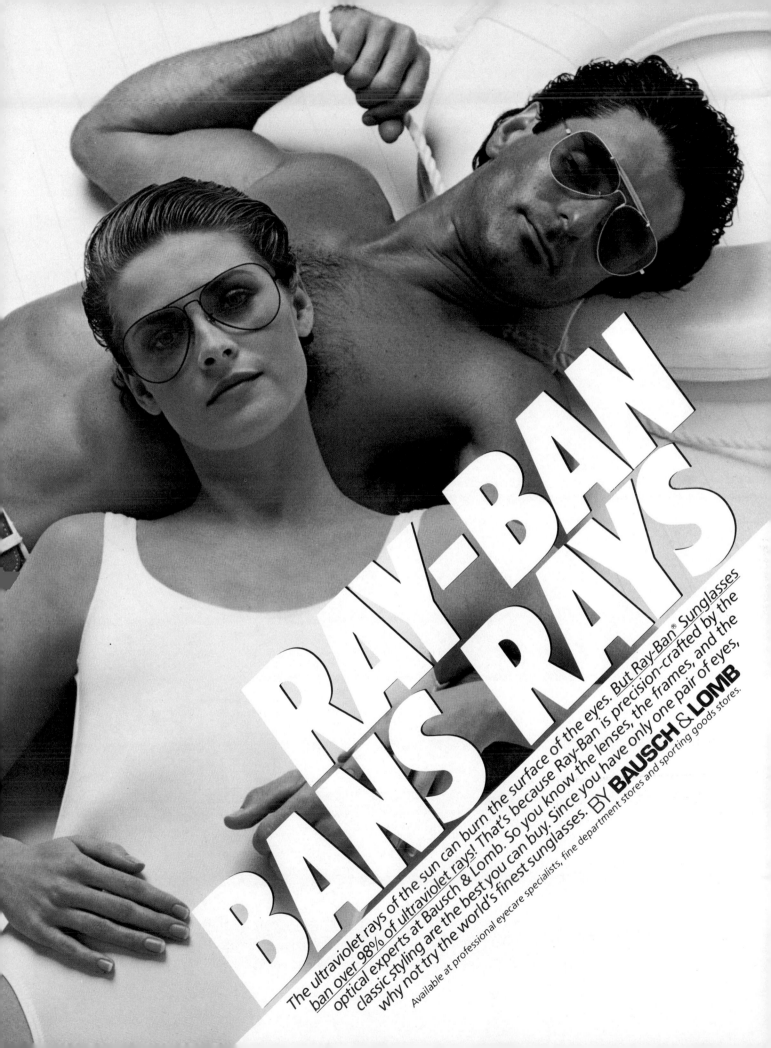

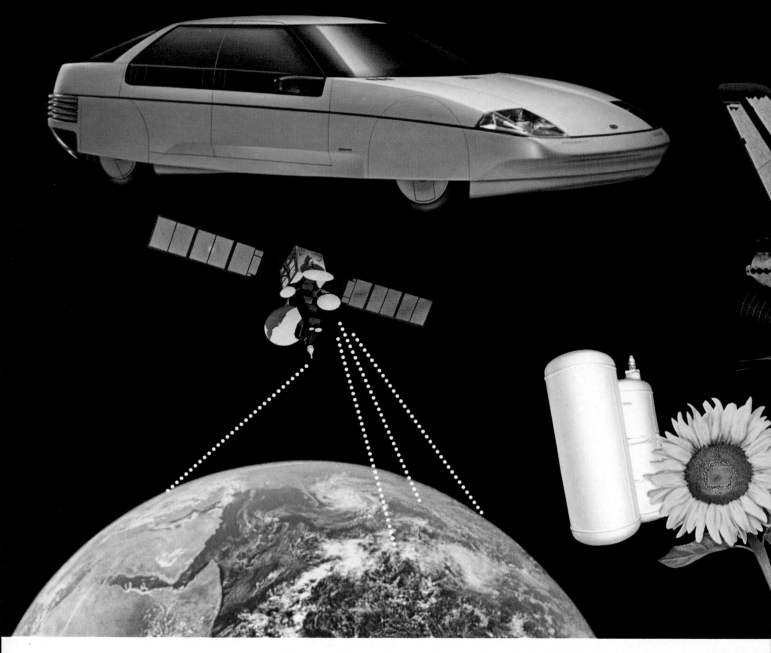

No Other Company In The World

- *Aerospace*
- *Communications Satellites*
- *Alternative Fuels*
- *Electronics*
- *Automotive Manufacturing*
- *Experimental Engineering*
- *Aerodynamics*

*Ford Is A Leader In
All These Technologies.*

Soon, two-thirds of all overseas communications and almost all intercontinental television programming will travel by satellites built by Ford Aerospace & Communications Corporation.

Our technology helped guide the Columbia space shuttle home, and bring back pictures from Saturn.

Ford is a leader in alternative fuel technology; fuels which can be derived from abundant organic matter, coal, and natural gases.

Our newest electronic brain takes the

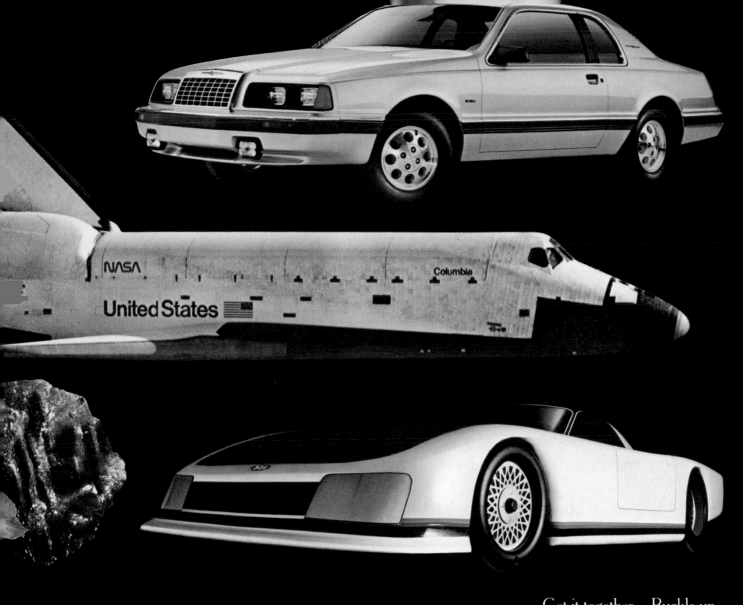

Get it together — Buckle up.

Can Make This Statement.

automobile to a new level of sophistication. It saves fuel and improves and refines total driving performance.

We've built a laboratory on wheels, a prototype vehicle made almost entirely of a graphite fiber reinforced plastic, that's lighter than aluminum, stronger than most steel.

We've designed the most aerodynamic passenger car in the world. The incredible Probe IV. (Cd .15)

Being a leader in all these diverse technologies can pay immense dividends for a company whose main pursuit is building cars, trucks, and tractors.

It gives us invaluable knowledge and insight, enabling us to build more sophisticated and efficiently performing vehicles. And staying on the leading edge of these technologies not only helps us build better vehicles today, but it assures that we can and will build better vehicles tomorrow.

Ford

Quality is Job 1

Ford · Mercury · Lincoln · Ford Trucks · Ford Tractors

MONTREAL 1976
*Three golds, a silver, a
bronze, seven
unprecedented perfect 10s
on the balance beam and
the bars. A soaring style.
An elfin charm. All made it
certain that the
performance of Nadia
Comaneci, 14, of Romania,
would be among those
chosen by an international
panel of sports experts for
inclusion in this gallery of
unforgettable Olympic
moments.*

*"Physically she has
strength, speed and
flexibility," said Nadia's
coach, Bela Karolyi, who
first spotted her talent when
she was six. "Mentally she
has intelligence,
phenomenal powers of
concentration—and
courage." He might have
been describing the essence
of the spirit that infuses all
of the athletes whose
accomplishments are
honored here or—as with
Jim Thorpe, Emil Zatopek
and Abebe Bikila—in
following features.*

ments

A selection by experts of performances which reflect the best in Olympic achievement

MUNICH 1972

Tanned, dashing, movie-actor handsome Mark Spitz won seven golds, a number never before amassed in a single Olympics by any athlete. Swimming at Mexico City in '68, Spitz, then 18, had earned two golds, a bronze and a silver. That, someone wrote, "would have been a stunning achievement" for anyone else but, in light of the expectations held by and for Spitz, represented "a flop." Training for Munich, as shown here, Spitz had not lowered those expectations. "I'd rather win even four out of four than six of seven," he said. "I just don't want to lose." And he didn't.

In Hitler's arena, a cotton-picker's son
from Alabama triumphed over the competition—
and the Nazi myth

BERLIN 1936

Blacks, according to the Nazis, were subhuman. But here was Jesse Owens, 22, black, American, proving otherwise with his repeated appearances on the victory stand (bottom). *The smooth sprinter from Ohio State won the 100 meters (below). He won in the broad jump, with a world-record leap of 26′ 5¼″ (left), and in the 200-meter* dash. *He also ran on the 400-meter relay team that set a world record. His mother's reaction:* "Jesse was always a face boy. When a problem came up, he always faced it."

MONTREAL 1976
*With an effort almost
beyond belief, the
incomparable Vasily
Alexeyev, a 34-year-old
mining engineer from the
Soviet Union, lifted a 562-
pound barbell. With that
world-record lift and
earlier ones, such as the
snatch shown here,
Alexeyev, who weighed in
at 345 pounds—evident in
his large tummy—won the
gold among the super
heavyweights. "A medal is
a medal," said the world's
most renowned strongman,
"but a world record is
something else." Then,
Alexeyev added somberly,
"Maybe now my wife will
show more respect."*

Neil Leifer/SPORTS ILLUSTRATED

Paavo Nurmi and Wilma Rudolph,
The Flying Finn and La Gazelle,
two effortless striders who struck gold

ROME 1960

To the Italians, she was "The Black Pearl"; the French called her "La Gazelle." To her friends back in Tennessee, she was Skeeter, the girl who had been crippled by childhood disease and had to wear a brace and special shoe until she was half-grown. She was Wilma Rudolph, the 20-year-old runner from Tennessee State who had amazed her coach with her effortless stride and an unflappable cool that let her fall asleep between heats. Utilizing that stride in Rome (far left), she took home golds in the 100- and 200-meter sprints and in the 400-meter relay.

PARIS 1924

With hardly a break in his step after finishing first in the 1,500 meters, Paavo Nurmi, "The Flying Finn," vanished into the locker room. An hour later he started the 5,000-meter race, another gold-medal performance (above). In only two hours, Nurmi had broken two Olympic records. The next day, he led Finland to the championship in the 3,000-meter team race, and the day after that he took another gold in the 10,000-meter cross-country run. At 27, Nurmi accepted his victories with the aplomb that might be expected of an athlete who as a youth had raced the mail train—and often had to wait for it to catch up to him.

MUNICH 1972
*Using the "Fosbury Flop,"
Ulrike Meyfarth of the host
nation, West Germany,
hurled her body backwards
over the high-jump bar to
equal the women's world
record of 6′ 3½″—and to
make herself, at age 16, the
youngest track-and-field
champion in the history of
the Games.*

Six decades apart, but driven by the same relentless will to win, Akii-Bua and Kolehmainen made their marks

MUNICH 1972

John Akii-Bua, 22, was a son of a Ugandan tribal chief with eight wives and over 40 children. He learned English from magazines and comic books and took up competitive sports at 15. Arriving at Munich, Akii-Bua first worried about the threat of an African boycott to protest Rhodesia's participation. Then he went without much sleep the night before the 400-meter hurdles, fretting about his inside-lane position, which would require him to turn tightly into the first hurdle. But at the start of the race Akii-Bua's fears ended and his training paid off: He had been working out six days a week, running 1,500 meters over hurdles while wearing a 20-pound vest. He took the gold, finishing in 47.82 seconds, and accepted the crowd's cheers (left) as Uganda's first Olympic champion.

STOCKHOLM 1912

Bursting into a finishing sprint, Hannes Kolehmainen (near right) of Finland won the 5,000-meter run a step ahead of Jean Bouin of France, in the world-record time of 14:36.6. Kolehmainen, 22, the first of a line of dominant Finnish long-distance runners, took another gold in the 10,000-meter run and won the 12,000-meter cross-country. His performance inspired another young Finn—Paavo Nurmi—to take up running.

IBM's Arena At The 1984 Olympics.

Before all the pageantry and the ceremony; before the exhilaration and the anguish; before the world turns its attention toward a competition whose roots lie in ancient Greece, the Los Angeles Olympic Organizing Committee will be working hard in its arena.

An office.

But not just any office.

An office where time is the enemy as the clock ticks inexorably toward the July 28th starting date.

An office responsible for the welfare of 10,000 athletes from 150 countries, speaking 51 languages.

And, fortunately, an office equipped with IBM Office Systems:

Item: IBM Office Systems prepare letters, reports, presentations and other office work in a fraction of the time that it would normally take on conventional office equipment.

Item: IBM Personal Computers simplify thousands of details that would otherwise take hundreds of hours—from arranging housing and transportation for athletes, to keeping track of equipment.

They will also provide judges and commentators with on-site access to detailed statistical information at selected events.

Item: IBM Displaywriters and an IBM 6670 laser printer type, print and distribute technical manuals with detailed specifications for every Olympic event.

Item: An IBM Audio Distribution System sends, receives and stores messages, virtually eliminating "telephone tag" at the Los Angeles Olympic Organizing Committee.

So, long before the Olympic flame is ignited, before the most skilled athletes in the world assemble in Los Angeles to bend the limits of human endurance, IBM will be helping to make the XXIII Olympiad a success. **IBM**

Ken Regan / Camera 5; bottom, Wide World Photos

MOSCOW 1980

In a dramatic turnabout, Steve Ovett, 24, upset Sebastian Coe, 23, in the 800 meters with a time of 1:45.4—a full three seconds slower than Coe's world record. Then, six days later, British rivals Coe and Ovett went up against each other again, in the race Ovett had declared himself "really prepared for," the 1,500 meters. This time, in another upset, shown above, Coe (254) pulled away from Ovett (279) in the final 180 meters to win the gold. Coe's reaction to his victory: "Such a bloody, marvelous relief!"

LOS ANGELES 1932

She was 21 and on her way to becoming the greatest woman athlete in U.S. history. What happened in the Games was no small part of the legend. First a gold in the javelin, an almost flat trajectory of 143' 4". "I could've throwed it farther," Babe Didrikson explained, "but I slipped." Then another gold in the 80-meter hurdles (near left) and a silver in the high jump, losing a tie for first because her style violated the rules of that time.

85

FALL IN LOVE IN SECONDS FLAT.

Two years ago, Volvo introduced a turbo-charged 4-cylinder automobile that could hurtle you from a standing start to the legal speed limit in a scorching nine seconds.

This year, there's something faster. The Intercooled Turbo from Volvo. By designing a device to cool the air before it enters the engine, Volvo engineers increased the horsepower of our stock Turbo by 24%.

The result is what *Car and Driver* calls "a missile." A car that can outaccelerate a BMW 318i, blow the doors off a Saab 900 Turbo and leave an Audi 5000s in the dust.*

So if you're looking for a great handling, great-performing car, check out the Intercooled Turbo from Volvo.

And if you already own a Volvo Turbo, don't despair. You can have an intercooler retrofitted at your Volvo dealer. Then you can fall in love all over again.

THE TURBO
By Volvo.

*Based on test conducted by Car and Driver.

MEXICO CITY 1968
"The Olympic long jump," Time *magazine reported, "was supposed to be a two-man contest between the U.S.'s Ralph Boston and Russia's Igor Ter-Ovanesyan, co-holders of the world record (27′ 4¾″)." A third contestant, Bob Beamon, had an "unpolished jumping style" that "made purists shudder. . . . In the qualification trials, he fouled on his first two jumps and barely made it to the finals on his last try."*

But in the finals Beamon managed to achieve tremendous altitude as he took off, flapping his arms like a bird, his body jackknifed and his legs spread-eagled. Then, upon landing, he fell to his knees and clasped his hands in prayer. He said afterwards, "I was thanking that man up there for letting me hit the ground right here." Beamon's mark, an incredible 29′ 2½″, exceeded the world record by more than 21 inches.

Courtesy of U.S. Olympic Committee

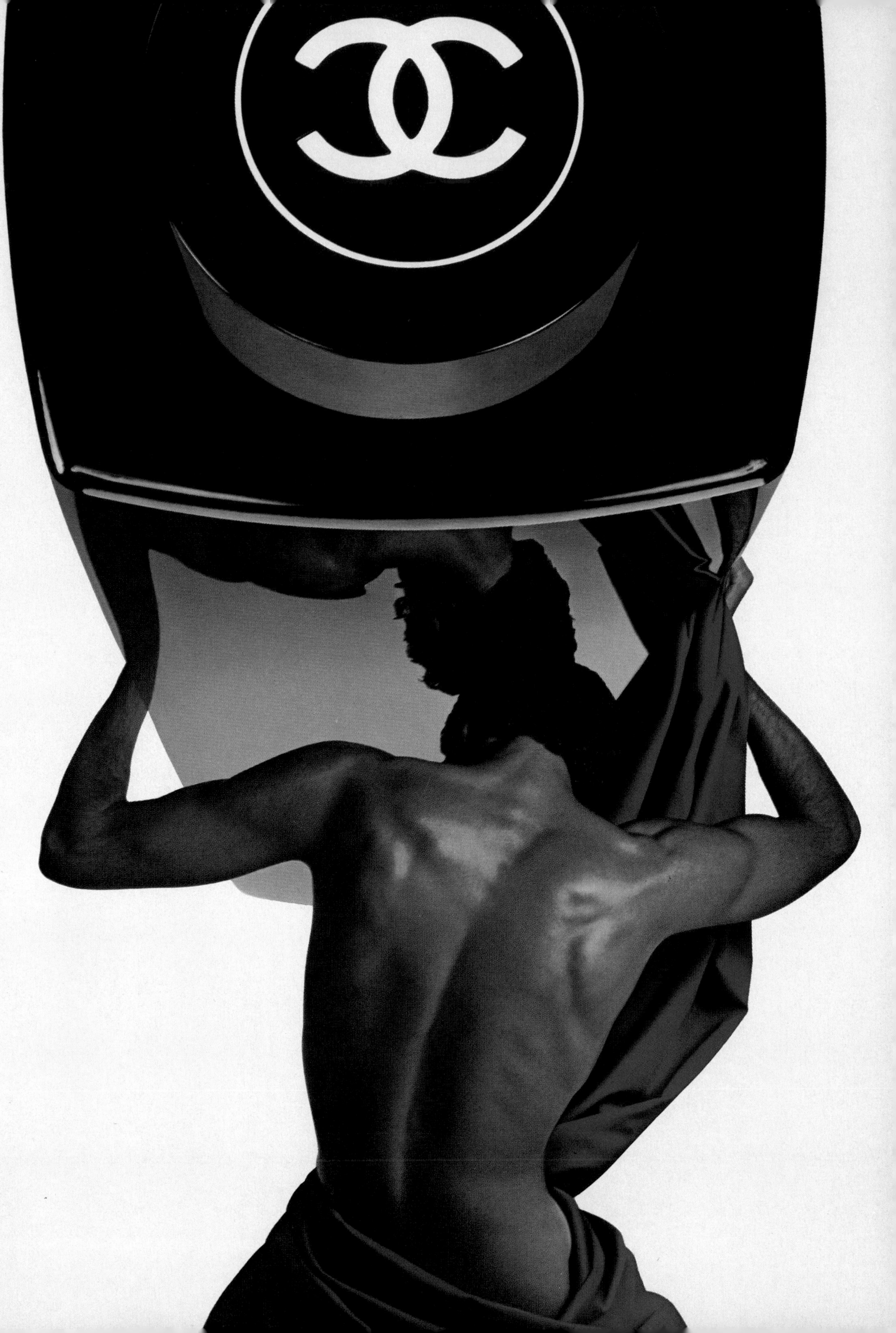

A REFLECTION OF STRENGTH AND SENSITIVITY.

ANTAEUS

THE FRAGRANCE FOR MEN.

CHANEL

Seiko gave you the world's first analog quartz chronograph.
Now we give you the moon.

Every phase of the moon. Or the day/date. Or the elegantly thin all gold-tone.
All analog quartz chronographs. All born of history-making technology. All governed
by four independent step motors to measure elapsed time in minutes, seconds, 5/100th
seconds up to 30 minutes. All with tachymeter. Moon and day/date models
water-tested to 300 feet. Gold-tone to 100 feet.

SEIKO
Setting the standard for the world, for the future.

MONTREAL 1976

As a youth in Maryland, he began boxing in 1971 and honed his style—swift jabs and hooks, cutting uppercuts and crosses, dragonfly footwork. He had been named after Ray Charles, the singer, and he was called Sugar after the Sugar, Ray Robinson, who reigned over several classes in boxing for years. And now, he was beginning his own reign. Having won championships in the Golden Gloves and the Pan American Games, Sugar Ray Leonard next earned a place on the U.S. Olympic team, whipped the international competition and stood there (above) a gold-medal winner, the Olympic light-welterweight champion.

MUNICH 1972

Olga Korbut of the Soviet Union was 17—a tiny, 4' 11" gymnast who weighed only 84 pounds, pigtails and all. But how she soared! She won two golds for her stunning acrobatics on the balance beam and her floor exercises and earned a silver on the uneven bars.

PARIS 1924

Harold Abrahams was a tall, laconic, 24-year-old Cambridge University student with a penchant for ale and cigars. He started the 100-meter sprint for gold unimpressively. But then, at 25 meters, Abrahams (later to be the model for a central character in the film Chariots of Fire) seemed to shift gears, sped out front and thrust his No. 419 across the finish line ahead of a trio of favored Yanks.

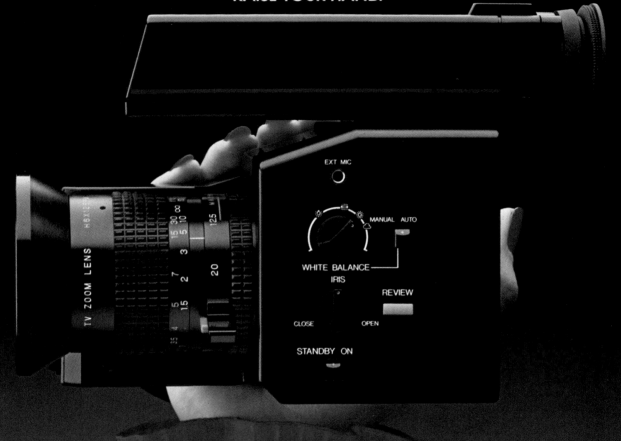

MEXICO CITY 1968

Kipchoge Keino (above) had already competed in the 10,000-meter run (where he collapsed three laps before the finish) and the 5,000 (taking a silver) when the 1,500-meter race began. This time the plucky 28-year-old Kenyan took a large early lead, withstanding a surge by American Jim Ryun, to win in Olympic-record time.

ANTWERP 1920

John B. "Jack" Kelly, 29, a bricklayer from Philadelphia, had been excluded from the prestigious Diamond Sculls at Henley, England, because, he reportedly was told, the strength built up by laborers gave them unfair advantage over "gentlemen competitors." But Kelly rowed in the Olympics. His mighty arms and artful starts won two golds—in doubles with his cousin, Paul V. Costello, and (left) in single sculls.

LONDON 1948

There were suggestions that at 30 she was too old to win and indications that her concentration continuously drifted to her children at home in Holland. But Fanny Blankers-Koen won four golds, more than any other woman in Olympic history: in the 100-meter dash, the 80-meter hurdles (right), the 200-meter run and the 400-meter relay. Then the mother of two went back to Amsterdam and her family.

MICHELOB
USA

Some things speak for themselves™

James Drake/SPORTS ILLUSTRATED; far right, T. Tanuma/SPORTS ILLUSTRATED; bottom, Brown Brothers

MONTREAL 1976

How dedicated was Bruce Jenner to training? Well, as a hint, consider that he kept—and worked out on— a hurdle in his living room. And now, his single-minded quest to win the decathlon title was near the end. Jenner, 26, strained (above) to make a 15' 9" pole vault (equaling a personal record). Two hours later he was trotting a victory lap, owner of the world decathlon record of 8,618 points and a forthcoming medal of Olympic gold.

TOKYO 1964

Nobody, said U.S. Marine Lieutenant Billy Mills, had even said hello to him, much less interviewed him before the 10,000-meter run. Then Billy (center, above), 26, part Sioux Indian, made history by threading through the crush of runners to set an Olympic record of 28:24.4. He was the first American to win the event.

PARIS 1900

Ray Ewry, 26, won golds for the standing broad jump, standing hop, step and jump and a nearly supernatural standing high jump—all in one day. Paralyzed as a child in Indiana, he had jumped to exercise his withered limbs. Ewry (left) managed to levitate his 6' 3" frame over a bar 5' 5" off the ground.

SHOULD THE REASSURANCES OF BUYING THE RIGHT CAR COME FROM THE CAR ITSELF OR THE APPROVAL OF OTHERS?

It isn't easy to buy a Saab.

Other cars offer the reassurance of status. Or the security of practicality. Or the image of performance.

The reassurances that come from buying a Saab, on the other hand, come mainly from the car itself, as perceived by the buyer.

The right car should tell you about itself.

If you view a twisty road as a challenge, a Saab will stimulate you with the poise of its front-wheel-drive traction and the grip of its 15″ Pirelli radials.

If, on the other hand, you view the same road as a potential hazard, a Saab will calm you for precisely the same reasons.

The Saab fuel-injected, two-liter engine accelerates in a manner that puts many alleged symbols of performance to shame.

The Saab APC Turbo engine leaves some of them positively mortified.

Its seats will help keep you alert and untired after hours of driving. Its controls are laid out to keep you well-informed about your Saab's relationship to driving conditions.

A Saab's structure will communicate its integrity to you over every jounce and pothole in the road.

A Saab communicates all these things to you without shouting to the world that it is a performance car or a luxury car of eminent practicality.

The right people will tell you about a Saab.

There has always been a hard core of Saab followers who've appreciated Saab's unique design philosophies.

But today there are a lot more people in it.

One reason for this growing acceptance might be that in the 27 years since the first Saabs pulled themselves onto American shores with front-wheel drive, just about every other carmaker has followed suit with front-wheel-drive cars of their own.

It might be that Saabs don't happen to look that different anymore.

It's possible that Saab's idea of using turbocharging for maximum performance from minimal fuel has taken root in the collective psyches of the public.*

Whatever the reasons, in some circles, Saabs have become rather fashionable.

So that today, if you look for them, you will actually find other people who will approve of your purchase of a Saab.

Not that that, as you know, should ever be a reason for buying one.

The most intelligent car ever built.

Saab 900 5-speed APC Turbo. 21 EPA estimated mpg, 34 estimated highway mpg. Use estimated mpg for comparison only. Mileage varies with speed, trip length and weather. Actual highway mileage will probably be less. Saabs range in price from $11,110 for the 900 3-door, 5-speed to $17,400 for the 900 4-door, 5 speed APC Turbo. Manufacturer's suggested retail prices. Not including taxes, license, freight, dealer charges or options.

Neil Leifer/SPORTS ILLUSTRATED; bottom, UPI

MUNICH 1972

Lasse Viren, shown above running his 10,000-meter victory lap, became the fourth man to win both the 5,000- and 10,000-meter runs in a single Games. So powerful a competitor was the 23-year-old policeman from Finland that he broke the world record for the 10,000 after falling near the halfway mark. Four years later, at Montreal, Viren became the only runner to repeat wins in both the 5,000 and the 10,000.

LONDON 1948

Bob Mathias (left) was 17, a California high school kid who had excelled in the hurdles, high jump and discus—but who, just months before the Olympics, had never pole-vaulted, tossed a javelin, or run a 1,500 meter race, had scarcely ever broad-jumped or tried the 400 meters. Now here he was having to do all that and more in the decathlon. Incredibly—and conclusively—he did it well enough to win.

George Silk / LIFE Magazine © Time Inc.; bottom, Monkmeyer

MELBOURNE 1956

Vladimir Kuts, 29, a Soviet naval lieutenant, set a killing pace at the outset of the 10,000-meter run, paused and then waved, inviting his nonplussed British competitor, Gordon Pirie, to pass. Pirie warily declined, then reluctantly passed when Kuts slowed to a taunting walk. Kuts then blitzed past, taking command over the last five laps to win his gold. Five days later, Kuts did it again, with a hard, steady race in the 5,000 meters (above), earning his second gold medal.

ATHENS 1896

The first modern Olympic marathon traversed the very course that provided the race with its name: Marathon to Athens, nearly 25 miles away. Winner of this first modern marathon was a Greek shepherd and former soldier, Spiridon Loues—shown at left during the victory ceremony—who had fasted and prayed most of the day before the race. His time, 2:58:50, was a full seven minutes ahead of his closest competitor, a margin that continues to stand as the widest in Olympic marathon victories.

IF YOUR VIDEO INVESTMENT IS SHOWING DIMINISHING RETURNS,

your picture could be suffering from dropouts, bleeding colors, and other annoying problems. Before you point the finger at your video deck, think about this! An inexpensive video cassette can turn your investment into a loss.

That's the way the system works. Friction can cause oxide particles to shed, and drag parts of the picture along with them. You're left with dropouts. Or bleeding colors caused by poor signal-to-noise ratio. Or even worse.

THE SOLUTION IS SUPER AVILYN.

For the first few plays, all quality video tapes usually perform well. Crisp images. Bright colors. A steady picture. But after they're played time after time, the problems can start. That's when one video cassette really starts to show its worth. TDK.

Its Super Avilyn high energy tape particles are densely packed and secured on the tape surface, which is polished mirror-smooth. The particles are there to stay. Your picture is there to stay. Play after play. In any mode, especially the slower speeds. Because TDK video cassettes are designed to perform best under all conditions.

BLEEDING COLORS

DROPOUTS

Surrounding the tape is TDK's super precision mechanism. It gives jam-proof performance and excellent tape-to-head contact.

With all this going for us, it should come as no surprise that TDK knows video inside out. And it stands to reason Super Avilyn is always compatible with any VCR you can buy.

TDK video cassettes are available in VHS and Beta formats, with a wide range of recording times and lengths, in two formulations: Standard Super Avilyn and Extra High Grade.

Look at it this way. The future of your video investment really depends on the video tape. With TDK Super Avilyn, you'll see the dividends, again and again.

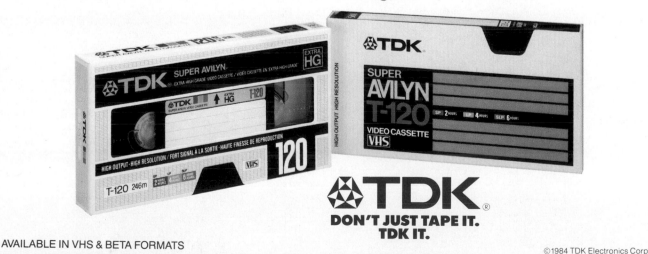

◈TDK.
DON'T JUST TAPE IT.
TDK IT.

AVAILABLE IN VHS & BETA FORMATS

©1984 TDK Electronics Corp.

Temporarily paralyzed in 1980 from a broken neck, Mark Caso nevertheless was in the fight for a spot as a U.S. Olympic gymnast in 1984, his resilience reflecting that of the past Olympians — James B. Connolly, Karoly Takacs and Joe Frazier — whose photos he holds here.

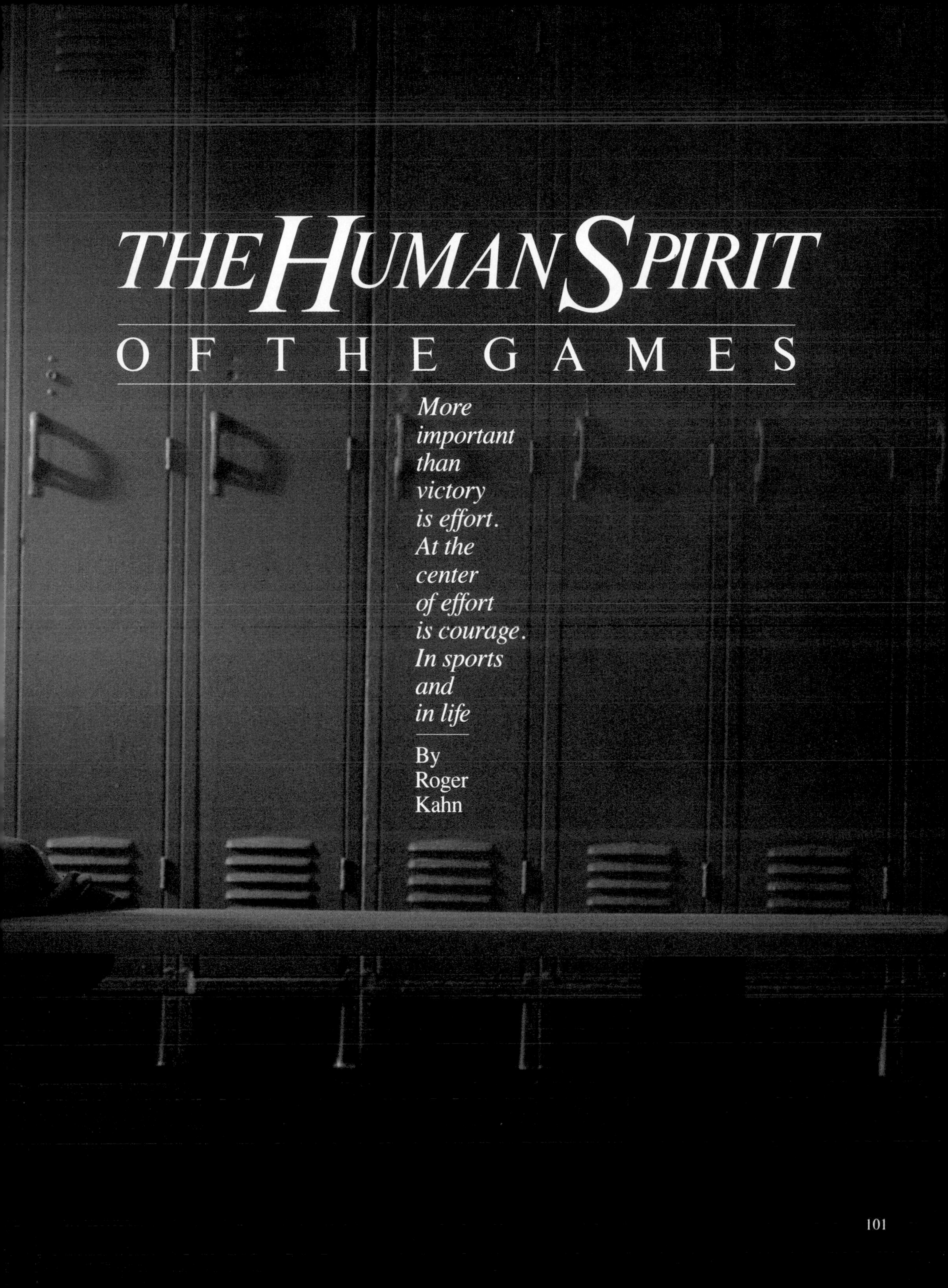

THE HUMAN SPIRIT
OF THE GAMES

*More
important
than
victory
is effort.
At the
center
of effort
is courage.
In sports
and
in life*

By
Roger
Kahn

To compete in the 1896 Games, James B. Connolly was forced to leave Harvard where he was finally welcomed back at a 1949 class reunion

Preceding pages and this page: Robert Peak Jr.; inset: Yale Joel / LIFE Magazine © 1949 TIME Inc.

COURAGE, THE WHITE PLUME that beckons us on through suffering, is an old story with writers, athletes and warriors. The word traces from the Latin noun for heart and the concept all but hypnotizes us as—not subliminally but consciously—we aspire to possess courage in all its vivid shadings. Mettle and fortitude and resolution and bravery and backbone and tenacity and, quite simply, guts.

You find courage in old men, whose voices crack even as their spirits sing. You find it in small children, as they experience grievous ailments and confront the premature suggestion of death. You find it in artists, who have the courage to be new, in surgeons who dare once more to touch a scalpel and in certain great musicians who brave audiences and themselves after 70 years of constant performance. You find courage, too, in less exalted places: men and women working at joyless jobs. Anonymous cops patrolling violent neighborhoods at night. School counselors putting forth long days with hostile, disturbed youth. To go back to roots, you find courage wherever you discover a boundless heart.

A modern Olympic roster of courage surely dates from 1896, when one James B. Connolly, a 19th-century Harvard Irish-American, abandoned The Yard and all its promise to make his own way to the Ath-

Roger Kahn, author of The Boys of Summer, *is writing a book,* Diamond in the Rough, *on his experience as a minor league baseball club owner.*

ens Games. There Connolly competed in the hop, step and jump.

He was a 27-year-old undergraduate, who had worked at a variety of hard jobs before he entered college. Harvard authorities in those days did not recognize Olympic competition as a valid reason for interrupting study and they rejected Connolly's application for a leave. Still he went, paying his own way. And still he won, with a triple jump of 44′ 11¾″ and also came in third in the long jump.

More than half a century later, Harvard conceded its error by granting Connolly a major letter—his crimson "H"—in 1949 at the 50th reunion of the class with which he did not graduate. By then, having set off on a life governed by his own terms, Connolly was comfortably established as a writer of sea stories. That same year, he was nominated to be Boston's official Censor of Comic Books. "Never read a comic book in my life," Connolly told the infinitely political Mayor James M. Curley. "But I care what children read, so I accept."

A forgotten band of overweight aldermen turned him down, deeming him to be too old for the position. Still, at Jim Connolly's death, he was honored and remembered for 25 novels, 200 short stories and his Olympic triple jump. Sung to a slightly discordant version of "Fair Harvard," this strikes me as a marvelous early version of "My Way."

Against that joyous tale is the darker adventure of a Hungarian pistol shooter named Károly Takács. During the European disasters of the 1930s, Takács found

himself a sergeant in the Hungarian army, with the Nazi hordes not far away. Takács was a superb marksman with his pistol, a weapon about as effective against a Panzer division as an air rifle. While he was participating in maneuvers in 1938, a grenade exploded prematurely and destroyed his right hand, which had brought him such acclaim as a shooter.

Takács, a handsome, high-cheekboned Magyar, survived World War II. He appeared at the London Olympics of 1948 and, firing his gun with his left hand, won a gold medal for the rapid-fire pistol-shooting event. Then, demonstrating that his remarkable comeback was no fluke, he won another gold medal at Helsinki in 1952. Imagine, to put this in more conventionally American terms, a great righthanded pitcher, a Tom Seaver or a Bob Gibson, suffering a dreadful injury and then recovering to win the Cy Young Award as a lefthander.

The distinction between the accomplishments of Connolly and Takács, set more than 50 years apart, suggests some of the disparity embodied in courage, the word and the concept. In literature older than the ancient Olympics, writers constantly fence with courage as a theme. The Bible gives us a pure young David going forth with a slingshot to battle a giant and, of course, defeating him. This, according to a friend of mine in the boxing business, "is the lightweight goin' out to take on the heavy, but he's helped because the heavyweight don't even have a featherweight brain. They had shields in those days, didn't they?"

Homer is obsessed with courage, writing of kings and generals (but few common foot soldiers) and describing an intricate society of deities who meddle in the affairs of men. Most agree that the greatest Homeric tale is his story of the wanderings of Odysseus. A bearded king of Ithaca, Odysseus wants to return after the Trojan wars to his kingdom, his wife, his son. The gods offer him apparent ease and power, threaten him with terrors and present him with women of infinite seductiveness. But Odysseus perseveres against temptations and the gods over many years.

In other times writers as varied as Shakespeare, Tolstoy, Kipling and Robert Frost have chosen courage as a theme. Hemingway was positively obsessed by it. To Hemingway, we owe the most often quoted definition of the word. Courage, he said, is "grace under pressure."

As literature holds a mirror up to life,

continued

THE LUXURY CAR FOR THOSE WHO REFUSE TO RELAX THEIR STANDARDS.

Anyone who pays $40,000 for a luxury sedan should not be asked to do so in a spirit of forgiveness for its deficiencies.

The BMW 733i makes no such requests. And one of the world's most unforgiving production processes makes certain that none is ever needed.

That process mandates over 3 million operations for the assembly of the body alone. It controls chassis alignments to within 4/1,000ths of an inch. And it assesses the corrosion-resistance of structural metals by submerging them in salt water for at least ten days.

It also endows the BMW 733i with such technological innovations as an optional four-speed auto-matic transmission that doesn't force you to sacrifice the precision of a manual gearbox, but rather "gives the best of both worlds" (Auto-sport magazine).

But the 733i is freer of compromise than even that implies. Of its more than 4,000 parts, none ever suffers from inattention because it's judged 'minor.'

The electrically-powered leather bucket seats are orthopedically molded to the contours of the spine. And because they're infinitely adjustable, being uncomfortable is all but an anatomical impossibility.

Human anatomy even dictates the design of the buttons that operate the power windows and the two-position electric sunroof:

They are precisely shaped to fit the natural curvature of the fingertip.

The 733i, in short, is an automobile in which nothing has been left to chance, in which luxury is the result of—rather than a substitute for—genuinely superior design and craftsmanship.

Providing something life commonly denies the perfectionist: Vindication, instead of disappointment.

THE ULTIMATE DRIVING MACHINE.

sports does the same, though on a lesser scale. The Olympic Games challenge sinews and spirit, often in excruciating ways.

Dressage, that sport of guiding horses through classical movements, was closed to women until 1952. Such rules were not only primitive, they were cruel. (As my own daughter once demonstrated to me in the Canadian Rockies, women sometimes ride more skillfully than men.) In 1944, Lis Hartel, one of Denmark's foremost women riders, awoke on a September morning with a headache and a stiff neck. Within a few days physicians made the diagnosis. Polio. To make matters more trying, Mrs. Hartel, 23, was pregnant.

*G*old-medal pistol-shooter Karoly Takacs of Hungary perfected shooting with his left hand after his right was destroyed by a grenade in 1938

Paralysis spread through her body, but in time she was able to give birth to a healthy daughter. After that, under the guidance of physiotherapists, she learned to crawl and finally to walk with crutches. In those days before the Salk vaccine, recovery from polio was an act of continuous discipline and determination. The muscles most severely affected often became useless. The patient—and Lis Hartel was a patient before she could hope to become an Olympian—was taught to substitute surviving muscles for the ones that were destroyed. No one who has seen that teaching process is likely to forget it.

The victim struggles awkwardly, as though wading in a bog, merely to ambulate across a room. The process repeats a hundred times, a thousand times. The therapist calls out the names of the muscles that have to be re-educated. The therapy is as harsh as dressage can be graceful.

At length Lis Hartel made a limited recovery. Then she decided she would ride again. In the 1952 Games at Helsinki she had to be helped to mount a horse called Jubilee. Nine years after she felt the first symptoms of polio, Lis Hartel won a silver medal. The gold medalist, Henri Saint Cyr of Sweden, helped her onto the platform for the presentation. Many who were in Finland for the Summer Games say they can remember no more moving moment.

Often courage is invisible from the grandstands. Joe Frazier, born in the coastal plains of South Carolina, won the Olympic heavyweight boxing championship at Tokyo in 1964. Frazier later grew renowned as a professional world champion, onrushing—"smokin'" he called it—with an attack powered by punishing left hooks. He was more a brawler than a stylist but his three fights against Muhammad Ali are respected as classics of modern boxing.

Frazier was working as a butcher at the Cross Meat Packing Company of Philadelphia when he made the Olympic team, a backup to big Buster Mathis. While the two fought an exhibition at an Air Force base, Mathis landed a right hand on Frazier's skull and broke a finger. The finger had to be placed in a cast—and Mathis missed the Tokyo Games.

"I didn't think I'd even get to fight in the Olympics," Frazier says. "I was mostly afraid I'd lose my job in Philadelphia and I didn't exactly have extra money back then. But after Mathis got hurt, they didn't have no choice. There was one heavyweight left, and that was me."

In those years, the Philadelphia Phillies, long ignominious as the Phutile Phils, began assembling ball clubs that were good enough to give fans hope. They were not, however, quite good enough to win a pennant. On the way to Tokyo, Frazier got a message from his wife and sisters: "Don't let us down, like the Phillies." That is not a classic Homeric war cry, but Frazier says the words helped him keep going.

He won two fights by knockouts, then took on a large Russian named Vadim Yemelyanov. Frazier twice knocked down Yemelyanov with left hooks. Driving for a knockout, he threw another hook that landed heavily. Pain flared from his hand up his left arm. He had fractured his thumb. Frazier says the pain was so intense at that moment that he could not have delivered another punch. He did not have to. Soviet seconds threw a white towel into the ring. The fight was stopped at 1:59 of the second round.

Frazier told the team physician that his hand was sore, but not injured enough to warrant X-rays. "I'd gone all that way," he said to sportswriter Phil Pepe, "and I couldn't let one hand pull me back. I'd seen what happened to Mathis. I figured, if I didn't take the gold medal, I'd have to forget professional fighting."

In the final, Frazier, using only one hand, fought a German named Hans Huber. It was neither an artful fight nor a very good brawl, but Frazier won it minus his best weapon. He won it on guts and a mediocre right. The Cross Meat Packing Company had lost one hard-working young butcher for good.

Sometimes courage, beyond victory over the immediacy of pain, spans a young life. Wilma Glodean Rudolph, the fifth of eight children born to a porter and a domestic worker, knew much of the illness, the deprivation, the naked struggle to exist that was for many years the lot of Southern blacks. When she sprinted her way to three gold medals at Rome in 1960, *The New York Times* described her as a lady of "charm and poise." She emerged as a gracious, sporting champion.

Some long-legged runners appear to glide. Watching them you miss the fierce effort of a sprint and observe instead the athlete's grace, as you do with certain birds in flight. Wilma Rudolph moved in a gliding way, but effort was a touchstone of her person.

She entered the world on June 23, 1940 in St. Bethlehem, Tenn., before the family moved to Clarkesville. Corn and tobacco

continued

Earth's First Quencher

Naturally Salt-Free *

Official mineral water of our
U.S. Olympic Team and the 1984 Olympic Games

Fighting toward an Olympic gold in 1964, Joe Frazier ignored the pain of a fractured thumb to win the heavyweight title

Robert Peak Jr.; inset: Wide World Photos

country. The Rudolph household included 14 siblings from her father's former marriage. That made for a very full house of 22 offspring.

Wilma weighed four-and-a-half pounds at birth and her parents said there was a period when they doubted that she could survive. At the age of four she contracted, successively, double pneumonia, scarlet fever and polio. She lost the use of her left leg after the sicknesses. For two years she had to be taken weekly to a clinic in Nashville before she improved to a point where she could limp about in a special shoe and a brace.

That is scarcely a childhood designed to encourage a girl toward anything more strenuous than sewing, but Wilma worked and willed her body back to health. When she was 11, one of her brothers set up a backyard basket. "After that," her mother said, "it was basketball, basketball, basketball. Whenever I'd call her in to clean up around the house, she'd be out in the yard, having herself a time."

After years of illness, good coordination came slowly to Wilma. When she was 13 and dribbling a basketball she managed to stumble, trip on the ball and land in a skinny tangle at a coach's feet. "A skeeter," the coach called her, using the Southern term for the annoying bug. "You're fast, you're little and you always get in my way." Seven years later, all speed and grace, Skeeter Rudolph won her three Olympic medals.

The roster of courageous Olympians runs long. Al Oerter, the first man to throw a discus 200 feet, won gold medals in four consecutive Olympics, from 1956 through 1968. He has continued to scale the ancient plate past his 40th birthday, a geriatric wonder in the foreshortened careers of athletes. Along the way Oerter has survived an injury compilation that would make the eyes of a young orthopedist gleam. Miscellaneous damages from an automobile accident. A pinched nerve in his neck, a specially punishing variety of agony for a discus thrower. A torn adductor muscle, which runs inside the thigh, and ripped cartilages in his rib cage. You would expect Oerter to tell interviewers not much more than, "Ouch." Instead he says, "There is something about the Games that gets into your blood."

An athlete in almost any sport looks out upon confusing possibilities: pain, humiliation, glory. The late Branch Rickey, discoursing on the role fear plays in sport, suggested that a professional ballplayer's greatest fear is not the hard, fast-moving baseball that thins Little League ranks so quickly. "Major leaguers are beyond that," Rickey said. "They *have* to get beyond that, or they won't reach the major leagues. The fear that I observe is something else. Fear of failure. Fear of looking ridiculous—in front of your teammates, the fans, the manager. And that fear is a very considerable thing."

"Choking" is the American colloquialism for surrendering to this fear. The symptoms are trembling hands, a dry mouth—and defeat. If there ever was an Olympic team with an excuse to choke, it was the 1980 U.S. hockey team. That it did

not choke against the slicker, more mature, faster Soviets is a glory of the modern Games. It is a story too often told to bear repeating, but it is not a story that fades.

Sports test you. They test your body, your mind, your being, and of all the athletes I have known, the one who stood up most dramatically against all tests was Jackie Robinson. Jack was extraordinary at almost every sport he tried: basketball, football, golf, Ping-Pong, track. He probably would have been an Olympic long jumper if World War II had not intervened. As it was, his great fame came when he was chosen by Branch Rickey's Brooklyn Dodgers to become the first black player in modern organized baseball.

It is difficult to imagine today, when blacks are major league managers and presidential candidates, but Robinson's appearance in a Brooklyn uniform drew terrible fire from old armories of hate. He had to hear a lexicon of gutter words. White pitchers threw at his head. White baserunners hurled their spikes at his legs.

In William Faulkner's term, Jack did not merely survive. He prevailed. At first he was under orders of restraint, but later he responded with fiery counterattacks. The hate persisted. His 10 years in the major leagues were as battering a gauntlet as any modern athlete has ever run.

Death came to Robinson at the age of 53 after a long, disabling illness. A combination of diabetes and high blood pressure severely damaged his legs, his kidneys, his retinas. Each time I saw him in his later years, he was a little more hobbled, a little less able to see. But he did not give in. He did not complain. He did not retreat.

A few months after Jack's funeral, I found myself sitting with Carl Erskine, the fine old Dodger pitcher, in Erskine's hometown of Anderson, Ind. We were talking seriously about serious things and Erskine asked me how Jack took the approach of death.

"The same way he took life," I said. "Heroically."

Erskine thought for a time. Then he said, "Do you think surviving all the terrible things he had to survive in baseball prepared him? Do you think going through all that in sports made him better able to face death?"

Now *I* was left to think, of sports and athletes, pain and frustration, and boundless courage, that beckoning white plume. I mark as one of my more sensible moments a time of silence.

For I would not presume to answer Erskine's question. ∎

THE QUEST

Some would not make it
to the victory stand.
Some would not make it
to the Games. But as
they worked to
exhaustion in 1984, each
of these top athletes
from around the world
had a chance for a
medal and the
dedication to sacrifice
for a dream

*BEST OF U.S.
men's gymnasts,
Mitch Gaylord
does handstand
on the rings.*

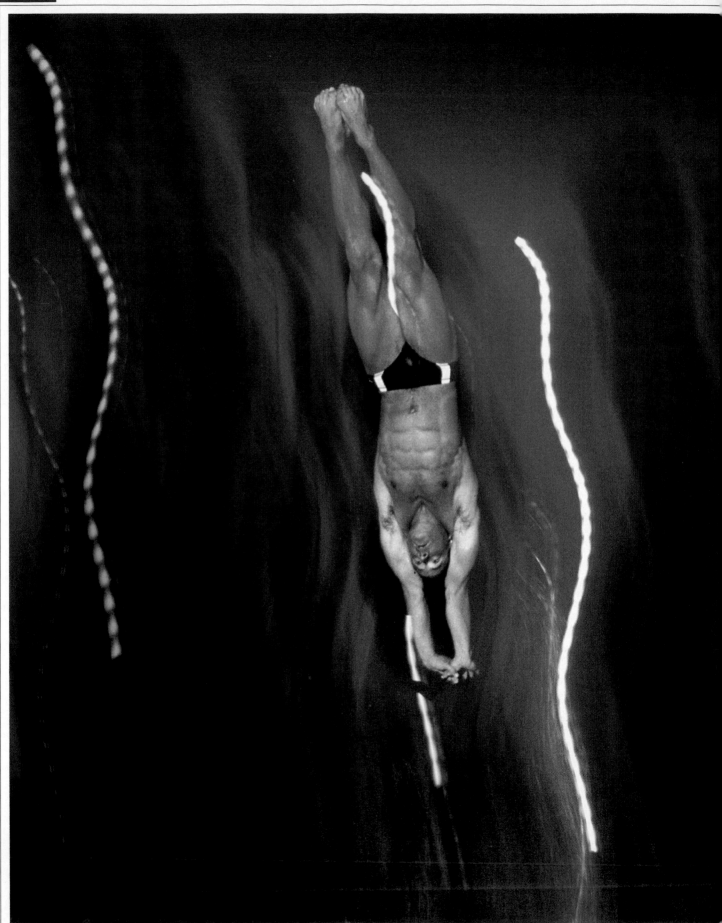

A *champion's dive to perfection, a Chinese jumper's victory lap, one runner's exotic workout in the wilds*

DIVING WITH flair, Greg Louganis of the U.S. aims for a double at the Games.

HIGH JUMPER Zhu Jianhua of China twice celebrated record leaps last year.

DISTANCE runner Zola Budd, 18, here in her native South Africa, moved to England to make an Olympic bid.

EDWIN MOSES, on the following pages, has dominated 400m hurdles since 1976.

*T*he uphill training grind in England, a prayerful reaction to a long leap, bursting around a turn to the finish

ABOVE THE River Thames, Sebastian Coe trains for another gold.

© Mark Shearman

CARL LEWIS, waiting for the measurement, prays his long jump is a record one.

SPRINTER Evelyn Ashford, the fastest in the U.S. at 100 and 200 meters, here takes the relay lead.

Walter Iooss Jr.

Britain's Daley Thompson defends his decathlon title

A CHARISMATIC
CONTRADICTION

He is on his nation's honors list with this medal and competes to become the best decathlete ever

By
Dick
Schaap

DALEY THOMPSON IS A fiercely private extrovert. He is also a truly modest braggart. He is, in other words, the ideal man for the decathlon, the most contradictory of track and field disciplines. The decathlon, combining ten different events in two days of competition, stresses speed one moment, strength the next, then spring, then stamina. A perfect decathlete would have to be both short and tall, wiry and massive. Daley Thompson, who comes as close to perfection as any decathlete has ever come, is neither short nor tall, wiry nor massive. He is, at 6′1″ and 190 pounds, a very sturdy, handsome and charismatic contradiction within a contradiction.

Thompson, who is both black and British, the London-born son of a Scottish mother and a Nigerian father, will celebrate his 26th birthday the week before he defends his Olympic decathlon championship in Los Angeles. He will, soon afterward, celebrate his tenth anniversary as a decathlete. "I've always thought that everybody can be good at something," Thompson says, "and it's just a matter of finding it. Most people don't find the thing they're good at till it's too late. I happened to find it when I was sixteen."

How good is Thompson at the thing he found? The best ever.

From 1978 right up to the brink of the 1984 Olympics, he did not lose a decathlon competition. His victories included the Olympic championship in Moscow in 1980 and the first world championship in Hel-

sinki in 1983, and on three separate occasions, he broke the world record. In his four strongest events, he has sprinted 100 meters in fewer than 10.4 seconds, pole-vaulted higher than 17 feet, high-jumped above seven feet and long-jumped farther than 26½ feet, and as impressive as those statistics are, it is far more impressive to watch Daley Thompson in action. He

brings to mind the most regal thoroughbred, the most graceful panther. He doesn't run, he prances, yet at full speed. His whole body shouts athlete.

Although he's been called the greatest athlete in the world, Thompson doesn't think so. "I'm probably just the world's best decathlete at the moment," he says, "and at every competition, there's the possibility that might change." So much for the modest side of Daley Thompson. He also says, of the decathlon competition, "Everybody *thinks* they might win, or *hopes* they might win, but there's always one guy who toes the line and *knows* he's going to win."

"Do you *always* know you're going to win?" I ask, falling into the trap.

Thompson winks and laughs. "So far so good, Dick," he says.

Considering how good he is, and how glib, it is remarkable how little known Thompson is in the United States. But obscurity is common among decathletes, especially between Olympics. And the condition is certain to be remedied, in Thompson's case, during the Los Angeles Games. Barring catastrophe, Thompson promises, he will deliver "*the* performance of the Games" and become the second man to win two Olympic decathlon championships. (Bob Mathias, in 1948 and 1952, was the first.) Then, Thompson says, in 1988 in Seoul, in honor of his 30th birthday, he will become the first man to win *three* Olympic decathlons.

Thompson has no problem remaining in the decathlon long enough to collect three

The Spirit of Excellence

It is the essence of the Olympic idea. The world's finest athletes striving to be the very best at what they do.

General Motors salutes these outstanding men and women—not only for the determined ability of those who will wear the gold, but for the dedication of all who take up the challenge.

They are all winners.

For theirs is the spirit of excellence.

Chevrolet • Pontiac • Oldsmobile
Buick • Cadillac • GMC Truck

Thompson, who has run 100 meters under 10.4 seconds, pushed himself for five or six hours in daily Olympic workouts.

gold medals because he competes at a time when amateur athletics is a profitable profession. His income probably does not approach that of, say, Carl Lewis or Mary Decker or Sebastian Coe, but it is in six figures. He hosts a television fitness show, turns his chest and feet into billboards for Adidas in Europe and does "adverts," commercials, for Lucozade, a British soft drink that is supposed to be good for anything that ails you, and Brut, the Fabergé line of men's toiletries. Thompson is the athletic spokesman for Brut in Britain, as is Joe Namath in the U.S., and for precisely the same reason: He is a symbol of boldness, of skill and of extraordinary appeal to the opposite sex.

The similarities between Namath and Thompson go beyond the qualities that sell after-shave lotion. The two men share sly senses of humor, each willing to mock his own image, his own ego. I ask Daley if he has improved his technique in his weaker events, and he says, "You mean, the other nine?" Or, outlining his training schedule, Thompson says, straightfaced, "I'm going to practice the long jump this afternoon. Just the landing."

Or, recalling his earlier training, Thompson says, "I was a real ass. I used to not even talk to guys I was training with."

"But you would always talk to the girls," I remind him.

ABC Television's Dick Schaap also contributed the article on the lighter side of the Olympic Games, "Did You Hear the One About' " on page 282.

"Hey," Daley says. "I said I was an ass. I didn't say I was a complete fool."

In the middle of the interview, he turns on me suddenly, out of nowhere, and says, "Are you still snorting coke? Your nose looks terrible."

"I have to," I lie. "To talk to athletes. In order to be on their level."

Thompson laughs. "Well, that's the only thing you have in common," he says.

Daley himself disdains drugs. "If you start taking drugs," he says, "you never know how good you are. It might be just how good your chemist is, and that would tarnish everything." Less seriously, he adds, "Most drugs, I'm told, get you to work harder, and the last thing I want to do is work harder."

Thompson's sense of humor can be misinterpreted. I ask him, for instance, about the latest injury to a mutual acquaintance, Steve Cram, Britain's brilliant middle-distance runner, and Daley says, "I hope he doesn't get better."

"Why not?"

Thompson beams. "Because then I'll be the only British gold medalist," he says, clasping his hands over his head like a winning boxer.

Daley is kidding. He likes Cram, wants him to be healthy and to win, but he can't resist a joke. He wouldn't dare crack the same joke, however, in front of British reporters. He fears he would end up in bold tabloid headlines: DALEY GLOATS WHILE STEVE SUFFERS. Thompson does not trust the British press, which has a reputation for glorifying British athletes, then, when

those athletes fail to live up to exorbitant hopes, pounding on them, skewering them. So far, the British press has been unable to fault Daley for failure. Reporters have attacked his personality, his social life.

When he and his longtime girl friend broke up last year, the British tabloids tripped all over themselves trying to get her to sell the inside story of the relationship. She refused. She is a lovely and sensitive young woman who even now has great feeling for Daley. She knows his virtues, knows his flaws, one of which she revealed to me: The current version of the world's greatest athlete can't lift a spider or a daddy longlegs. "At home, he wouldn't touch them," she said. "I had to remove them, but I wasn't allowed to kill them. I had to pick them up and put them outside."

She also recalled the time they were on a safari in Kenya, sleeping in a small tent in separate cots, and she heard very heavy breathing. "Is that you, Daley?" she said.

"I thought it was you," he said.

"Shouldn't you see what it is?" she said.

"I'm not opening my eyes," said Thompson.

She got up and saw the head of a water buffalo outlined against the tent. "There are water buffalo outside the tent," she said.

Daley responded immediately. He retreated deeper under his blanket. That's probably not the sort of inside story the scandal sheets were looking for.

Thompson did create a mild scandal a few years ago when he won an award as

continued

the outstanding athlete in Britain. He was invited to a dinner to receive the award and was told that dress for the occasion was informal. To Thompson, informal meant jeans and a T shirt. Everyone else wore three-piece suits, shirts and ties, and when a microphone was thrust in front of him, and he was asked how he felt, Daley, clearly out of place, responded, live, on national television, "I really do feel like . . . ."

The reaction was understandable.

"A few people died," Thompson says, "but my friends loved it."

Thompson is fanatically loyal to his friends. "I would rather have pizza with my friends," he says, "than steak with anyone else." When he is invited for steak, or for lobster and smoked salmon at one of the fancy hospitality tents during the tennis championships at Wimbledon, he brings his friends along, shares the good life with them. Often, he brings Clifford (Snowy) Brooks, a former decathlete who is now a professional bodybuilder, or Doreen Rayment, a woman whom Daley calls "my auntie." A small but energetic woman with grown sons of her own, Doreen is not really Daley's aunt. She was a friend of his mother's, and when Daley graduated from boarding school at 17, determined to devote himself to athletics, and his mother refused to encourage him, Doreen encouraged him. He moved into her home, and she became, in effect, mother, cook, social secretary, friend and cheerleader. She cheered for Daley in Moscow and Helsinki, and she will cheer for him in Los Angeles. The bond is special. "She's always on my side," Thompson says, with obvious affection, "if I'm right or wrong."

Doreen happens to be white, just as Daley's mother is, just as his former girl friend is, just as most, but not all, of his friends are. Race hardly ever enters into Daley's thinking, which dismays some black activists in Britain who feel Thompson could, and should, do more for blacks. But he is not a Muhammad Ali. He has great difficulty in thinking in terms of color. Thompson went to a boarding school at which he was the only black student. "Has it had much effect on you," I asked him recently, "being black?"

"Am I black?" Daley glanced at his skin, then let out a scream as if he had never realized his color before. He had to be funny first, but then he turned serious. "Some people say I should stand up for black kids," he said, "but if I'm going to stand up for any group, why can't I just stand up for kids in general? I've never considered myself either black or white."

One of Thompson's newer friends is an American decathlete named John Crist. They met in competition in Europe, and Daley saw that Crist had considerable natural ability, and several weaknesses. "Why don't you come to England and spend a few weeks with me?" the Olympic champion suggested to the little-known American. "I've got a coach who could help you." Crist was amazed. "I'd never had an opponent offer to help me like that," he said. Crist accepted Daley's invitation, went to England and the friendship flourished.

During the year leading up to the Olympics, Thompson and Crist trained together

Striving to improve his pole-vault high of over 17 feet, Thompson hopes to deliver "the performance" of the L.A. Games.

in Southern California, at the University of California in Irvine, prodding each other, encouraging each other, advising each other. Their skill levels were markedly different, but Thompson never played the star, never acted condescending. He gave advice, and he listened, too, and when Crist competed in a decathlon early in the spring, Thompson was more nervous than if he were competing himself.

Thompson knows he's *good*, but doesn't think he's *special*, and that may be what makes him, among athletes, so special. In a restaurant, he seems embarrassed if he is recognized, but he is not at all embarrassed to hold a friend's baby, and to toss the baby in the air for half an hour, till Thompson pleads fatigue, the great strength drained, temporarily, from his arms. A few days later, when he wins a pole-vaulting competition, he hands his medal to the baby. She tosses it on the ground, and Daley laughs.

Thompson, like Namath, may not take life, or himself, very seriously. But Namath, despite his image, spent much more time studying football-game films than anatomy, and Thompson subscribes to the same work ethic. In Irvine, aiming at the Olympics, Daley worked out five or six hours every day, seven days a week, expanding and refining his skills. After one particularly grueling stretch this spring, Thompson says, "I sat down and said to myself, 'No one in the world could work as hard as I've worked in the past 10 days.' "

Yet a few days later, during another workout, he pushed himself beyond exhaustion, then collapsed on the grass, gasping for breath for perhaps 10 minutes. "It felt like I was giving birth," he said. He was sharing a house with several other athletes on the beach at San Juan Capistrano, but the house wasn't his home, the training field was. The training field was his home, his office, his retreat, the center of his life. He thought of the decathlon when he drove to the field each day; he thought of the decathlon when he drove away. In between, he drove himself. "I hate to work so hard," he said. "It hurts so much. But it hurts even more not to hurt."

But Thompson refused to allow a cameraman from ABC Sports, shooting an "Up Close and Personal" feature, to take pictures of him looking tired, looking pained. "I don't want anybody to know how difficult this is," he insisted. "If they knew, nobody would want to do the de-

continued

cathlon." A more reasonable explanation is that Daley does not want his rivals to see how hard he works. He would prefer that they think the decathlon is a lark for him. He wants to project an image of invincibility, and of indefatigability.

In fact, the decathlon itself, the two days of competition, *is* a lark for Thompson, far easier than his training. "The actual decathlon is the most fun thing you can do," he says. "Physically, it's pretty simple. The hard thing is the mental thing, to get yourself to try to reach the highest level you've ever reached in every event. You're not going to be able to do that, of course, but you can't let up. You've got to do better than the other fellows *think* you can."

Thompson has worked that psychological ploy to perfection on the man who figures to be his chief rival in Los Angeles, Jürgen Hingsen. "Hollywood," as Thompson likes to call the striking 6′ 7″, 225-pound West German, is, on paper, a more gifted decathlete than Thompson. With the Olympics two months away, Hingsen held the world record, a record he set, significantly, in a meet Thompson did not enter. In eight head-to-head confrontations, including the 1983 world championship—a meet Thompson entered with only three weeks of training after nursing a pulled groin muscle—Hingsen has never beaten Thompson, a fact Daley will not forget when the Olympics begin. He suspects Hingsen will not forget it, either.

"I think it makes him feel, or I hope it makes him feel," Thompson says, "that whatever he does, it's not going to make any difference."

"How does he look at you?" I ask.

"I hope he's envious."

"Do you see fear in his eyes, psychological fear?"

"I don't know."

"Do you look at him?"

"Of course. I look at him often. But, it's funny, we look at each other often, but we never see each other looking at each other. I mean, he always looks when I'm not looking. But I know he's looking."

Thompson stops and laughs. "I know the answer to your question," he says. "But I'm not going to tell you. I'll tell you after. *After.*"

During each of his major decathlon competitions in recent years, Daley has shared a room with a British discus thrower named Richard Slaney, a gentle giant, and even though in the past year Slaney has become, on a more regular basis, Mary Decker's roommate, Daley hopes to bor-

row him back for the Olympics. Thompson needs an experienced, understanding roommate for the night between the first five decathlon events and the final five.

"I go straight home as quickly as I can," Thompson says, "and I have a quick something to eat, and then I sit down and think first about what's gone on and then about what's going to go on. Then I get about an hour's sleep, and then I start thinking again about what's gone on and what's going to go on.

"And I know that no matter what happens, in the middle of the night I can start talking to Richard and he'll always be awake because he knows I'm going to talk to him so there's no sense in going to sleep. And we just chat away for an hour or so, and then I go back to sleep, and he stays awake in case I wake up again. At the end of the two days, Richard looks terrible."

In his bid for a second Olympic championship, Daley Thompson was doing *almost* everything to prepare himself mentally and physically for the most important competition of his life, except one thing. Unlike his tennis-playing friend, Martina Navratilova, who has made proper diet almost a fetish, Daley ignores nutrition. He split his Irvine training meals between a Del Taco drive-in and a Shakey's pizza parlor. On Monday nights, he never passed up Shakey's all-you-can-eat-for-$3.65 special. He loved the pizza with pineapple on it, with gallons of Sprite on the side. His concession to conventional wisdom was that he neither drank nor smoked.

For relaxation, Daley practiced the

standing long jump, from the edge of the patio to the beach behind his temporary home. He set the San Juan Capistrano record of almost 11 feet, marked by a small stick. He also, on occasion, played a video game called Track & Field, an electronic mini-decathlon featuring six events, instead of 10, and two competitors, one black athlete and one white. Once Daley, operating the black athlete, played against a nine-year-old white boy, and while Daley didn't mind losing all that much, he did resent the fact that on the screen, after each event, the electronic white athlete waved his hands victoriously, while the electronic black athlete hung his head. "I was useless," Thompson admitted.

He expected to do better in the Los Angeles Coliseum in August, in front of 100,000 spectators and hundreds of millions of television viewers. He realized that victory in the Coliseum would bring him recognition and wealth far beyond what he had known, and yet he insisted, convincingly, that he would not be competing for fame or fortune or for the entertainment of the crowd.

"It makes no difference to me whether there's one person there or one million, I'm not going to run any faster," Thompson said. "I don't have anything against being rich—I'd rather be rich and unhappy than poor and unhappy—but that's not why I compete. I compete because I want to be the best, and I compete at the decathlon because I am the best. And I wouldn't give that up—that particular feeling—I wouldn't give that up for anything." ∎

"I compete because I want to be the best," says Thompson, and he is already in a class with the best high jumpers in the world.

Douglas Kirkland/Sygma

U.S. boxer Mark Breland coolly eyes a knockout career

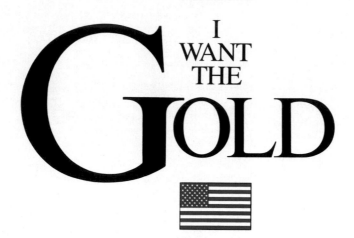

I WANT THE GOLD

"I don't think about pressure— it's just me and the other guy and he might keep me from getting what I want"

By
Pete
Hamill

IN THE DAMP BROOKLYN mornings, the young man runs among the wooded hills of Prospect Park. He's a tall, lean figure in a dark blue sweatsuit, and usually he runs with a few friends. They stay on the rich black earth of the horse trails, and for several years, in all seasons, this is the way they've begun their days. The others subtly defer to the lean young man. Sometimes he turns and runs backwards for 100 yards, firing sudden bursts of punches at the air. He runs five miles each morning, until the sweat begins to blister his face, and although the horse trails go in an endless circuit through the 526 acres of the city park, the true finish line is more than 3,000 miles away. For this young man is Mark Breland and his destination is Los Angeles.

"Everything comes down to this," he says. "All the running, all the training, all the boxing, everything. It all ends up at the Olympics. We yell at each other in the park, 'For the gold, man! For the gold!' We know what's up there over the hill."

Mark Breland is probably the best amateur fighter in the United States. In over 100 amateur fights, the 6′ 3″ welterweight has lost only once. He has knocked out 70 of his opponents, and in March he won his fifth consecutive New York Golden Gloves championship, a record unequalled in the 58 years of that tournament. In those five Golden Gloves tournaments, he faced 22 opponents, knocked out 20 of them, 14 in the first round. In 1982, he won solid decisions over two of the toughest opponents he might have faced in the Olympics: Can-

delario Duvergel of Cuba and Serik Konakbaev of the Soviet Union. His home in Brooklyn is crammed with medals and trophies from other contests. He is cool, poised, confident.

"I don't even think about losing," he said one day this spring. "I just want to get in there and do what I do best. What I've been doing all my life."

That life began on May 11, 1963, when

Breland was born in the Bedford-Stuyvesant section of Brooklyn. There were five brothers and sisters, two of whom still live at home, as does Mark. His father, Herbert, is a roofing and construction worker, who was born in Harlem, but raised in Allendale, S.C. His mother, Luemisher, was born in Denmark, S.C., and is a nursing-home attendant.

"They're good people," Breland said. "They work very hard, they raised me right. In that neighborhood, some kids were not raised right, and they paid the consequences."

The family was living in the Tompkins Houses, a housing project on Brooklyn's Park Avenue, when Mark Breland first put on gloves. At seven, he went to the first Muhammad Ali–Joe Frazier fight with an elderly neighbor and, betting against his friend, picked Ali to win. He also predicted to the old man that even if Ali lost to Frazier, Ali would go on to win the world championship. Breland lost the bet when Frazier floored and defeated Ali, but the second part of the prediction came true.

"I remember the excitement that night," Breland says. "I'd never been anyplace so exciting, seen anything so exciting, in my life."

As so many other kids did in those years, Breland began sparring with friends outside his home, imitating Ali's moves and styles. Upstairs in the Tompkins Houses, there lived a professional fighter named Kevin Isaac. He let some of the boys try sparring with boxing gloves. And Isaac saw immediately that Breland had a

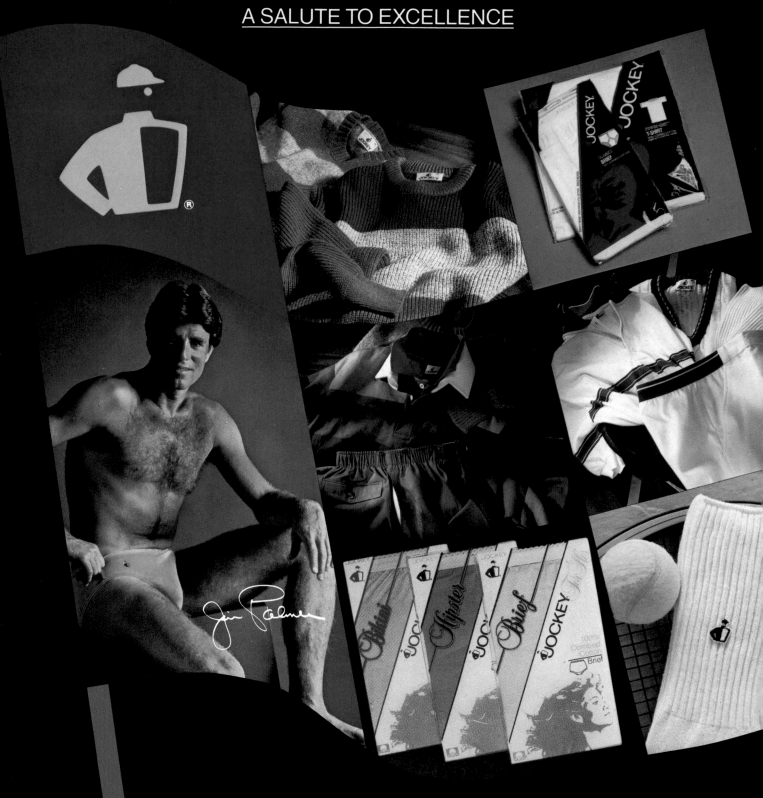

Breland (right) moves in with a style modeled on Sugar Ray Robinson— "He's my graduate school."

gift. He urged the boy to go to a real gym, and Mark Breland, age 9, first walked into a place called the Broadway Gym.

"In a gym, kids come and go," says trainer George Washington, a rotund man who had been the Armed Forces heavyweight champion of the Pacific theater during World War II, and later was a sparring partner for Joe Louis. "Some want to lose weight. Some want to get even with some bully. Some want to show off. Some think they can be bad, or *badder*. But most of them don't stay around. Most of them don't have it, the moves, the intelligence. Or the heart. Mark stayed around."

He started in a series of street tournaments organized by Madison Square Garden to keep kids out of trouble during the hot city summers. Washington soon realized that Breland had "the makings." He spent time with the young man, teaching him the fundamentals: the jab, the hook, the straight right hand. "I didn't try to make him something he wasn't," Washington says. "You have to watch a fighter, see what he does naturally, then refine that."

What Breland did naturally was knock people out with his right hand. In 1979, when he was 16 and a student at Eastern District High School, Breland entered his first tournament, knocking out Everett Copeland in one round in the finals of the national Junior Olympics. The following

---

Pete Hamill, who writes for the New York Daily News, *is the author of six novels and a number of screenplays. The hero of his novel* Flesh and Blood *was a boxer.*

---

year, he won the first of his five Golden Gloves championships, flattening Angel Garcia in one round to become the 139-pound sub-novice champion.

"The thing you've gotta remember is that he was always learning," Washington says. "If you showed him something, and he couldn't do it, he'd keep trying until he could. The best fighters are also the smartest. They think, they anticipate, they learn from mistakes. No real dummy was ever a great fighter."

Breland was also looking at films of other fighters, and learning from them. "Roberto Duran was great," Breland says. "I don't fight like him, but he's so smart, so good. And Ali, of course. But then George showed me Robinson. That was the greatest."

Today, Breland continues to study videotapes of Sugar Ray Robinson's fights with Carmen Basilio, Gene Fullmer, Jake LaMotta and Randy Turpin. "Robinson doesn't know it, but he's my teacher. I've learned more from him than from anyone. Doubling the hook. Hooking off the jab. How to set a guy up with the jab, sucker him in, bring him at you, then knock him out while you're backing up. I'd say about 20 percent of my knockouts, I scored them while I was backing up. But Robinson was also thinking in there, he was seeing what the guy was doing, he was cool, he could box or punch. He's my graduate school."

When the Broadway Gym closed, a new gym opened on Sumner Avenue, a few blocks from Breland's home. It is called the Bedford-Stuyvesant Boxing Association,

and George Washington is its resident professor. It's also Breland's second home. One afternoon this spring, Breland arrived at the gym with his friend, 26-year-old Yoel Judah, the U.S. Professional Karate Association lightweight champion. Judah was carrying a ghetto blaster, and turned it on full volume in the area of the gym where about a dozen fighters were shadowboxing in front of full-length mirrors. And while singers Shannon, Lionel Richie and Rick James performed on a tape (which Breland had made at home), Breland made an imaginary fight for three rounds: He jabbed, backed up, fired the right hand; he threw a volley of punches at an imaginary opponent who was crowding him; he set up patterns, then varied them, never missing a beat. After this warmup, he strapped on headgear and gloves and went into the ring.

"I haven't worked out for two weeks," he explained. "Since the last tournament. So I'm taking it a little easy."

Taking it easy meant boxing six hard rounds against a 16-year-old amateur light heavyweight named Riddick Bowe. George Washington watched, shouting instructions to Bowe, but not to Breland. "Hands up, comin' out. Hands up! Keep that chin down . . . now!" Bowe was willing, and had 30 pounds on Breland, but he was really a sparring partner. When he closed with Breland, the lighter man ripped hooks and right hands to the body; when he boxed at long range, the Breland jab whipped out and jolted his head back.

continued

Introducing the *1985*

Ninety Eight Regency

Precise road management engineered in a luxury automobile.

High-tech engineering, luxury for six. That's the new Ninety-Eight Regency Brougham. Each wheel has its own independent suspension to give you a smooth, controlled ride. You feel the road, but not the bumps.

A spirited new 3.8 liter multi-port fuel injected engine is standard on Brougham models. A fuel metering system precisely regulates fuel for optimum performance. An optional electronic instrument panel for precise read-outs is available after June, 1984. Even a voice information

Four-Wheel Independent Suspension

3.8L Multi-Port Fuel Injected Engine

system and auto calculator can be added to give you additional assists while driving. An electronic load leveler automatically keeps your Ninety-Eight level, with varying passenger or trunk loads.

Electronic Instrument Panel

This Ninety-Eight also features a new 3-year/36,000-mile, limited new-car warranty. A deductible may apply. See your dealer for details and a test drive.

Some Oldsmobiles are equipped with engines produced by other GM divisions, subsidiaries or affiliated companies worldwide. See your dealer for details.

Electronic Load Leveler

There is a special feel in an *Oldsmobile*

But an observer saw some of Breland's weaknesses. He pulls back from punches in Ali-style, instead of bending under them, and this often leaves him out of punching position and vulnerable to leaping hooks. He carries his left hand low, as Robinson often did, but still doesn't cover his chin completely with the left shoulder or the right glove. The result: He can be hit with right hands. And while most fighters are taught to keep the chin clamped tightly to the chest, Breland's chin hangs out in a way that alarms some traditional boxing people.

"Someone is going to drop one on his chin," said former light heavyweight champion Jose Torres, who won a silver medal at the Melbourne Olympics in 1956. "Then we'll see if he's a champion. He's an amazing amateur. But he can't hang that chin out like that with the pros. And some guys in the Olympics are virtually pros."

In his more than 100 amateur fights through April, Breland had been floored five times. He got up in all those fights, and won four of them. In his only amateur loss, in 1981, he was knocked down by a fighter named Daryl Anthony, got up, rallied, but lost a split decision. The following month, he entered the National Sports Festival, hoping to get even with Anthony. But Anthony got knocked out by Darryl Robinson of Houston, and Breland had to be content with knocking out Robinson in one round to win the tournament.

"I really wanted Daryl Anthony bad," Breland says. "But I never did get the chance."

In the gym this afternoon, Breland was clearly the star attraction. Young kids drifted in from the street to watch him, alerted to his presence by the fighter's brown Datsun parked at the curb. A camera crew was there to shoot an interview. Other fighters, shadowboxing, doing their push-ups, punishing the heavy bags, glanced at Breland when he boxed. Earlier that day, walking with Breland in midtown Manhattan, I observed two people ask for his autograph. In all the years I've been around prizefighters, nobody ever asked an amateur for an autograph while I was around. Until Breland. And for many people, fame is a heavy form of pressure.

"I don't think about this kind of pressure," Breland says. "It's nice, and I'm used to it. But when I fight, it's me and the other guy. That's all. I don't care if there're 20 people watching or 20,000. It's me and him. And he might keep me from getting what I want—the Olympic gold. Then a professional career, a world championship,

a lot of money, and then out of boxing."

Breland's clarity about his goals, and his poise, have shown themselves in a number of ways. He is, for example, a talented movie actor, having starred in *The Lords of Discipline*, a movie about the first black cadet to enter a military college in the South. A Paramount Pictures casting director, Ellen Chenoweth, saw Breland's picture in a magazine article about young fighters, and invited him to read for the part. The movie people were impressed, and for four months in 1982 he worked as an actor.

"It's hard work, acting," he says. "It's not as easy as it looks. And I'd like to do some more, particularly after I'm through

An amateur welterweight with professional poise, Breland has won over 100 fights, most by knockouts.

with boxing. I'm planning to go to college after the Olympics. Take a major in business administration. But maybe acting is something to pursue, too. I don't know. First, it's the Olympics."

Part of the preparation for the Olympics was Breland's decision to train for a while at the famous Kronk Gym in Detroit. "I was running out of sparring partners," he says. "I couldn't get people to box with me I could learn from. They had them there."

When he first showed up at the Kronk, Breland sensed immediately that he would have to prove himself. "They're all warriors in that gym," he says with a smile. The first day, he was put in with the WBC welterweight champion, Milton McCrory. The professional champion moved in on Breland, pressing hard. And Breland stepped back and let his right hand go. Down went McCrory. In came the trainers. The round was over. "After that, they

respected me," Breland says. "And I was able to learn a lot."

One of his teachers at the Kronk was Tommy Hearns, a fighter Breland physically resembles. Hearns helped Breland refine his left hook, particularly to the liver; urged him to be more economical with his punches; talked with the younger man about strategy and tactics.

"He's a great fighter," Breland says of Hearns, "and a good guy. He taught me a lot."

Breland clearly enjoys his widening fame, but realizes that it has drawbacks, too. If Breland's plans work out, he will not stay in Bedford-Stuyvesant much longer.

"I've got friends here, guys I grew up with, and I don't want to lose them," he says. "There's girls, too, girls who wouldn't talk to me in school and now want to talk to me all the time." He smiles. "And I make them *suffer*." There are also people who resent Breland for his fame. He's had weird phone calls, damage done to his car, remarks made as he walked past groups of older men whose dreams were already dead. "I understand where they're coming from," he says. "But I don't have to like it. It just makes me feel bad."

But neither fame nor the resentments of strangers have changed Breland's dedication to a sport that has changed his life. Each morning he runs; every afternoon he's at the gym. A shot at Olympic gold is ahead, and after that, riches that could be vast. Asked to describe himself, he says: "Mark Breland is a young man, a fighter, a Brooklynite and hungry." He smiles in an ironic way. "Real hungry." ■

In Brazil, Hortencia rules the basketball court

THE QUEEN

She never considers failure or missing a shot — her fiery will presses the possibility away

By
Jeremy
Larner

WHEN I HEAR OF A new athletic star, I imagine a godlike being, come along to break with ease the barriers that no one else has broken. But if I get to know that individual, I'm soon impressed by a struggle which is anything but superhuman, and by the price each performer must pay, whether he knows it or not, to be what he is and do what he does.

My first news of Hortencia Maria de Fatima Marcari stirs up the old images of more than mortal powers. She has scored 36 points against the United States women's basketball team in the 1983 World Championships, then followed with 46 points against the same team in the Pan American Games a few weeks later. Further, I learn that this Brazilian phenomenon is only 5′ 8½″—and that in each game the deeper U.S. team was able to keep switching fresher, taller players to guard her. "She can shoot on anybody," says U.S. star Cheryl Miller, who has a good six inches in height on Hortencia. "She sure could shoot on me. She has to be one of the most powerful offensive players I've ever seen in my life."

And so, as the '84 Olympics approach, with Hortencia rated possibly the best woman basketball player in the world, the chance to go to Brazil and discover the real person is compelling.

My assignment takes me to a town near the Paraguayan border, 300 miles inland from São Paulo. There, Hortencia—known by her first name, as are all athletes in this sports-mad country—plays five months a year for the local club team, the Prudentinas, funded by the merchants of the town of Presidente Prudente. In a land of startling contrasts, Presidente Prudente is a long way from the hectic Brazilian cities or the poverty of the jungle and mountain areas. It is a trading center of 160,000 where TV sets and tape recorders are plentiful, and where one can't get away from American pop music, which is even piped outdoors.

The club has seen to it that Hortencia has everything she needs, including a new car, a motorcycle and a modest apartment in the town's newest, brightest little highrise building. I am taken to the apartment by Beverly Crusoe, a woman from the United States who has learned Portuguese in order to play for "Prudench."

Hortencia meets me with her wonderful flashing grin. She is a handsome young woman who moves about her apartment in white hip-hugger pants and a leopard blouse, physical and intense even in her relaxation. She talks about herself in rapid bursts of emotion. As translated by Beverly, I hear the story of a young woman who, like so many of her contemporaries, has been cut off from the traditions of her family's past. Hortencia knows her grandparents came over from Italy, but she doesn't know what section they were from or what they did. Her father was a small farmer who early in Hortencia's life moved into a nearby town to take work as a laborer. When she was 10, her family moved again, to São Paulo, a chaotic metropolis of

133

XEROX

Fortunately, the athletes at the Olympics won't be slowed down by paperwork.

The competition among the athletes at the 1984 Olympics has never been stiffer.

Team Xerox The paperwork, never as awesome. And while the world awaits its new champions, one team, Team Xerox, will be content to stay out of the limelight; quietly doing what we've done in the past. Making short work out of producing the 70 million pieces of paper the Olympics needs to function.

Xerox facsimile systems will also be busy transmitting the results worldwide.

Many new records will be set at this year's Olympics.

And some of them, we're proud to say, will be broken by Team Xerox.

OFFICIAL COPIER AND FACSIMILE SPONSOR OF THE 1984 OLYMPICS.

around eight million at the time, where Hortencia sought release through her natural talent for sports.

At first her parents tried to prevent her, feeling she was wasting time that could be better spent contributing to the family's survival. Of course, her parents didn't stand a chance—Hortencia claims they have influenced her in no way whatever. Her father before long had to leave his job and draw disability pay—but Hortencia cannot even remember what he worked at.

This admission is striking because Hortencia's father is in the room—and she does not ask him. Her parents have come in to see the big game the Prudentinas will play against their main rivals. Unlike their daughter, Hortencia's mother and father have bulky peasants' bodies. The father stands against the wall, smiling a proud and baffled smile. In the kitchen Hortencia's mother, in a shapeless print dress, stirs a country stew in a big old battered pot that sits on a modern range.

When she was 13, Hortencia began to play basketball in her school gym. At 14—11 years ago—she was spotted by Waldir Paga Perez, who was then the coach of Brazil's women's basketball team. At 15, Hortencia was playing on Brazil's national team. While she was still a teenager, she became known throughout the land as *la Rainha*, the Queen.

What Perez saw was a skinny ragamuffin who started her jump shot with the ball resting on her right shoulder. But obviously he saw more—because he insisted that the girl drop handball, track and volleyball and do nothing but play basketball. Perez changed Hortencia's shooting motion and drilled her relentlessly. "He was very hard on me," says Hortencia. "He wanted me to be a star right away." Yet she was no less hard on herself. With single-minded intensity Hortencia worked all day, every day, developing the sure grip and flawless release that soon fulfilled her coach's vision of her. Even now Hortencia shoots 600 practice shots a day, often coming back to the gym alone at night after two daily sessions with her team. "I always do more," she says. When she is not with the Prudentinas, she is playing for the Brazilian national team, which means that she has to play games every week on a year-round basis. Sponsorship by her club and by Adidas eliminates the need for another job, but

Jeremy Larner, author of Drive, He Said *and the forthcoming novel,* On Top of the World, *won an Oscar for the screenplay of* The Candidate.

Hortencia goes to town on market day in Presidente Prudente where she stars on the local club team

Miguel Rio Branco/Magnum

there is little time left for anything other than basketball. She has a serious boyfriend who is a world-class volleyball player in São Paulo, yet when Hortencia is in Presidente Prudente she can see him only two or three times a month.

When it comes time to interrupt our conversation for the Prudentinas' afternoon practice, Beverly and I travel by Beetle to the sports club; Hortencia zooms through the streets on her motorcycle. People along the sidewalks turn as she goes by, and when the Queen strides into the club lounge her court quickly gathers around her. The style is friendly raillery, and she loves it, tossing her head and flinging her hands about, responding with total body language as she returns every jibe.

When practice begins, Hortencia seems to send out shock waves each time she moves up the court. She is like the U.S. football player O. J. Simpson: Her body each time she gets the ball is charged with pure possibility. Once her moves begin, there is no telling in what direction they will continue. Usually she prefers to take the ball off a pick, near the top of the key. In heavy traffic she will do a series of pivots as she dribbles. She can explode upwards at any moment, tucking her legs beneath her at the level of an opponent's shoulders. All she needs is an inch to clear her shot. Or without warning she may blow by the opposition, and even as they leap to surround her, she will *lean* through a thicket of arms to ease the ball to the basket. Or she may with equal fluidity pass off to a teammate left in the clear.

But Hortencia reacts badly when she passes and a teammate misses a setup. She tends to scream at the other players in tight situations, unnerving them and causing them to freeze. In some ways Hortencia's temperament has suffered from her early and continuing uniqueness. For example, she will continue to fire away on an off-night, and there is no chance the coach will bring her to the bench to cool down. Hortencia supersedes her coach. When she screams, he will tell the other players they should be used to her. She has a status in her country unattainable in the United States, where there are so many great players. In every game Hortencia plays, the response of the crowd is telling her that all eyes are upon her, that it is up to her alone to carry the day or to fail.

But Hortencia doesn't consider failure. Her fiery will presses that possibility far away where it cannot affect her actions. She is ready to charge right into the most extreme situations and get up her shot, but she is not ready, finally, to miss. Losing, or falling short in any way, is very hard for Hortencia.

I see her put to the test the night the Prudentinas play their archrivals from Unimep. Between the two teams, most of Brazil's national team is on the floor—including Paula, Hortencia's main Brazilian rival, another backcourt whiz who is exactly the same height. In a previous encounter this year, Unimep beat "Prudench." With another victory tonight, the Unimep team will finish the

continued

Skill. Commitment.
Unrelenting effort.
And the indomitable
desire to excel.
These are the
qualities that make
a champion.
And make champions
a breed apart.

Merrill Lynch
Merrill Lynch. Pierce. Fenner & Smith Inc.
A breed apart.

season as the best club team in Brazil.

It seems the whole town tries to pack into the little club gym, creating among a few thousand people enough noise to fill a large American arena. At moments of emotion the fans take whatever is close at hand—cups, papers, programs, water-bombs—and throw them down on the playing floor. And as the game unfolds the fans are constantly provoked, for the international style of play is rougher and meaner than the game U.S. fans are accustomed to, and the referees more capricious and careless. It is not uncommon to see a woman player slugged in the stomach, or a man in the groin.

On this night it seems at first that "Prudench" is going to get blown off the court. Hortencia is firing and missing, while the calmer Paula drives doggedly for baskets. Hortencia pulls herself together on defense, soaring a good foot above Paula to jam a shot. But it is the American, Beverly Crusoe, who gets the team back in contention, repeatedly stealing the ball and hitting clutch shots. Before halftime, Hortencia begins to hit, too, and the Prudentinas draw well in front. At one point Hortencia dribbles through the entire Unimep team, spins full circle at the foul line, and gets off her shot as two defenders crash her. The ball goes in, but Hortencia is on the floor howling in agony. She has wrenched one of her "jumper's knees," where she has chronic tendinitis, and which are protected not by braces but by narrow bands of elastic bandages. Every time Hortencia goes down, her career might be over. But this time she gets up, and stays in the game, her face drawn and tearful as she hits the free throw and continues to play with full-out fury.

As halftime ends, Hortencia is the first player out of the locker room, taking extra shots all alone on the littered floor with her face still streaked and haggard, her dark eyes like two rivets.

But the second half goes badly. Hortencia cannot get a streak going, and slowly Unimep wears down "Prudench" with the strength of its heavier front line. Under pressure Hortencia takes over her team's offense, flinging herself down the court and into the air again and again. On defense she presses and fouls, throwing her arms out in agony, thrusting her sharp chin at the referee, holding her hands upward as if to appeal to God. With three minutes left and her team four points ahead, Hortencia fouls out. She shakes the referee's hand and stalks off, her face gone white. It is clear to everyone in the house that Unimep

can now break down the home team. Each time they get the ball, they push in close for scores. But Beverly Crusoe, in the right place all night, hits for six more points. Still pressing to tie, Unimep jams up seven offensive rebounds—and misses every one. The crowd noise is piercing beyond belief, like a sheet of white sound. Hortencia is on the edge of the court, screaming at her teammates. Finally a jump ball is called. Unimep controls the tip, but Beverly grabs the ball and in one motion wings a floor-length pass to a streaking guard. The Prudentinas win by two.

After the crowd begins to clear, I find Hortencia chatting side by side with Paula; for the moment, no one dares approach

Near São Paulo, a young admirer gets an autograph from la Rainha, as Brazilians proudly call her

these royal persons. Paula is calm; Hortencia's eyes are snapping angry. One would think the outcome of the game had been exactly otherwise. Even as reporters ask her questions, Hortencia cannot suppress an occasional sob. She is saying the right things—how pleased she is that her teammates were able to make up for what she considers an off-night, never mind her 32 points. But she cannot quickly recover from the tempest of emotion in which she plays, or forgive herself for failing to be at her greatest.

In a private interview, Paula expresses doubts that Brazil will make the final six in Los Angeles. Brazil will have to survive an elimination tournament in order to qualify for the Games. Paula's cold-blooded assessment is that Brazil lacks the up-front power and will likely be worn down by taller, more disciplined squads from Asia and Europe. Paula plays very well with

Hortencia—but she's not sure that Hortencia's knees will hold up all the way to Los Angeles.

There are experts, I learn, who agree. There is a chance Olympic fans will not set eyes on the highest flying woman basketball player.

Hortencia, however, will not accept the chance of that outcome even for a moment. She tells me she intends to be in Los Angeles, and she will not damage her effort by admitting the merest flicker of a negative thought. I am not surprised by this denial. Stardom in sports rarely comes by accident. The very few who become stars will allow themselves no such reasons. They are usually people of narrow and intense focus. They have a tremendous will to triumph that sees them through hours of boring and painful practice. Above all they will gear themselves not to accept the fact of loss until it is shoved down their throats—and if possible, not even then.

And so as I watch Hortencia limp from her small-town gym, surrounded by clamoring Brazilian children, throbbing with energy even though she is dog-tired, I do not count her out of the '84 Olympics. She will be there or collapse in the effort. I recall what her teammate Beverly said of Hortencia that very day: "She could be in big trouble when she has to quit. Being a star—it lasts for a moment, then it's over." That is the iron law that is written into Hortencia's body. She is not going to quit; she will go till she snaps, and if Brazil is at Los Angeles, hers is the demon force the world of women's basketball will have to deal with. ∎

In China, Li Ning rises as the nation's gymnastic star

TRYING THE UNTRIED

> "*He is working on movements that have never been done by gymnasts— we expect they will be a big surprise*"

By
Michael
Parks

WITH THE MESMERizing speed of a whirling dervish, Chinese gymnast Li Ning mixes sweeping leg circles, scissors movements and handstands on the pommel horse, turning a normally dull event into one of the most exciting routines in gymnastics today.

Not quite perfect, not quite fast enough, Li says to himself, catching his breath during a practice session, and then he does it again, a third time and a fourth, picking up speed and increasing the fluidity of his movements. The gym fills with the whistling sounds of Li's faster and faster twists up and down the pommel horse until he dismounts with a feather-light landing.

Li's pommel horse routine has become one of his specialties, earning him top marks in international competitions for the past two years, but Li is not satisfied with it and wants to incorporate bolder movements and do it even faster.

"Difficulty, originality—that is what I strive for," the 21-year-old Li said in an interview in Peking while he trained for the Summer Olympic Games in Los Angeles. "Originality means trying the untried, difficulty means risking the impossible.

"Gymnastics is a sport where you are always trying to push yourself to the limit and then to go beyond it. What was good enough last year will probably not be good enough this year, and it certainly will not be next year."

For superior gymnasts like Li, who took an unprecedented six of seven gold medals at the 1982 World Cup Gymnastics competition and helped the Chinese team defeat the Soviet Union at the World Gymnastics Championship last year, technical perfection is only the start, and the real competition lies in attempting ever more difficult routines.

"Li is working on movements that have never been done by gymnasts," one of his coaches, Feng Jibai, said. "He is practicing hard and will show them at the Summer Olympic Games in Los Angeles, particularly on the rings, in the floor exercises and on the pommel horse. We expect they will be a big surprise."

Li himself would only say, "In gymnastics, to stand still is to fall—you have to keep moving, keep innovating." For example, his breathtaking new floor-exercise routine starts with a double spin, double backward, tucked somersault and finishes with two tucked backward somersaults. It earned him a perfect 10 from all five judges at the Peking International Gymnastics tournament in April.

But Li has also found that what is newer and harder must still be done with the same precision and perfection achieved in old routines: In the McDonald's American Cup competition early this year in New York, a warmup for the Olympic Games, Li came in only fourth, after faltering in a handstand on the parallel bars and falling from the horizontal bar while incorporating new moves into his routines.

Underlying Li's innovations is tremendous raw courage. To do Li's swings and twists on the horizontal bar, a circus acro-

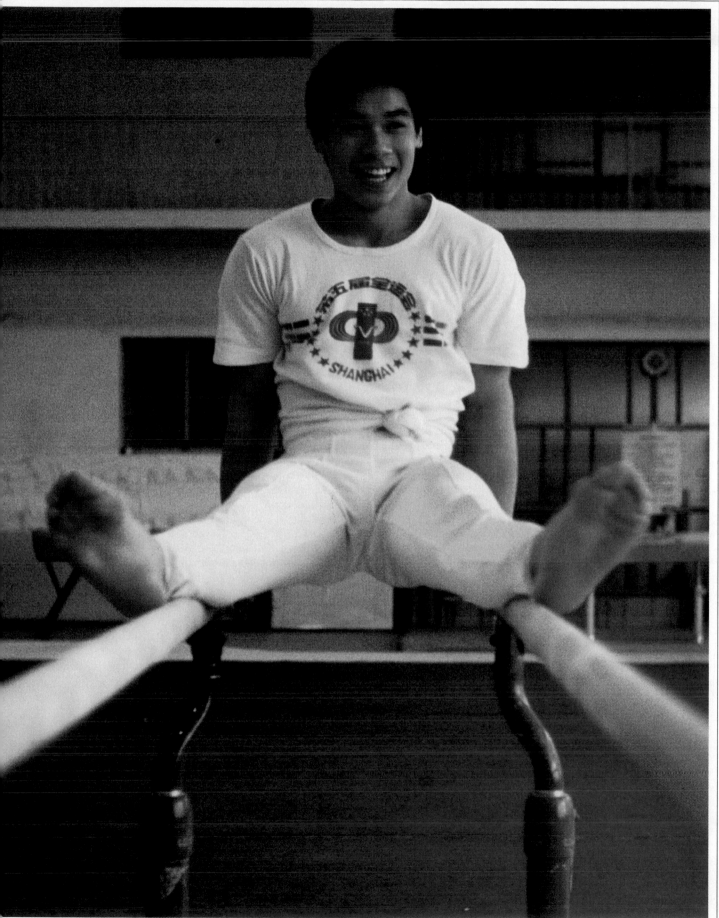

Taking large risks, Li Ning uses routines designed for the pommel horse and adapts them to the parallel bars.

James Drake

bat would probably require a safety net below. Li further increases risk by taking movements used on the pommel horse and adapting them to the parallel bars and by adapting those of the parallel bars to the higher rings. Jack Rockwell, a trainer for the U.S. men's and women's gymnastics teams, said recently, "Li Ning's courage is unmatched—he is totally fearless."

And there is the sheer virtuosity of a powerful and well trained athlete. On the rings, for example, Li uses his great arm and shoulder strength to achieve a smoothness that makes the breaks almost imperceptible and the exercise wholly elegant. In floor exercises, Li has stunned his competitors with his tumbling ability, particularly the height that his tremendous leg power gives him on his flips. On the horizontal bar and the parallel bars, where Li is weaker, it often is just a matter of a tenth of a point between him and first place.

But Li knows the gold medals that he and other Chinese gymnasts hope to bring home from their first Olympic Games will be theirs only if they overcome American competition. "One does not win an Olympic event easily," Li said in Peking. "True, Chinese gymnasts have done well in the past few years, but the sport is still not very well developed in China and we do not have as much experience as the American gymnasts."

Michael Parks is a foreign correspondent for the Los Angeles Times *and he is currently based in Peking, China.*

For most athletes, the Olympics are the peak, the goal toward which they work for a decade or even longer. That is true for Li, too, but this summer will also be an attempt at a comeback after several disappointing performances following his dramatic victory at the 1982 Sixth World Cup Gymnastics in Zagreb, Yugoslavia. He has not done quite as well since, and there is open concern here over Li's ability to pull everything together for the Olympics.

Zhang Jian, who has coached Li since 1980, recalled recently how he began to worry about his protégé after the huge success in Yugoslavia. "You have now captured six world titles, and I should congratulate you," Zhang told his new star, then 18. "But I have misgivings that it may be difficult for me to work with you in the future now that you are a world champion."

"No, no, Coach," Li replied. "I will follow your instructions just as I did before. If I do anything wrong, you must criticize me, scold me. . . ."

But Li did prove more difficult to coach, according to Zhang, and for a time became complacent about improving his routines. "He will be absolutely superb in three or four events and then slip badly in one or two," says a Chinese sportswriter who covers gymnastics. "Sometimes he is nursing an injury from training, sometimes he is just a little unsure of himself." After his 1982 triumph at Zagreb, Li was overwhelmingly chosen China's top athlete of the year, but last year he was not even in the top 10.

Li began training hard last autumn,

however, and believed he would be in his best shape yet for the Games in L.A.

"Gymnastics is not just in your body, but in your mind too," he recently said, as if he were quoting an old coach's pep talk. "I believe in confidence, calmness and, of course, blazing new trails. . . . The gymnast's motto should be, BE INVENTIVE AND DO THE DIFFICULT."

Like most Chinese athletes, tutored to credit others for their achievements, Li, although personable and widely popular here, is modest and almost reticent in talking about himself. "China has much better athletes than me," he says. He is sincere about that.

What he has achieved, Li attributes to his coaches—particularly to Liang Wenjie, who discovered him when Li was eight, and to Zhang Jian, who has prepared him in Peking for international competitions for the past four years.

"Zhang is very strict, very demanding, but that is good," Li said. "This is a sport where the goal is to reach perfection and even beyond perfection. The coach really decides on new routines, not me," he pointed out. "Of course, we talk things over—what I think I can do, what he thinks—and then experiment and practice, but the coach decides because he is the better judge."

Like most other top international gymnasts, Li now uses videotape recordings to improve his routines ("You can see exactly what you did wrong, particularly in slow motion," he says.) and includes supple-

continued

A HOT TIP FOR BETTER MILEAGE FROM MOTORCRAFT.

Motorcraft Extended Tip Spark Plugs are engineered to save gas in any properly tuned, normally driven car. As you drive, they actually burn away sooty carbon deposits that sap your car's performance and power. They're also designed to handle power surges of up to 38,000 volts — twice what your car should ever experience. For more protection and better gas mileage, get the Extended Tip Spark Plug from Motorcraft. Quality parts for all makes of cars and trucks.

Motorcraft
EXCEEDS THE NEED

35,000V

30,000V

25,000V

20,000V

15,000V

10,000V

5,000V

Get it together — buckle up.

ONCE IN EVERY
FOUR YEARS, a weary
world looks away from
familiar scenes of crisis
and conflict. For a few
short weeks, our atten-
tion shifts to a single
arena, where young ath-
letes strive to find the
best within them. And
in so doing, encourage
us to look for the best
within ourselves.

Since the first foot-
race was run on the
Elean plain twenty-seven
hundred years ago, the
example of Olympic
competition has inspired
mankind to do better,
to reach farther, to excel.

We believe that the
inspiration of the 1984
Olympic Games will
be felt by the men and
women of Southern
Pacific, as they help our
company achieve its
own goal of excellence.
And we hope it will be
remembered by all the
men and women of
the world through the
next four years, until
the Games begin again.

SOUTHERN
PACIFIC

Official sponsor for the 1984 Olympic Games

mental weightlifting in his training regimen to build up his arm and leg strength. He gets help from other Chinese gymnasts anxious to see their country do well in international competition. The ring routine that Li has made a specialty, for example, is based on movements first developed by a provincial coach.

"Chinese have a special style of competition," Li said in Peking, where he trains with Tong Fei, Lou Yun, Li Xiaoping and China's other top gymnasts. "We are very united, and we encourage each other and help each other all we can. We don't see each other as rivals, though we do compete hard against each other."

Li Ning dazzles audiences with his constant boldness. "To stand still is to fall— you have to keep moving."

Li began his training at age seven when he started primary school in Liuzhou, a medium-size industrial center in South China's Guangxi province. His father, a music teacher at the school, arranged for him to practice with its gymnastics team even though he was too young. "My father wanted to keep me out of mischief, I think, because I was always spreading the family's padded cotton quilts and other bedding on the floor at home to do tumbling," Li recalled. "I loved to do somersaults and handstands and cartwheels, and all the way to school I used to practice handsprings. My parents wanted me to be a musician, but I kept trying to fly."

Liang Wenjie, the gymnastics coach at a special sports school in Nanning, the Guangxi provincial capital, spotted Li in 1971 while scouting for recruits in Liuzhou. Impressed by Li's quickness and

fearlessness, Liang was excited by the boy's potential and enrolled him in the special provincial athletics school, one of more than 40 that China has established to train promising youngsters in a variety of sports.

As the youngest gymnast at the school, Li got little attention, but followed the training Liang gave boys five and six years older. "This let me start very difficult events at an early age," Li said. "It was really a big head start. While others my age were learning basic tumbling, I was getting ready for competition."

But Li's fondness for pranks earned him a reputation in Nanning—during the autumn moon festival one year, he climbed

James Drake

to the gymnasium roof to get a clearer view and to eat his mooncakes—and some staff members wanted to send him home as too troublesome. "I really was one of those naughty boys," Li said. "People wonder why my mother named me Ning," which means quiet and peaceful.

In 1973, when he was 10, Li took first place in the floor exercises at the national junior gymnastics tournament and then began regular training under Liang. But he then had to stop all but the most basic exercises for two years because of serious injuries to both of his elbows. When Li recovered in late 1975, Liang plunged him into intensive training—a team session in the afternoon after class, additional individual sessions during lunch breaks, in the evenings and on Sundays.

"Whatever free time Liang had, he spent on me," Li says, "and we became like

father and son. He was very demanding. Whenever he found there was something I disliked or that was difficult for me, he insisted I do more and more of it. Even when my floor exercises were up to world competitive standards in 1978, the coach said that it was not enough and that I needed more training, more practice."

Third place in the men's all-around event in China's 1980 national gymnastics competition won the 17-year-old Li a place on the national team and brought him to Peking. Then, in less than a year of international competition, he made it to the top, surprising both himself and his competitors.

Although he still has a boyish grin, Li now looks every inch a mature, experienced gymnast. At 5′ 4″, he has a powerful V-shaped torso on stocky legs, rippling arm-and-shoulder muscles, thick wrists and heavily calloused hands. His large, dark eyes are clear and quick. And his inch-and-a-half brush cut stands straight up ("the result of my spending so much time upside down," Li jokes).

Zhang is now his principal coach. But Li still trains with Liang when Li is in Nanning, where he has continued his studies in physical education while coaching at Guangxi Teachers College.

"What I have managed to achieve, I owe to those men as much as to my own efforts," Li said. "How else could a boy from Guangxi go to Zagreb and Budapest and Los Angeles?" ∎

We're helping the 1984 Olympics run a little faster.

The 1984 Los Angeles Olympics. The excitement keeps building day by day. Fourteen thousand athletes from 150 countries will compete. Los Angeles' population will swell to nearly twice its normal size. Events will be staged at 23 different arenas and stadiums, spread across 300 miles. And Suzuki motorcycles will be there, serving as escort vehicles and helping with crowd control. Suzuki's rugged all-terrain vehicles will be there, too, moving officials and materials around the many Olympic sites. As the Supplier of Motorcycles and ATV's to the 1984 Olympics, we're proud to be doing everything we can for this year's Games. And when you stop by your Suzuki dealer and see the quality and innovative engineering that's built into every Suzuki, you'll know just how far that pride can go.

SUZUKI

The Supplier of Motorcycles and All-Terrain Vehicles to the 1984 Olympic Games.

© 1982 L.A. Olympic Committee

The Sensation of Suzuki.

MORE OF THE BEST

*Closeup
reports on
dozens
of top
contenders*

LONG JUMPER and sprinter Carl Lewis has world records on his mind.

Alan D. Levenson

147

New Techniques, Old Rivalries, Fierce Goals

By James Dunaway

TRACK AND FIELD (ATHLETICS)

CARL LEWIS (U.S.A.)
Men's 100 and 200 meters and long jump

When Carl Lewis won three gold medals in the 1983 track and field world championships in Helsinki, his coach, Tom Tellez of the University of Houston, was not surprised. "Carl has total concentration," he said. "He can do anything he wants to do." One of the things America's celebrated track force wants to accomplish is to leap over Bob Beamon's 1968 long-jump record (29′ 2½″). This past winter in the Millrose Games he made an impressive run on the mark with a world record indoor jump of 28′ 10¼″.

Lewis, a former communications major at Houston, needs such concentration to fit in his daily workouts with interviews, TV assignments, public demands and business decisions. An exuberant, sometimes demonstrative winner, Lewis also likes to celebrate the victories of sister Carol, the best woman long jumper in the U.S. "Carl embraces competition," says coach Tellez. "He loves it. And the better his competitors perform, the more he enjoys it."

EVELYN ASHFORD (U.S.A.)
Women's 100 and 200 meters

Why has Evelyn Ashford of Los Angeles, who set a world record in the 100-meter dash of 10.79 seconds, been hopping up a flight of stairs on one leg? "We're trying to strengthen her left leg," explains coach Pat Connolly. "Her right leg is stronger and does all the work when she runs—and that causes injuries." One of the world's top sprinters since 1976, Ashford has suffered several serious right hamstring pulls. The most critical occurred at the halfway point in the 100-meter final of the 1983 world championships while she was running even with eventual winner Marlies Göhr of East Germany.

When Ashford trains she runs as many as 100 100-meter dashes in a single workout; in the weight room, she bench-presses more than her body weight. She trains so hard because, Ashford says, "I want to be the best sprinter of all time."

continued

POWERFUL
Michael Gross
(right)
hopes to win
West Germany's
first gold
in swimming.

SHOTPUTTER
Dave Laut (far
right)
made a style
change—and
set a U.S.
record.

CYCLIST
Nelson Vails (left)
sprinted from
a New York City
messenger job
into world-class
1,000m speed.

TIFFANY
Cohen (right), *18,*
has trained
four years
with the Mission
Viejo team.

Brazil's Joaquim Cruz (on right), here battling Steve Scott, is now a middle-distance star at the University of Oregon

Walter Iooss Jr.

BERTLAND CAMERON (Jamaica)
Men's 400 meters

Bert Cameron used to attend a lot of parties, trained no more than four days a week and never worked out on Saturday or Sunday. That didn't stop him from winning the 400-meter run at the 1983 world championships in Helsinki. But according to 1952 Olympic gold medalist Herb McKenley, Jamaica's national coach and national idol, Bert, now 24, went into high-gear training for the first time as he readied himself for the L.A. Games. Instead of partying, he stayed home and watched videotapes of his running form. Besides doing his regular weekday sprinting workouts with a new intensity, he added weightlifting and special "form drills" which helped him stay relaxed while running at top speed. "A lot of times when I am running I think of McKenley," Cameron says. "I want to do what he did."

JOAQUIM CRUZ (Brazil)
Men's 800 meters

Joaquim Cruz was an unknown 18-year-old when he set a world junior record of 1:44.3 for 800 meters in June 1981. That fall, Cruz and Luis Alberto de Oliveira (his coach since Joaquim was 11) left Rio to find a setting where he could train and compete with the best. They ended up in that city of runners, Eugene, Ore. While studying English so he could enroll at the University of Oregon, Cruz underwent a foot operation, which slowed him in 1982. But in 1983, training twice a day, Cruz set

Brazilian records for 800, 1,000 and 1,500 meters and finished a close third in the world championships at 800 meters after leading much of the way. He's a firm believer in sheer speed. Much of his training is done at world-record tempo, and he grabs the lead and pushes the pace in every race he runs. In Los Angeles he will try to stay in front all the way—in front of Willi Wulbeck of West Germany and Rob Druppers of the Netherlands, who beat him in the world championships, and especially in front of Great Britain's Sebastian Coe.

SEBASTIAN COE (Great Britain)
Men's 800 meters

The scene is a familiar one on a country road outside Sheffield, England: Sebastian Coe runs while his father and coach, Peter, drives alongside, timing each run and shouting encouragement. Unlike many middle-distance runners who cover more than 100 miles a week in training, Coe rarely runs more than 60 and sometimes as little as 30. But it is *quality* running. In one workout he did a set of six 800-meter runs in 1:52 or under for each, with the last one in 1:48. Compact training like this has enabled the 27-year-old Briton to break world records at 800 and 1,000 meters and run the fastest mile (3:47.33). He has a 1980 Olympic gold medal for the 1,500 meters.

In 1983, a glandular infection prevented him from competing in the world championships. As a result, he told *Track & Field News*, "I'm hungrier in 1984 than I was in

1980. And I know how to channel my emotions and my nerves better."

MARY DECKER (U.S.A.)
Women's 1,500 and 3,000 meters

Since Mary Decker won world championships at 1,500 and 3,000 meters in 1983, coach Dick Brown has had to keep reminding her *not* to train so hard, *not* to run so many miles (no more than 60 per week), *not* to compete too much. And each workout on the roads in and around Eugene, Ore., has been followed by a thorough massage to help prevent any more of the leg injuries that have plagued Mary since she was a pigtailed, 14-year-old record-setter in 1973. "I tend to overdo things," Decker explains, "and Dick keeps me from hurting myself." Much of her Olympic preparation has been psychological: Sometimes she runs with men, who bump and jostle her to simulate the racing conditions of championship middle-distance running.

EAMONN COGHLAN (Ireland)
Men's 5,000 meters

After missing competition during 1982 with Achilles tendinitis in his left leg, Eamonn Coghlan came back in 1983 and set a world indoor record in the mile (3:49.78) and won the 5,000 meters in the world championships. But last December he suffered a stress fracture of the right tibia, and had to stop running again. Eamonn didn't stop training. He just moved his workouts indoors, using a stationary bicycle and a cross-country skiing machine to keep up

continued

The most difficult goals are the ones most worth achieving.

 **Rockwell International**

...where science gets down to business

**Aerospace/Electronics
Automotive/General Industries**

the cardiovascular exercises a distance runner needs. The fracture mended, and he returned to his running—through Dublin's hilly parks, and in the U.S. on golf courses in Rye, N.Y. and on the miles of trails in nearby Pocantico Hills.

Coghlan expects his strongest Olympic opposition will come from Thomas Wessinghage of West Germany, and one or more East Africans. But he says, "We all have to run the same schedule, three tough races in four days. I feel fortified in having been in two Olympic Games and knowing how to handle the pressure."

ALBERTO COVA (Italy)
Men's 10,000 meters

The devastating finishing kick that carried Alberto Cova to victory in the final 10 meters of both the 1982 European championships and the 1983 world championships in the 10,000-meter races was the result of special speed training he puts in shortly before every major race. On the track of his club—Pro Patria Pierrel of Milan—he runs repetitions of distances from 200 to 600 meters at near top speed and takes very short recovery periods. At the end of the week, Alberto runs eight 400-meter dashes, each in 57 seconds, with a 100-meter jog in between.

ROBERT DE CASTELLA (Australia)
Men's marathon

Arriving at a friend's house in New Jersey after a flight from Italy, marathoner Robert (Deek) de Castella wasted no time: He changed into running clothes, grabbed a map and set off on a 10-mile run at a fero-

cious pace. The training system developed by de Castella and his coach, Pat Clohessy, kept him on a week-long diet of road runs in hilly terrain and over flat country, mixed with sessions of uphill sprinting and interval running on the track. Although de Castella's home is Canberra, Australia, he has spent three or four months a year pitting himself against the world's best on their home grounds. It seems to work: The 27-year-old runner has been a steady winner since he finished tenth in the 1980 Games. Last August he won the world championship. He sees his toughest Olympic foes as Japan's Toshihiko Seko, two Tanzanian runners, Juma Ikangaa and Gidamis Shahanga, and Ethiopia's Kebede Balcha.

JOAN BENOIT (U.S.A.)
Women's marathon

Other world-class runners went south to avoid the New England winter but Joan Benoit, who thrives in the rugged climate, ran more than 100 miles a week on the country roads of her native Maine. When she wasn't running, she worked at restoring the 19th-century house in which she lives, and chopped wood for the fireplace. On April 25 Benoit underwent knee surgery and, with the U.S. Olympic marathon qualifying trials less than three weeks away, it was feared she would not make the team. But on May 12 she ran in the trials and finished first. "Joan," said her coach, Bob Sevene, "is the toughest athlete I've ever seen." Her chief rival, Norwegian schoolteacher Grete Waitz—who put women's marathoning in the headlines

with her five New York City Marathon victories—has also trained tough for the 1984 Olympics, covering 100 miles a week on the icy hills around Oslo.

GREG FOSTER (U.S.A.)
Men's 110-meter high hurdles

Greg Foster has a unique problem for a high hurdler: His legs are so long that he has to "chop," or shorten his stride between the hurdles to keep from hitting them. Afternoons at the UCLA track, where he competed as a student, Greg has concentrated on bringing his lead leg down quickly to give him more room to run between hurdles. Weightlifting sessions, he says, have helped build the base of strength he needs to run the last five hurdles as powerfully as the first five. Having won the 1983 world championship, Foster believes he will win the Olympic high hurdles, too. But he says, "I sometimes wish my legs were an inch shorter."

EDWIN MOSES (U.S.A.)
Men's 400-meter hurdles

Even when not "in training," Edwin Moses ran several miles cross country every day on the brown terrain around his Laguna Hills, Calif. home. "You can't be successful in any phase of running unless you have that distance base," he says. Moses' Morehouse University degree is in physics and he approaches his training scientifically. He uses a computer to record workouts, breaks practices down into strength work (distance runs), speed work (short sprints), and work on technique (running the high hurdles to sharpen his intermediate hurdling skills). His objective? "To battle the last five hurdles—the most important part of the race." Moses has been the dominant force in hurdling ever since he won the 400-meter event in the '76 Games. He

continued

Lanky world champion Greg Foster has increased his closing power in the hurdles by weightlifting

---

James Dunaway has covered every Olympic track and field competition since 1956.

Richard Levin, who played on UCLA's first two NCAA champion basketball teams, is co-author with Magic Johnson of Magic.

Bill Bruns, who covered the 1960 Olympics as a schoolboy reporter, is a former sports editor of LIFE.

Len Albin, a free-lance writer based in New York City, is working on a novel.

LAS VEGAS

A HOP, SKIP AND A JUMP

FROM THE OLYMPIC GAMES.

The single most important spectacular in the world of sports, the Summer Olympic Games, takes place July 28 - August 12, 1984.

While you're enjoying the grandest of all sporting events, why not take the time to visit Las Vegas, the city of games.

Las Vegas is the perfect way to make your Olympic stay a winner by a wide margin.

Las Vegas is so close, why not jump at the chance to go.

For your Las Vegas visit select from column "A". Then it's your choice of column "B".

Column "A" (from Los Angeles)	Column "B" (in Las Vegas)
• 50 minutes by air	• 53,000 hotel / motel rooms
• 37 flights daily	• Superstar entertainment
• 5 hours by car or bus	• Dine from gourmet to buffet
• 7 hours by train (Daily schedule via Amtrak)	• 11 golf courses
	• 100 tennis courts
	• Gateway to the Grand Canyon
	• Hoover Dam and Lake Mead

For reservations or information call or write:

"Everything's mental," says Tom Petranoff, the U.S. javelin champion, whose 1983 world mark was over 327 feet

ALL SPORT / Tony Duffy

hadn't been beaten at his specialty in eight years as he bore down in training this past spring. His goal is simple. "I would like to break 46 seconds while everybody else is trying to break 48."

WILLIE BANKS (U.S.A.)
Men's triple jump

"I'm not very systematic in my training," says a smiling Willie Banks of Los Angeles, who set an American record in the triple jump (57′ 7½″). To break the monotony of weightlifting, sprinting and hopping the length of a football field on one leg and then the other—which is the heart of a triple jumper's training—Willie has retreated to the UCLA pool to try an in-air "triple jump" off the high board. Or he has pedaled 30 or more miles on his bicycle. He doesn't practice a full triple jump. "But everything I do," he says, "is focused toward the triple jump." He has had to fit his training sessions in between his studies to become a lawyer and a part-time job in a Los Angeles brewery.

DAVE LAUT (U.S.A.)
Men's shotput

"My dad kept a set of weights in the garage," says Dave Laut. "He got me started lifting when I was 12." Laut, who at 28 became the American record holder in the shotput (72′ 3″), has spent hours each day in the weight room, "trying to get as strong as I can." After injuring his left knee in 1980, he changed his shotputting tech-

nique from the conventional "glide" style to the newer "spin." It took time for him to master the discus-like spin technique, but now he feels comfortable with it. "I must have looked at a thousand miles of videotape to get it right," he says. Laut is optimistic because recently he bench-pressed a personal high of 530 pounds. "Every year that I've improved my best in the bench press," he says, "I've improved my best in the shotput, too."

TOM PETRANOFF (U.S.A.)
Men's javelin throw

Tom Petranoff's Olympic training is full of the physical output one would expect of a world record holder. But equally important, he believes, are the mental aspects of his event. "Everything's mental," Petranoff says. "When 100 million people are watching you, it's all in your head." So he has been devoted to control training—a breathing technique that reduces the tension in his neck muscles. In 1983, he set an astounding world record of 327′ 2″ in May—9′ 10″ over the previous mark.

FATIMA WHITBREAD (Great Britain)
Women's javelin throw

When Fatima Whitbread was 14, she read about Atalanta, the Ancient Greek princess of legend, who could throw a spear farther than any man. Whitbread asked her mother, an international-level javelin thrower, to teach her how—and her mother has been her coach ever since. "You've

got to do the work and punish the body to reach the top," says Whitbread, who has endured as many as five different training sessions a day. "Fatima trains a lot harder than I ever did," says Mrs. Margaret Whitbread, who admits that the sessions she has planned for her daughter would have discouraged *her* from competing. Whitbread lost the gold medal in the 1983 world championships to Tina Lillak of Finland on the final throw of the competition. But Fatima has improved her best distance every year since she started throwing, and in 1984, she says, "The sky's the limit."

Jordan, Patrick and The Baby Bull

by Richard Levin

BASKETBALL

While it is generally acknowledged that the talent gap in international amateur basketball has diminished considerably over the last decade, it is unlikely that the United States—where the sport was born and where it has flourished—will be surpassed so long as it continues to produce players with the skills of Michael Jordan.

A star guard/forward for the University of North Carolina three straight seasons, the 6′ 6″, 20-year-old Jordan is generally considered the best all-around amateur player in the world. In 1984 he received the John Wooden Award as the nation's best college player, he was named to every All-America first team, and he was the consensus NCAA Player of the Year.

About the only honor remaining in his illustrious amateur career is the Olympic gold medal. He's already won an NCAA championship, scoring the game-winning basket as a freshman in the 1982 championship final against Georgetown.

Jordan played on the U.S. national team at the Pan American Games in Caracas, Venezuela last summer and won a gold medal there. Jordan led the team with a 17.3 scoring average.

"This is just the start," he said at the time. "Everyone wants to be part of the Olympics. That's been my dream ever since I started playing." That dream began when he was a seventh-grader in Wilmington, N.C., his hometown.

Jordan averaged 17.7 points, more than five rebounds, and has shot 54 percent from the field during three years at North Carolina. Last season, he averaged 19.6 points and shot 55.1 percent. The key to

continued

PROUD SPONSORS OF THE 1984 U.S. OLYMPIC TEAM

Tony Tomsic/SPORTS ILLUSTRATED

College player of the year, Michael Jordan has dreamed of Olympic glory since he began playing in North Carolina

"You Feel Like You're Swimming With People On Your Back"

by Bill Bruns

SWIMMING AND DIVING

In diving, one of the intriguing questions is not whether the Olympics will confirm Greg Louganis's reputation as the best diver in the world—experts already concede him that distinction—but whether he can pull off a double win. Since 1928, no male diver has been able to win both the three-meter springboard and 10-meter platform events at an Olympics.

Blessed with a performer's flair and unrivaled physical gifts ("He's the closest diving has ever come to perfect," his coach has said), Louganis, 24, views the Olympics as more than a personal quest for gold medals. "I don't want to be somebody who only cares about winning," he says. "I'm out there to put on a performance." Ever since he won a silver medal in platform diving as a 16-year-old in the Montreal Olympics, Louganis has been stretching his talent and testing his limits in both events. This past year, rather than take a conservative path to Olympic gold, he has been experimenting with numerous high-difficulty dives, honing them in practice, as he strives to score more than 700 points from the platform in the Olympics, and more than 800 in the springboard. "That would be near-perfect diving," he admits.

In their first Olympic Games, the Chinese will be fielding a strong team that may include Li Kongzheng, one of the only non-Americans to defeat Louganis in the past eight years. But the stiffest competition for Louganis in the platform event could come from teammate Bruce Kimball, 20. They have been friendly competitors for 12 years, continually pushing each other to improve, and Kimball has won six national platform titles. He placed third behind Louganis and Vladimir Alemik of the Soviet Union at the 1982 world championships, just eight months after surviving an automobile accident in which he suffered severe injuries.

One of the feistiest gold-medal contenders in women's diving should be Wendy Wyland, a 19-year-old American who can

continued

his success: old-fashioned hard work. Dean Smith, Jordan's coach at North Carolina, says he is the hardest working player he's ever coached. Jordan plays non-stop throughout the year. There are no vacations, he has learned, when you're motivated to leap one step ahead of the competition. The day after one season ended at North Carolina, he was spotted working out in the gym. "I couldn't wait for the next game," he explained. And when the next semester opened, Jordan was the first to begin working out. "The freshmen were already talking trash," he said. "I had to see what they had."

Other reasons why the U.S. is favored to win the gold medal are Patrick Ewing, Georgetown's towering center, and Wayman Tisdale, a power forward at Oklahoma. Known as the "Baby Bull," Tisdale is a 6′ 9″, 259-pound sophomore who played on the winning U.S. team at the most recent Pan American Games.

Tisdale is a fast worker. It took him only two seasons to become the leading scorer in Oklahoma history. A two-time consensus All-America, Tisdale was the first player ever to make the Associated Press All-America first team as a freshman. He also broke Wilt Chamberlain's Big Eight Conference single-game scoring record when he scored 61 against Texas-San Antonio last December.

"I've won quite a few awards and honors," he says. "And I'll admit that most of them are stuffed away in a drawer somewhere. But I guarantee that the Olympic gold medal won't be going in any drawer if I'm fortunate enough to bring it home. I'll probably hang it on my front door where everybody can see it."

As a youngster, Tisdale had visions of entertaining people with a bass guitar, not a basketball. He was a member of a band that played "Muddy Waters stuff," he says. "I loved it, but I saw I wasn't going to make any money playing the bass."

He turned to sports, but picked the wrong one as far as his father was concerned. His dad wanted him to play football. "You know how it was back when he was growing up in the days of covered wagons," young Tisdale says. "Basketball was for girls. The boys played football."

Detlef Schrempf, a 6′ 9″ forward, is one of a growing number of players from West Germany who have migrated to U.S. schools. As a result, the West Germans are on the verge of joining the Soviets and Yugoslavs as the elite of European basketball. Schrempf led the University of Washington to the Pac-10 title as a junior last season.

Another West Coast player, 20-year-old Cheryl Miller, the flashy 6′ 3″ sophomore from the University of Southern California, has helped her school gain two NCAA championships and may well lead the U.S. to gold in the women's basketball competition.

156

The Stegemanns on their 20th visit to Bermuda.

It's not whether you win or lose, it's where you play the game. Bermuda.

Golf is a unique experience on Bermuda's seven spectacular courses—with fairways that border the blue Atlantic, and greens that tower above the sea. Our tennis is no less spectacular on almost 100 superbly-groomed, flower-scented courts. But the sporting life is only the beginning of a Bermuda vacation—a quality vacation that's worth so much more than what you spend.

Miles of pink beaches.

If you value beauty, you'll love Bermuda. Our soft sands are almost as pink as this page. Our waters are liquid turquoise. Our emerald hills are dotted with pastel-coloured houses and flowers in dazzling variety. Even our shops are beautiful—with tempting prices on international merchandise. (Here, as everywhere in Bermuda, you'll be welcomed with a genuine smile and gracious manner.)

Our historic values.

We have 3½ centuries of historic sights for you to explore. Just getting to them is a delight—in spotless taxis, breezy motorbikes, or quaint little ferries that afford magnificent views of our island.

Comfort you'll value.

Bermuda sees to your comfort with a wide range of quality accommodation—from cozy guest houses, to uniquely Bermudian cottage colonies, to the most luxurious of resorts. See your Travel Agent and plan a visit with us soon.

Experience the values of

Bermuda

2204

WRITE FOR A FREE BERMUDA BROCHURE:
Bermuda Department of Tourism,
Post Office Box 4300, Woburn, MA 01888.

Name_____
(please print)
Address_____

City_____

State_____ Zip_____

The Barton family on their 2nd visit.

A favorite to win a 1980 medal in the butterfly, Mary Meagher of Louisville, Ky., is happy with another chance

expect tough competition from China—notably Li Yihua, the world's top springboard diver last year. When she was 10, Wyland had such boundless energy that her parents allowed her to compete simultaneously in three different sports throughout the year—swimming, gymnastics and diving. Knowing she needed to find better coaching and competition, she left her family in Rochester, N.Y. and moved to Mission Viejo, Calif., where current Olympic coach Ron O'Brien was working with Louganis and other hopefuls. "I want to be known as Wendy Wyland, the diver who made it to the top," she vowed in 1981. "I want to be the best."

American long-distance swimmer, Jeff Kostoff, 18, has undertaken some rather remarkable workouts to strengthen his endurance while bolstering his inner confidence. Last December 31, for example, as a symbolic send-off for the Olympic year, he swam alone for 3 hours and 20 minutes, covering 20,000 yards (11½ miles) with barely a minute's rest after every 5,000 yards. At the end, he hung onto a lane line, smiling, knowing he had accomplished his goal—to swim each 5,000-yard set in less than 50 minutes.

The most formidable swimmer in the Games will likely be West Germany's Michael Gross, who turned 20 in June. His country has never won a gold medal in Olympic swimming, but the 6' 6" Gross is an awesome presence in three individual events and anchors an 800-meter freestyle relay team that broke the world record in 1983. Gross, who set world records in the 200-meter butterfly and 200-meter freestyle, faces a strong challenge in the 100-meter butterfly from American Matt Gribble, 22, winner of the event in the '82 world championships.

While most world-class swimmers feel they must train in a highly competitive environment to gain and maintain their preeminence, Gross has taken the unconventional approach. He is the only swimmer of national stature at his swim club near Frankfurt—"I compete against myself in each workout"—and trains only once a day during the school year (except for double workouts on weekends), because he doesn't like to get up early. Besides, he believes that excessive training in the pool could ruin his body and his motivation. "I have got long limbs which are strong and sensitive at the same time," Gross explains. "I'm a racing car and not a lorry. I don't believe in wearing myself out."

American Rick Carey, 21, last summer broke John Naber's backstroke records that had stood for seven years, only to inherit typical Olympic-year pressure: the expectations of a public hungry for gold medals. "You feel like you're swimming with people on your back," he said. "It's not something I enjoy." Despite the distractions, Carey retained a single-minded focus on his swimming while attending the University of Texas, continually pushing himself to improve. A muscular 6-footer, he is physically gifted for the backstroke,

with hyper-extended knees and extraordinary flexibility through the shoulders, and is willing to drive himself unmercifully in workouts. One of his favorite training routines is to swim 10 "descending sets," where each set—400 yards of the backstroke and 100 yards of freestyle—is swum at a faster pace, with only a brief rest between sets. "Everyone hates to lose," noted one veteran U.S. swimmer, "but no one hates to lose more than Carey."

Among the women the distance ace is America's 18-year-old Tiffany Cohen. Cohen's rise to swimming prominence typifies one approach being taken by American teenagers anxious to fulfill their athletic potential. At the age of 13, eager for a no-nonsense training regimen, Cohen moved south from Los Angeles to join the famous Mission Viejo swim team. She lived with a local family until her parents were able to relocate a year later, and began swimming 10 to 12 miles a day, six days a week, 11 months a year. Ever since, school has been sandwiched between a morning workout from 5:15 to 7:30 and a session from 2:30 to 5. Most days also include an hour or so of weight training.

Two other American hopefuls, Mary T. Meagher, 19, and Tracy Caulkins, 21, typify the aspirations of those swimmers who saw their 1980 Olympic dreams eliminated by the boycott, but who continued to compete with Los Angeles as their goal.

Louisville's Meagher, after being fa-

continued

Swimming is good for your body. Bad for your hair.

The UltraSwim® solution.

Chlorine chemicals attack the life and lustre of your hair. That's because chlorine reacts with hair's natural protein and eats away at the hair's surface. Weakening it. Leaving hair dull, dry, brittle and broken. Hair can change colors. Tinted hair turns brassy. Hair gets that chlorine smell.

UltraSwim® shampoo has a patented formula that works to renew chlorine-damaged hair. Gently and quickly, UltraSwim washes away damaging chlorine like no other shampoo. Look. Special chlorine-sensitive test liquid on left shows the amount of chlorine in

Without UltraSwim.   With UltraSwim.

hair after swimming. The same liquid on right shows virtually no chlorine remaining after an UltraSwim shampoo.

After you swim, UltraSwim.

Used on a regular after-swim basis, UltraSwim can help restore chlorine-damaged hair to its original beauty. No more dryness. No further discoloration. And no more smell. Only fresh, manageable hair.

For a complete after-swim beauty shape-up, use UltraSwim shampoo, hair conditioner and moisturizing body bar.

Official Supplier to U.S. Swimming National Teams
USA SWIMMING

UltraSwim® Gets chlorine out. Puts beauty back in.

SIO-4139-38

vored to win gold medals in the two butterfly events in 1980, set world records in both in 1981. That year she took time from college and moved to Mission Viejo in order to focus her life completely on swimming. "I don't look at it as a sacrifice," she said. "I look at it as something I want to do. It's fun to train with people who have the same goals."

Although the 1980 boycott might have cost Caulkins at least four gold medals and international acclaim, she was able to overcome the disappointment, knowing she was young enough (17 at the time) to try again. Still regarded as the greatest all-around woman swimmer in U.S. history—she has won national championships and set American records in all four strokes, plus the individual medley events—Caulkins has stayed in college while training for 1984. "Having other things to think about helps my swimming," she says.

Samurai Ceremonies, Assorted Psyching, Maneuvering Through Traffic For "Operation Gold"

by Len Albin

ARCHERY

"You have to be a good daydreamer," Rick McKinney of the U.S. was saying, as he described his recent Olympic preparation. For two hours a day, McKinney, the 1983 archery world champion, practiced "visual imagery"—imagining the bull's-eye as much larger than it really is, or pretending that he was "looking down a tunnel" at the 10-circle target. And then he kept staring until little could distract him, not even his coach, Sheri Rhodes. "It's all through the mind," McKinney explained.

And what about the body? As a 30-year-old physical education major at Arizona State, McKinney learned firsthand that there is hardly any relationship between athletics and archery. To nourish his 5′ 7″, 120-pound frame, McKinney's choice of food is "whatever's in the fridge." Breakfast usually consists of cookies or a slice of cold pizza. He does spend several hours a week shooting arrows, but his most strenuous exercise consists of running a mile or two—four days a week. That helps keep his resting pulse rate around 64 beats a minute, and that's important. If McKinney had a faster pulse it wouldn't give him time to aim.

"The elite archers," McKinney said, "shoot *between* heartbeats."

CANOEING

For the better part of three years now, Ian Ferguson has been hauling his K-1 class kayak up to beautiful Lake Pupuke in Auckland, New Zealand. There—in water so fresh and clear he could drink it—he has paddled some 25 miles, seven days a week. For about four hours a day on this lake, which sits in the sheltered crater of an inactive volcano, city life seemed far away.

"I'm actually an accountant," says the 32-year-old Ferguson. "But I've been training in this sport, you see, and I can't hold a proper job down." In fact, since Ferguson got his degree from Victoria University (Wellington) eight years ago, he's *never* found time to practice accounting. So Ferguson taught himself an unorthodox trade—repairing video games and then leasing them to customers in Auckland. "It's a good business for me because it doesn't require much work," he says. "But it's enough to keep me solvent."

The 5′ 10″, 183-pound Ferguson first learned to paddle a canoe some 10 years ago when he trained as a surf lifeguard. But since 1974 Ferguson has doggedly pursued his goal of Olympic kayaking glory, undeterred by a poor showing in '76 at Montreal. At the Moscow Games, Ferguson finished seventh and last year he finished second to Vladimir Parfenovich of the U.S.S.R. in the 500-meter kayak race at the world championships. "He was only half a second in front this time," Ferguson recalls. "But he was on my mind all the time when I was training."

continued

Rick McKinney of Arizona State is only 5′ 7″ and 120 pounds, but he pulls his bow as a world champion

Duomo/Dan Helms

He has waited a lifetime for the next ten seconds.

This is the day he has worked for all his life. It is his moment. And ours. Because, for the millions of us watching from the sidelines, our hopes and our dreams go with him. That's the Spirit of the Games, adidas.

COLORSPORT

Lucinda Green worked with horses from her Hampshire stable for a place on the accomplished British equestrian team

CYCLING

When the DON'T WALK traffic sign flashed for the ninth time, the light itself turned green and Nelson (Cheetah) Vails, carrying six to eight packages and envelopes on his Bianchi touring bicycle, sprinted out of the intersection and up Sixth Avenue in midtown Manhattan. For months the Harlem-bred Vails had been pedaling 25 to 35 miles a day while working as a messenger, earning $60 daily and narrowly missing trucks, garment-district clothing racks and cabs making aggressive moves. Some pedestrians weren't so lucky. "I hit some people," Vails admits. "Knocked them on their *butts.*"

Two years later, this experience of looking over his shoulder while moving at top speed was a help to the 24-year-old Vails as he prepared for the 1,000-meter sprint event. That's the cat-and-mouse duel on a banked track that starts slowly but ends at top speed. Although he lacks the racing polish of his American archrival, Mark Gorski, the rapidly improving Vails has world-class speed, and used it to win the sprint at the 1983 Pan American Games.

Last November, the 5′ 9″, 175-pound Vails began what he called "my Operation Gold program"—riding up to 150 miles a week on his custom-built Raleigh bicycle and lifting weights for overall body strength. This training was done with the U.S. cycling team in the Southwest, and took him far away from his wife and two daughters in New York, but Vails was willing to pay the price: "I have a mission to accomplish."

EQUESTRIAN

Near the Hampshire town of Wayhill in England, Lucinda Green arose at dawn every day and rode her horse all morning. As the mist burned away on the spacious Salisbury Plain, Green would ride cross-country, then take her mount up into the hills. But since Green competes in the three-day equestrian event, she also had to devote time to schooling horses in the pin-point movements of dressage, or in the third discipline, show jumping. After lunch, Green did some jumping on her own—exactly 300 skips with a jump-rope. Then she plunged into the details of keeping a stable of several horses, and the grueling desk work that it demands. "We never stop," said Green, whose husband, David, was also preparing for a place on the British team. "You must be completely free of other commitments. Without sponsorship we wouldn't be around."

While in training, she rode several horses. But of all her stable, the horse she will ride in the Olympics is a 12-year-old gelding named Regal Realm, an Australian thoroughbred. This is the horse she rode in 1982 to win her world championship, and so she made certain that he was whipped into shape. But *gently.* "You can't put too much pressure on a horse," Green said. "They're human beings."

FENCING

For Dorina Vaccaroni of Italy, the preparation would begin with makeup. Then, "Baby Doll," as she's been called, would put on earrings, bracelets and rings. Finally, she would pick up her tools—fencing outfit, fencing mask and foil—and head for a match. Then she would win the match. Though the 5′ 6″ Vaccaroni has reminded people of a runway model out of place on a narrow 14-meter fencing strip, her performance last year in Vienna was worth a world championship.

Vaccaroni started fencing 15 years ago, at the age of five. Most of the time, she has practiced at a club in Mestre, near Venice, run by the strict coach, Dino DiRosa. At other times, she has joined the Italian team, and their trainers and doctors, at fencing camp—which in Italy is financed by the national soccer pool.

Formerly a temperamental competitor who fenced "on guts" and bellowed at judges, Vaccaroni has learned to control her temper and has polished her technique, too. Her feet are not only fast, but they belong to a pair of very long legs, ideal for fencing.

FIELD HOCKEY

In Amsterdam, Lisette Sevens, a 35-year-old veteran with the top-seeded Dutch women's field hockey team, has never lacked for opposition. Field hockey is a national sport in the Netherlands. Four nights a week and on weekends she covered her territory as a midfielder in workouts with members of the national team.

The emphasis was on speed and dazzling stick work. "And we did a little bit once with those medicine balls," Sevens says. "You know, those big balls?" During the day Sevens covered her turf as a sportswriter for an Amsterdam daily newspaper.

FOOTBALL (SOCCER)

As Kazbek Tambi has learned, competing for a place on an Olympic team involves much more than training. Last winter this 22-year-old sweeper for the U.S. soccer team was a member of the (New York) Cosmos *professional* soccer club, but stayed an *amateur.* While the International Olympic Committee and the International Soccer Federation (FIFA) were deciding who was eligible to play in the Olympics, Tambi was gaining much need-

continued

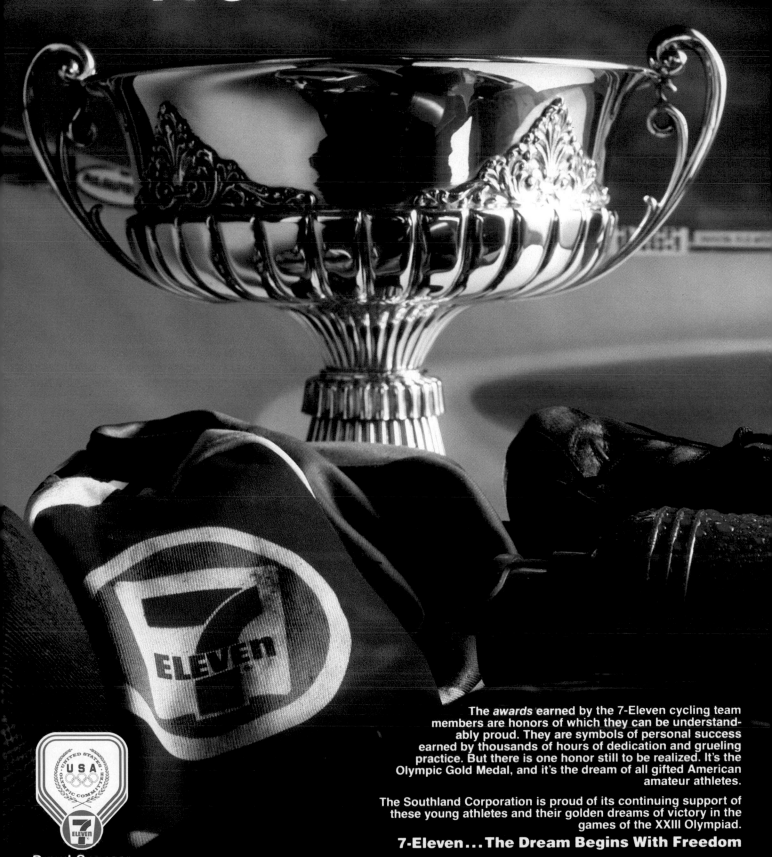

ed experience against professional players. During the winter, members of the Cosmos play *indoor* soccer, which isn't technically soccer ("It isn't even close," Tambi says). But the game helped him to stay sharp.

And Tambi made sure he kept his amateur status. He received no salary from the Cosmos, just expenses. Tambi lived carefully on savings.

JUDO

Before every judo match, Yasuhiro Yamashita of Japan thoroughly cleans his room. According to Samurai tradition, if a war-

Walter Iooss Jr.

rior dies in battle and leaves behind a shambles, he will suffer disgrace.

But it's unlikely that the 5′ 11″, 276-pound Yamashita will suffer disgrace in this violent martial art, in which a *shime-waza* (chokehold) can cut off blood flow through the carotid arteries. After more than 180 straight victories, the 26-year-old physical education teacher at Tokai University has been virtually untouchable.

Early this year, Yamashita prepared for the Games with more than four hours of daily weight training, running and practicing his technique. Meanwhile, in order to avoid him, judo coaches around the world waited to see whether Yamashita would enter the heavyweight (209+ pounds) or open (all weights) division. Yamashita has won the last three world championships in heavyweight, and in 1981, he also entered the open and won that, too.

ROWING

Running through the streets of London in the dead of night was one way Beryl Mitchell, 33, maintained her ranking as one of Britain's best in single sculls. Her training at a site near Hammersmith College, where she teaches physical education, also included workouts with weights to build leg power. And she took her single scull out on the Thames River twice a day, rowing between Putney and Maltlake, a course well-known to crews from Oxford and Cambridge.

But the waters haven't always been smooth for Mitchell. Two years ago, she

With ultimate and artistic effort, Rita Crockett exhibits her skills as a member since 1978 of the U.S. volleyball team

suffered a serious head injury—not in the river, but while tobogganing at some 80 kilometers an hour down a slope in Hampstead Heath, London. It took two operations to repair the damage done to her face.

Last year Mitchell was in top form again—taking a close second behind the current world champion, Jutta Hampe of East Germany, at the Lucerne International Regatta—and was determined to have a good show in Los Angeles. "I like winning," Mitchell says. "It's as simple as that."

SHOOTING

When Staff Sergeant Dan Carlisle, 28, would tote his 12-gauge shotgun out near the piney woods of Fort Benning, Ga., he wasn't looking for quail. His game was

skeet and trap shooting and his targets were clay pigeons. Three or four times a week, he would head up to the U.S. Army Marksmanship Unit's trap and skeet range and fire at 150 targets a day. In the case of "trap," he was shooting birds that flew out of their bunker at about 100 miles an hour. Even though he had plugged a world-record 200 out of 200 traps when he won his 1983 Pan American Games gold medal, Carlisle still spent the whole day on "The Hill." "It still takes practice to break 99 and 100 straight," he says. "And we need to shoot in all types of light we can. It doesn't take a Mr. Universe to be good—as long as you can see."

Carlisle, who is an Army Ammunition Storage Specialist and squad leader, also tacked on a weekly four-mile run in order to stay physically fit because it helps his concentration. "You more or less have to blank everything out on the shooting range," he explains. "Except the target."

TEAM HANDBALL

Vasile Stinga, 26, of the world champion Romanian team handball squad, played in weekly matches with his local club team in Bucharest as part of his pre-Olympic preparation. Now and then he would join the national squad and, for up to six hours a day, build his strength and speed through sprints, weight training and by throwing around a handball that weighed about three times that of a regulation ball. The 6′ 4″, 200-pound Stinga is the team's chief offensive weapon—he scored 36 goals in the '80 Moscow Games—and creates havoc for his opponents from the left backcourt position. "You don't go *near* him to shoot," says right backcourt player Jim Buehning of the U.S., who has competed against Stinga. "He is *everywhere.*"

WATER POLO

For Terry Schroeder, who plays the "hole man" position for the highly ranked U.S. water polo squad, teamwork has always meant taking plenty of abuse. In water polo, it's the hole man's job to position himself close to the opponent's goal and shoot, or get fouled in the act, which occurs much more frequently. With six years' experience on the national team, the 25-year-old Schroeder has suffered deep bruises, chipped teeth and a partially dislocated neck. By 1984 he was perhaps considered the top hole man in the world. And not surprisingly, given his injuries, he

continued

For four decades Best Western has provided travelers with more of the best places to stay. We still do.

Best Western
WORLDWIDE LODGING

To find the right place to stay
at the right price, pick up your free copy
of our full-color 300-page Travel Guide
at any Best Western.

Instant Reservations
*Make reservations at any Best Western, contact your
travel agent or call toll-free* **1-800-528-1234.**

3,000 independently owned and operated properties in 2,100 cities worldwide

Andorra, Aruba, Australia, Austria, Barbados, Belgium, Canada, Denmark, Finland, France, Great Britain, Guadeloupe, Holland, Ireland, Italy,
Liechtenstein, Luxembourg, Mexico, New Zealand, Puerto Rico, Sweden, Switzerland, United States, Virgin Islands, West Germany

was studying to become a chiropractor.

Nevertheless, Schroeder, who is a 6′ 3″, 200-pound ex-football player, survived the damage and continued practicing to meet the formidable West German squad. "The water provides a pretty good cushion," he says. "Unless you get kicked in the groin."

WRESTLING

Bruce Baumgartner, 23, of the U.S., did all he could to prepare for the super heavyweight (220+ pounds) freestyle wrestling competition. Over the past year, when not coaching wrestling as a graduate assistant at Oklahoma State, or working on his master's thesis ("An Analysis of Injuries in the Industrial Arts Woodshop"), the 6′ 2″, 260-pound Baumgartner was absorbed with workouts that keep him running, climbing stairs, weightlifting—and wrestling. And before his matches, Baumgartner did a lot of positive thinking—to help build some of the crucial "intensity" wrestlers need. "I find it easy right before I go to sleep," he says. "I lie back and just visualize myself wrestling a match—and winning." Particularly, Baumgartner liked to call up the scene of triumph after he won the NCAA title in 1982: "I want to re-feel that feeling when I get to the Olympics."

YACHTING

On freeways throughout America, a popular bumper sticker reads, I'D RATHER BE SAILING. Not Dave Curtis. "A lot of times I'd rather be playing golf," says the 38-year-old Soling-class yachtsman and sailmaker from Marblehead, Mass. "I just hate going out and practicing. It's boring." To practice during the past winter, Curtis had to load his 26′ 9″ Whip, weighing 2,300 pounds, onto a trailer and then drive 1,500 miles to Florida. Once in warmer waters, Curtis and his crew (Jamie Hardenbergh up forward with the jibsheet and Wally Corwin, sail-trimmer) set out at 9:30 every morning and sailed as long as there was breeze and sunlight.

Curtis would have liked more than 14 days a month, on average, over the past two years, to prepare for the 12.5-mile Olympic race. But unlike many yachtsmen, he had business to take care of: Curtis Sails and Curtis Boats. Curtis has also had the luxury of testing sails fresh from his factory. And since he won the 1983 pre-Olympic regatta at Long Beach, on the Olympic course, he has already tested the waters. His strategy is simple: Get a good start, get on a port tack and go *fast*.

Here on the balance beam, 16-year-old Mary Lou Retton soared into contention as one of the best in the vault

James Drake

Grooming Gypsy Munchkins

by Bill Bruns

GYMNASTICS

When Romania's Nadia Comaneci and her teammates returned home with three gold medals from the Montreal Olympics, a new generation of gymnastic munchkins was already being groomed at the national training center in Onesti. Head coach Bela Karolyi, a demanding, no-nonsense perfectionist, boasted that he had several young girls with greater talent than Comaneci had had at a similar age—including 9-year-old Ecaterina Szabo and 10-year-old Lavinia Agache. Both girls had moved to Onesti to attend school and train with him year round.

By the time Karolyi defected to the United States in 1981, Szabo and Agache were already emerging as Comaneci's potential successors. Last fall in the world championships, Agache won three individual medals and Szabo four, including a gold in the floor exercises with a bold, exciting routine featuring spectacular flips and spinning aerial movements.

Karolyi, meanwhile, was developing a new set of Olympic contenders, Americans, at a private gymnastics club in suburban Houston. His prized recruit, in this era of gypsy gymnasts who are willing to travel great distances in their pursuit of better coaching and competition, has been 16-year-old Mary Lou Retton, from Fairmont, West Va. A dynamic, expressive performer, she represents a new look in women's gymnastics—short (4′ 10″) but also muscular, with explosive power in her thighs that enables her to get an incredibly high trajectory when she vaults, and soaring height during the tumbling phase of her floor exercises. Indeed, she has the potential, especially in the vault, to become the first American woman to win an individual Olympic medal in gymnastics. Although she missed the world championships with an injury, she later defeated the vaulting winner, Bulgaria's Boriana Stoyanova, at the Chunichi Cup in Japan.

Retton was the only elite gymnast in her state when she moved south to Karolyi's club in 1982. "I wanted to go all out to bring out the best in me," she says. "It's a once-in-a-lifetime thing, and, while I may be missing out on things now, I feel I will have time later in my life to enjoy them."

One reason Retton progressed so well is that she was able to train last year with a competitive equal, Dianne Durham, the national all-around champion, who came to Houston from Gary, Ind. In competitions and workouts, they pushed each other to try new and more difficult elements and combinations within their routines.

Durham, an outgoing 16-year-old, likes to perform in flowered leotards—"*Definitely* an extension of my personality," she says, smiling brightly. ∎

167

THE DREAM DEFERRED

*These athletes, too,
devoted their lives to
being here. But
as their goal drew near,
they were told—
in the Soviet Union
and elsewhere—
that the Games would
go without them*

TRACK AND FIELD (ATHLETICS)

MARITA KOCH (East Germany)
Women's 200 and 400 meters

To be a great 400-meter runner, says 1980 Olympic champion Marita Koch, you must constantly work at the shorter sprints. In 1983, although nagging injuries prevented her from competing effectively at her favorite 400-meter distance, the 27-year-old medical student from Rostock improved her 100-meter time to 10.83 seconds (third best in history), and won the world championship at 200 meters. By using her time efficiently, Marita has managed to get in two hours or more a day of training while continuing her demanding studies in pediatrics. "I really don't like to get out of bed in the morning, but usually not a minute of my day is wasted," she says.

JARMILA KRATOCHVILOVA (Czechoslovakia)
Women's 400 and 800 meters

Even on everybody's holiday—New Year's Day—you could find Jarmila Kratochvilova doing her sprints on a frozen lake in Czechoslovakia. As a country girl, she learned about hard work early and at 12 was strong enough to throw a pitchfork of hay up into the loft. She lives in Golcuv Jenikov, the village where she was born, and trains in a park at nearby Caslav, a town of 10,000. Years of training that included a lot of weightlifting and sprinting while wearing a 22-pound vest have given

Kratochvilova, now 33, impressive muscles, world championships and world records at 400 meters (47.99 seconds) and 800 meters (1:53.28).

IGOR PAKLIN (U.S.S.R.)
Men's high jump

In his Olympic preparations, 20-year-old Igor Paklin, a computer science student at the Polytechnic Institute in Frunze, a Kirghiz city 2,000 miles southeast of Moscow, crammed workouts into two days because of his studies. After the physical high intensity, he let his body rest for 48 hours while he concentrated on computers. Paklin is a natural talent who has held the world indoor record of 7′ 8¾″. He knew he would have to jump even higher if he made it to Los Angeles, perhaps 8 feet, to beat China's Zhu Jianhua, the world outdoor record holder at 7′ 9¾″, and several talented Europeans and Americans.

TAMARA BYKOVA (U.S.S.R.)
Women's high jump

Like many student-athletes, 25-year-old Tamara Bykova had to plan her two or three hours of daily training around her studies (journalism and television) at Rostov University. In the winter, she combined 30-kilometer cross-country skiing excursions with weightlifting to build strength. As the competitive season approached, the emphasis turned to sprinting (to increase speed) and jumping (to hone her timing and form). In 1983, Bykova raised the world record to 6′ 8¼″ and won the world championship.

SERGEI BUBKA (U.S.S.R.)
Men's pole vault

Before he took up pole vaulting, Sergei Bubka was a soccer player, and there have been times when his coach wondered if he should have switched. But last year, in his first major international competition, Bubka became world champion by vaulting 18′ 8¼″ on a rainy, windy day when many of the world's best vaulters could not clear even a low height. Last winter he raised the world indoor record to 19′ 1½″. His training at the Institute for Physical Culture in Kiev, which emphasizes weightlifting and sprinting, has made him the strongest, fastest pole vaulter around. "Sergei runs as fast carrying the pole as most jumpers can run without a pole," says Soviet head coach Igor Ter-Ovanesyan. Asked how high he can jump, Bubka smiles and replies, "First do it, then say it."

ILONA BRIESENICK (East Germany)
Women's shotput

As Ilona Slupianek, she won the 1980 Olympic shotput gold medal, but at last year's world championships, competing despite an injury, she finished fourth. The defeat spurred her to train harder than ever—sprinting faster, lifting heavier weights—in coach Willi Kuhl's group of top weight throwers in East Berlin. There

East Germany's sprint stars Marita Koch (left) and Marlies Göhr, both medalists at the Moscow Games, were expected to win more in '84.

168

All-around 1983 world champion Dmitri Belozerchev is best of U.S.S.R. gymnasts

ALL SPORT/Tony Duffy

she met her husband, Hartmut Briesenick, a top competitor in the shotput in the early 1970s. Ilona Briesenick, who teaches kindergarten, says the undercurrent of competitive tension involved in training with other world-class athletes provides her with an important edge: "It gives me self-confidence . . . and nerves are what make the difference between being a top athlete and just another competitor."

BOXING

TEOFILO STEVENSON (Cuba)

No boxer training for the Olympics had more experience at the championship level than Cuba's super heavyweight Teofilo Stevenson. He won his first gold medal as a heavyweight in 1972, added two more and in 1984, at age 33, had his hopes set on a fourth.

The 6' 5", 220-pound Stevenson has a basic standup style and utilizes tactics that allow him to wait for the opening to throw his powerful right. His age and some losses in international competition raised suggestions that he had lost punching power and interest in amateur sport. However, Pat Nappi, coach of the U.S. team, said, "He's lost some of his reactions and movements, but he's made up for that with experience. He does what he has to do to win."

Stevenson's personal goal was to become the first to win four golds in boxing. "All athletes go after records," he said. "It's like the high jumper looking at a record height. He attempts to jump it."

GYMNASTICS

DMITRI BELOZERCHEV (U.S.S.R.)

Serenely self-confident and self-contained as he competed in the world championships in Budapest last October, Dmitri Belozerchev of the U.S.S.R. won the all-around competition (scoring 10, 9.95, 9.95, 10, 9.95 and 10 in the six events) and then captured three of the individual events, plus a silver. "He's the greatest gymnast ever," marveled one U.S. coach, but the 17-year-old Belozerchev took his successes stoically, waving perfunctorily to the audience and rarely smiling.

What seems to give Belozerchev a special dimension is his ability to perform with breathtaking skill and consistency under pressure. At 5' 6" and 145 pounds, he combines unusual physical strength with agility, flexibility and an unerring sense of where he is going as his body is spinning or flipping through the air. He's not flamboyant, but his routines include high-risk elements that he performs at near-perfection. And they are capped by landings that are almost invariably *solid*, without a misstep that will subtract points.

Gymnast Belozerchev is the prize result of a training system that helped mold his emotions and technique over the past 10 years, and yet he almost slipped away to another sport in the beginning. When he was about eight, he attended a gymnastics tryout at the Soviet army's sports club in Moscow, but the head coach thought he

was too heavy and tried to persuade him to take up wrestling. Belozerchev's father, a construction worker, wanted him to play ice hockey, but his mother preferred gymnastics and she won out. Young Dmitri worked on his basic tumbling skills and was eventually invited to join the army's sports school, where athletes receive their education, training and three meals a day, as well as specialized input from physiologists, biomechanics experts, nutritionists, physicists and psychologists.

Preparing for the Games, Belozerchev trained up to six hours a day in an effort to improve on near-perfection.

NATALIA YURCHENKO (U.S.S.R.)

One of the top challengers among the women was 19-year-old Natalia Yurchenko, a striking, dark-haired beauty (5' 1", 100 pounds) who won the world title last fall. Born in Norilsk, a Siberian city above the Arctic Circle, Yurchenko took up gymnastics when she was eight. Several years later, a coach saw her doing elegant cartwheels and flip-flops during a vacation on the Black Sea and urged her to apply to the famous gymnastics school in Rostov-on-Don, where coach Vladislav Rastorotsky had produced a succession of Olympic champions. Yurchenko was 11 when she was accepted with the coach's prediction that she would follow in the footsteps of the best. She became an alternate on the 1979 world championship team but, unfortunately, illness and uneven performances

continued

WE'RE GIVING HIM HIS FIRST SWING AT A GOLD MEDAL.

Right now, a lot of young men are anxiously hoping to make it onto a baseball team.

Not an American League team.

Or a National League team.

But the team that will represent the United States at the 1984 Olympics.

The General Electric Major Appliance Business Group is proud to be sponsoring these fine young men. We're doing it because we feel they believe in the same idea we do. That a lot more can be accomplished when people work *together* to reach a common goal.

We don't know if the U.S. team will win the Gold Medal at Los Angeles.

But, if they don't, we do know this.

It won't be for lack of trying.

WE BRING GOOD THINGS TO LIFE.

Two of the Soviets' most popular record holders: Leningrad swimmer Vladimir Salnikov; the "Bull of Kiev" Anatoly Pisarenko

plagued her during the next two years. In 1982 she had to start over with entirely new routines.

Yurchenko and her friends train twice a day for upwards of eight hours, including an early-morning run before school, an hour of choreography, an hour of acrobatics, and extended work on the beam, uneven bars and vault. "We practice the same exercises thousands of times, so they suddenly become part of ourselves," Yurchenko said. But she considers all these hard training hours to be a fair tradeoff for the benefits she says she has gained—"health, figure, beautiful trips and competitions. I owe everything nice in my life to gymnastics."

MODERN PENTATHLON

TAMAS SZOMBATHELYI (Hungary)

Tamas Szombathélyi of Budapest has a physical education degree from the Tesné-velsi Föiskola ("College for Coaches"). He has a wife and two children. But when Szombathélyi, 3l, trains for the modern pentathlon he is, in a sense, transported back into the Napoleonic era. Indeed, that's the general idea. This five-event, four-day athletic mix—consisting of a 600-meter horseback ride over a grand-prix style course, epée fencing, .22-caliber pistol shooting, freestyle swimming (300 meters) and a 4,000-meter run—was modeled on the skills that a 19th-century battlefield courier needed to deliver a message to the front lines.

In Hungary the modern pentathlon itself is a tradition. Fencing, which provides the stiffest challenge in the modern pentathlon, is a Hungarian specialty. Preparing for the Olympics, the 5' 7", 140-pound Szombathélyi, a member of the army-sponsored Honved ("patriot") sports club in Budapest and an expert in fencing and shooting, was spending over 40 hours a week in training.

Hungarian tradition demands that a pentathlete practice no fewer than three disciplines a day. Szombathélyi typically started his day at the riding stable on Budapest's north side, and took a hard two-hour ride. In the afternoon, it was a long workout in a municipal swimming pool and, in the evening, a few hours of combat in Honved's fencing salle. On some days, shooting and running were shuffled into the schedule.

SWIMMING

VLADIMIR SALNIKOV (U.S.S.R.)

For the man who has dominated world swimming since 1976, it's what you do after your body feels as if it can't do any more that counts. Then, believes Vladimir Salnikov, who had to struggle as a child just to learn to swim, is when the champion emerges. "The greatest difficulty is fighting the weariness that grips you about 300 or 400 meters before the end." Salnikov's ability to call upon his tremendous reserve enabled him to set world records at 400, 800 and 1,500 meters. Salnikov's domination in international swimming has made him a 24-year-old Soviet athletic hero, with a wife and small apartment in Moscow. One admirer, Mark Spitz of the U.S., told him, "It's a pleasure to watch you swim. And I'm glad I'm not swimming now—you're too strong."

WEIGHTLIFTING

ANATOLY PISARENKO (U.S.S.R.)

For the past four years, Anatoly Pisarenko of the Soviet army reported for weight training as often as two or three times a day and lifted about 25 tons. Gradually, the hard work paid off. The 6' 1", 277-pound "Bull of Kiev" set 11 world records in weightlifting's super heavyweight division (over 242 pounds). In 1982, at Dnepropetrovsk, he accomplished a 570-pound clean and jerk. In 1983, at Moscow, he hauled up 454 pounds in the snatch. On his days off, the 26-year-old Pisarenko usually went fishing. In his own mind his personal best sports record was the 20-pound fish he once pulled out of the Dnieper River.

Pisarenko has always relied not on bulk but on his fluid method and speed. He has kept trim and as solidly built as a brick *dacha*—thus realizing his original goal in weightlifting, which was to obtain "an impressive figure." Now Pisarenko proudly displays a 51-inch chest and a 36-inch waist—plus a sinister black mustache. "Sometimes when I see myself on television," he has remarked, "I get scared." ■

The mark of a champion.

Exxon salutes the American
athletes for all they have given,
their achievements, and the
commitment to excellence that
marks each one a champion.

EXXON

Quality you can count on.

We built Laser XE to outperform the competition.

We gave Laser XE world-class performance. In the slalom, Laser beats all entries— from Trans Am to Mustang GT. We built Laser XE to outperform the competition: Camaro Z28, Trans Am, Mustang GT, Toyota Supra, Nissan 300 ZX. Laser does it when you equip it with turbo, performance handling package and nitrogen-charged shocks.* Laser does it with front-wheel drive, new dual-path suspension system

Laser beats Nissan 300 ZX in the slalom.

Laser outperforms Trans Am in braking.

Laser is faster than Camaro Z28 from 0-50 mph.

and quick-ratio power steering. In the slalom Laser shows its spoiler to the competition and finishes No. 1.

We turbocharged it. From 0-50, Laser XE leaves Camaro Z28 with its shadow. Z28 is a powerhouse— but Laser XE is the sophisticated new wave. Its multi-point injection system "spritzes" fuel in at four points. Its water-cooled bearing reduces critical turbo temperatures to prevent oil "coking" and bearing failure. Its turbo engine boosts h.p. 43%. With 5-speed

your time to 50 mph is 5.4 seconds. Z28, Trans Am, Toyota Supra and 300 ZX are in your remote-controlled side view mirrors.

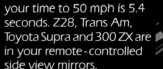

We gave it high-performance braking. Laser XE stops where Trans Am doesn't. We think total performance calls for performance braking. So we gave Laser XE semi-metallic brake pads, power brakes all around and optional wide 15" alloy wheels with Goodyear Eagle GT radials. Result: Laser stops quicker than Trans Am, Z28, Supra,

We gave it a turbo you can trust.

00 ZX. And the margin isn't minor. Laser XE stops 17 ft. before Mustang GT. We even gave it a brain. This is a car that thinks with you. Laser XE's 19-feature electronic monitor is like your sixth sense of the road. It even talks your language, while its color graphic displays make you a calculating driver. And Laser's self-diagnostic system is the nearest thing to an on-board mechanic. It even remembers one-time problems that may never repeat. But performing better isn't your only pleasure. Laser XE's AM/FM multiplex stereo remem-

bers what you like to hear on 20 stations and plays it through six premium speakers you can choose.

Even your performance seat performs. It cushions you with pronounced padding and holds you in position on turns with lateral "wings." You pump up pneumatic cushions for lumbar and

thigh support, and you can order a six-way power seat and a cockpit fitted with Mark Cross leathers. We gave it our best: even your turbo has a 5 year/50,000 mile Protection Plan. Chrysler believes a performer has to be a survivor. We build for that. And back your turbo engine and powertrain with a 5 year/50,000 mile Protection Plan, with outer body rust-through protection too.** What competitor gives you that? None. See dealer for details. Buckle up for safety.

35 Est. Hwy.
22 EPA Est. MPG†

The best built, best backed American cars.‡

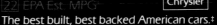

*Based on overall results of USAC tests against standard equipped models. Laser XE equipped with optional handling suspension, Turbo package and 15" road wheels and tires. **5 years or 50,000 miles, whichever comes first. Limited warranty. Deductible required. Excludes leases. †Use EPA est. mpg for comparison. Actual mileage may vary depending on speed, trip length and weather. Hwy. mileage probably less. ‡Based on lowest percent of National Highway Traffic Safety Administration recalls for '82 and '83 models designed and built in North America.

CHRYSLER LASER

"THE COMPETITION IS GOOD. WE HAD TO BE BETTER."*

Lee A. Iacocca

NEW EVENTS

The Games grow in size and spectacle with many more competitions for women.

THE NAME OF THE GAME SHOWN HERE IS RHYTHMIC GYMNASTICS, AN athletic ballet performed with colorful accessories, and it is part of an unprecedented expansion of the Olympic schedule. The '84 Games are enriched by the surging involvement of women in competitions such as this, in which they have specialized, and also in many long regarded as all-male strongholds. Of the 15 new events, 11 are for women, three are for men and one is open to both. Rhythmic gymnastics adds wide spectator appeal and a very unusual kind of athletic glamour.

KAYAKS WITH *four-woman crews race over a 500-meter course, an event new to the Games. In cycling, men will hold an individual points race for the first time, and a 79-kilometer individual road race (below) is set for women only. On the opposite page, synchronized swimmers Tracie Ruiz and Candy Costie apply a flourishing finish to their duet routine.*

OLYMPIC MEDAL EVENTS IN SWIMMING HAVE BEEN OPEN TO BOTH MEN and women since 1912, but it wasn't until 1928 that there was competition for women runners, jumpers and discus-throwers. Field hockey became a new event for women in the '80 Games at Moscow. This year women will be competing at nearly all Olympic venues, from canoeing and cycling courses to handball courts and rifle ranges. The kayak program for women expands to three events, and for the first time women will challenge each other for Olympic honors in cycling.

National champions Tracie Ruiz and Candy Costie are a couple of reasons why the U.S. is so enthusiastic about the introduction of synchronized swimming to the Games. The sport, which was popularized as water ballet in the U.S. by Esther Williams in the 1940s, generally offers competitions for singles, pairs, trios and teams of four to eight. But the event in this Olympics is limited to duets. Much in the manner of figure-skating pairs, the swimmers move to the sound of music that is made audible to them by underwater speakers. Their routines, lasting four minutes, are performed both above and below the surface of the water and are judged on execution, complexity of movements and, of course, degree of synchronization.

179

Y ACHT RACING, IN ONE CLASS OR another, has been on the Olympic scene since 1900. But this year a radically different category has been added—the highly individual discipline of boardsailing. Open to both men and women, it will be conducted in the Pacific Ocean off Long Beach. As in other sailing competitions, races will extend over a seven-day period with accumulated points determining the order of finish. The sport's booming popularity hastened its inclusion in the Olympics. In this year's official event, Windglider boards will be used; in the freestyle, long-distance and slalom exhibitions that follow the official schedule, contestants will ride Windsurfer boards.

FLASHING *across a bright sea, boardsailors race in an Olympic-class regatta at Long Beach. This sailing offspring of surfing becomes the seventh racing category in Olympic yachting.*

THE JAVELIN, *as thrown here by Corinne Schneider of Switzerland, has been a women's event since '32. Now it is also part of the heptathlon. At far right, a race new to the Olympics, the women's 3,000 meters: U.S. star Mary Decker leads the field in the 1983 world championships at Helsinki. Below, Mary Godlove of the U.S. in standard rifle competition—new for women in '84.*

MANY OF THE STRIKING RECENT ACHIEVEMENTS BY WOMEN athletes have come in long-distance running. This year they have their first Olympic marathon, 3,000-meter race and the 400-meter hurdles. The women's pentathlon has grown to a heptathlon with the addition of the 200-meter and javelin events. In other firsts, the Olympic shooting range will be the scene of men's and women's air-rifle competitions and women's pistol and standard rifle events. For men, boxing will add a super heavyweight category. ∎

Capture the Olympics

With Hitachi's VK-C1500 MOS color video camera. At just a touch over two pounds, it's designed for operation with just one hand. So recording any memorable moment, such as a breathtaking 100-meter dash, is ultra-easy.

We've replaced the ordinary pickup tube with our unique MOS image sensor, a solid-state semiconductor device that enables considerable reduction in camera size and weight. It eliminates distortion problems and improves color fidelity, too.

The VK-C1500 also offers a wide variety of automatic functions that take the worry out of shooting. Including fully automatic white balance control and auto-iris.

To complete the picture, our VT-7P includes a lightweight portable VCR—the perfect teammate for the VK-C1500. It's a total video performer, featuring a 5-head design which enables superior recording quality outdoors. Then indoors gives you special speed-play, slow motion and fine still effects in all modes by providing exclusive heads for SP and EP.

What's more, you can enjoy 8 full hours of continuous entertainment in EP mode, plus 7-program/14-day preset timer recording enabled by the VT-7P's tuner/timer.

You'll always have Olympic-sized thrills at hand with Hitachi—continually improving even the best of our 20,000-plus products, for ever greater convenience, higher quality and solid reliability.

Single-handed

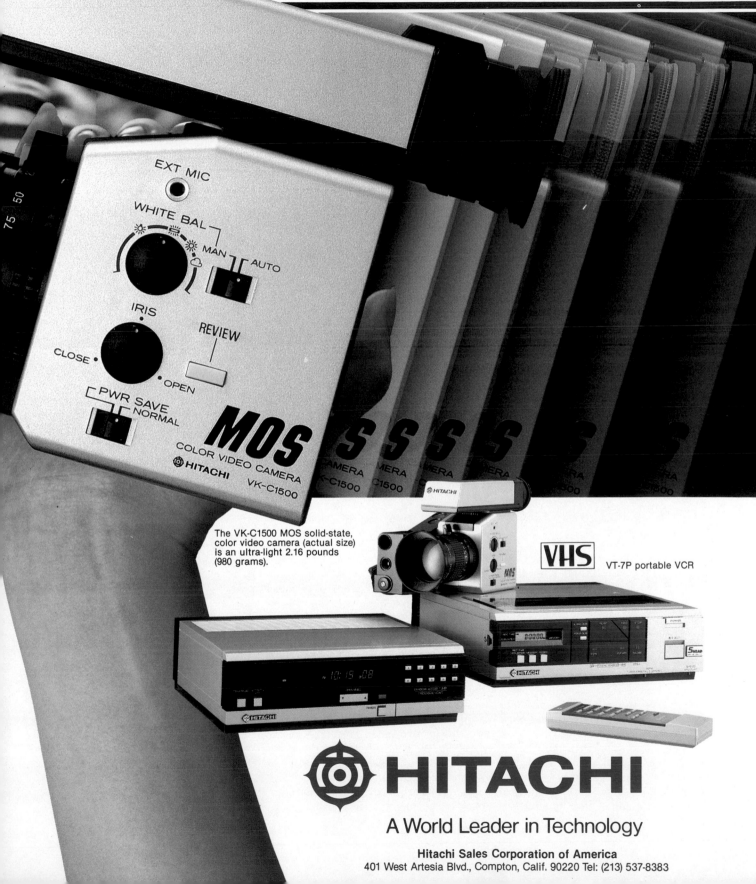

EXT MIC

WHITE BAL
MAN
AUTO

IRIS

REVIEW

CLOSE
OPEN

PWR SAVE
NORMAL

MOS
COLOR VIDEO CAMERA
⊙ HITACHI VK-C1500

The VK-C1500 MOS solid-state,
color video camera (actual size)
is an ultra-light 2.16 pounds
(980 grams).

VHS VT-7P portable VCR

⊙ HITACHI

A World Leader in Technology

THE Athletes Remember

*In their own words,
competitors offer
a rare look
at the interior of
the Olympic
experience.
An album of
photos from
the present and
recollections
of the past*

By
Donald
Dale
Jackson

Photography
By
Mark
Hanauer

MOST OF THEM LIVE comfortably, with late-model cars in the garage and grandfather clocks in the foyer and swimming pools in the yard. They were among the best in the world at what they did for a month or a year or a decade, and many of them are good at what they do now, because the lessons they learned best were discipline and the value of preparation. They did not, as a rule, suffer second place gladly, and it was not always easy to bank their competitive fires when they moved from the arenas to the marketplace, the classroom and the home. They were winners, they knew it and so did everyone else, and the expectations they satisfied so readily as Olympic athletes were more difficult to fulfill amid the complications and compromises of life after sports. "People expected me to achieve equal success in everything else," runner Billy Mills recalls, "and I tried to do it. But I had to find out who I was." "There's a real void in your life after a gold medal," says diver Pat McCormick. "One day you're a star and you're invited to the White House and the next day it's over, and I mean over."

In time almost all of them came to terms with the internal and external pressures to excel and the hollow sensation that commenced when the cheering stopped. They put the medals in a cabinet, to be enjoyed now and then but not flaunted, and they hung the plaques and ribbons and maga-

Dr. Sammy Lee, 63, the diver who twice came up with golds, soars into a dynamic reminder of his Olympic effort.

I FELT
*the tape
across my
chest—I
felt it in my
mind—and my
first thought
was 'Dad knows
I'm an athlete,'"
recalls Billy
Mills of his
feat in Tokyo.
The ex-Marine
from a Sioux
reservation
now lives
near Sacramento.*

zine covers on an out-of-the-way wall. "You have to get on with the program," Pat McCormick says. And when they were able to do that, they could gaze back on their Olympic moments with joy and an enduring satisfaction. "Every four years people come through here and bring me out and interview me," says swimmer Chris von Saltza. "It always amazes me. And then I'm put away again for another four years. But I don't mind, I'm proud of what I did even if it's not that much of a living reality for me anymore." Their memories are vivid, sharply etched and close to the surface; they cherish their achievements and enjoy reliving them.

A shared set of values underlies their memories: Victory goes to the best-prepared and the best-disciplined; luck is a by-product of effort; losers form their excuses before the starter's gun sounds; pain is just one more hurdle to leap. They are united as well by the remarkable clarity of their recollections, by the bond that links them to their fellow competitors.

But as they sort through the pictures in their minds to tell their stories they suffer

Donald Dale Jackson, whose books include Gold Dust, *is a California-born writer now living in Connecticut.*

from the same weaknesses that afflict the rest of us: They remember the good times more clearly than the bad, the successes better than the failures; if they lost they frequently have an explanation—the altitude, the weather, a virus; they are usually the heroes and heroines of their own tales. But none of this tarnishes their achievements or their memories, it simply stamps them as human. Here then is their testimony, their individual witness, here are the Olympic Games—their Olympic Games—as the athletes remember them.

BILLY MILLS, *a U.S. Marine officer who had grown up on a Sioux reservation in South Dakota, scored one of the most stunning upsets in Olympic history when he won the 10,000-meter run at Tokyo in 1964. The unheralded Mills bettered his own fastest time by 46 seconds while breaking the Olympic record. He remembers the following scenes from that extraordinary day:*

On the bus to the stadium I sat next to an attractive girl from Poland. She asked me what event I was in and I said the 10,000. "Oh, and today's the final," she said. "Who do you think's going to win?" I sat there in silence for a minute. I knew that if I said anybody else I'd lose. So I fi-

nally said, "I'm going to win." She said, "What's your name?" and I told her.

Nobody was aware of me in Tokyo. The track world had no idea who I was. Ron Clarke of Australia had the world record and he was the favorite. My strategy was to let him set the pace and to stay in contention, within 15 yards or so. He almost broke me at 5,000 meters. I was fourth or fifth and 15 yards behind but I was also within a second of my fastest time ever. I was thinking I was going to collapse, that in another mile I'd be exhausted, so I thought I'd take the lead and I did. If I had to quit at least I'd have been in front for a while. But I could see my wife Pat in the stands and when I looked at her I felt too embarrassed to quit, so I told myself "just one more lap" every time I came around.

Clarke took the lead back and then my attitude started changing. Now I was thinking I could win a medal and maybe the gold. I saw Clarke look back. I figured he knows I'm here and he's worried and I went ahead of him with two laps to go. He passed me again, and now we came up behind a runner we'd both lapped and I boxed Clarke in and got outside the other runner. But Clarke pushed me and I went out to the third lane. I felt I was going to

continued

EXPERIENCE MAZDA RX-7.

THE SPORTS CAR THAT TAKES THE HIGH PRICE OUT OF HIGH PERFORMANCE.

The Mazda RX-7 is the best-selling two-seat sports car in America. We think we know why.

For one thing, it is an exceptional value.

For another, it has remained true to its origins. It is still a real, bona fide sports car.

A high-revving rotary engine helps it accelerate from zero to 50 in just 6.3 seconds. And its suspension system is designed for high-performance driving—

29 EST. HWY. MPG	/	**19** EST. MPG*

independent struts in front, Watt linkage in the rear.

As for resale value, the Kelley Blue Book, Jan.-Feb. 1984, tells us that a 1981 RX-7 S has retained a healthy 93.4% of its original

sticker price, compared with 83.9% for a 1981 Datsun 280ZX.

Of course, a test drive will tell you even more. It will prove that while we've taken the high price out of high performance, we've taken the true sports car experience and made it come alive in the Mazda RX-7.

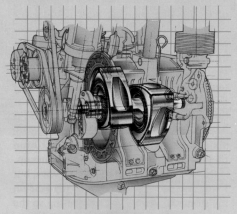

The rotors in the RX-7's rotary engine spin constantly in one direction instead of moving up and down like pistons. At high rpm it uses less energy fighting friction than a conventional reciprocating engine. This means that the rotary engine is smoother and more powerful for its size—the ideal power plant for a sports car.

1984 Mazda RX-7 S
$10,195**

Standard features include 5-speed overdrive transmission •Steel-belted radial tires • Power-assisted ventilated front disc brakes •Front and rear stabilizer bars •Full cut-pile carpeting • Driver's seat lumbar support adjuster •Electric rear window defroster •2-speed wipers/washer plus intermittent feature •Dual door mirrors •Lockable, lighted rear stowaway lockers •Quartz digital clock •Tinted glass.

Experienced drivers buckle up.

*EPA estimates for comparison. Your mileage may vary with trip length, speed and weather. Highway mileage will probably be less. **Manufacturer's suggested retail price. Actual price set by dealer. Taxes, license, freight, options (tires/al. wheels shown) and other dealer charges extra. Price may change without notice. Availability of vehicles with specific features may vary. Mazda's rotary engine licensed by NSU-WANKEL.

THE MORE YOU LOOK, THE MORE YOU LIKE.

*T*HE *world's best woman sprinter in the mid-'60s, Wyomia Tyus now concentrates on raising two children in Los Angeles. Lindy Remigino, high school track coach in Connecticut, was called a "Cinderella Kid" in '52 for his victory in the 100 meters, but he knows it was no fluke.*

to London and there the U.S. State Department transferred me from one car to another three times on the road before I flew back to L.A. It was like cops and robbers. What was really eerie is that I was actually home in Sacramento 48 hours after my last event, just sitting there like every other American watching the Games on television.

Georgia-born WYOMIA TYUS *is the only woman athlete in the history of the Olympics to win back-to-back gold medals in the 100-meter dash. Part of the reason for her successes in Tokyo in 1964 and in Mexico City in 1968, she believes, was a talent that all world-class athletes covet—the ability to relax under pressure:*

I could always relax. My coach used to say that the biggest problem with Tyus was that she slept too much. We played cards and told jokes and laughed the night before the finals in 1964. When the gun went off it was as though I was in a tunnel—I blacked everything out, and the next thing I knew it was over and I turned to my U.S. teammate, Edith McGuire, and said, "Who won?" She said, "You did." I gasped, "I did?" I was just in shock. Then we hugged.

In 1968 I remember there was a dance that was popular called the Tighten Up and I told some friends that if I got to the

finals I was going to do this little dance before the start, just when they told us to take our warmups off. I remember hearing bongos in the stands and I went into my dance. This time I got one of the best starts of my life and I knew I had it when I was 50 yards out. About a month later one of the Australian girls who ran against me asked me what that strange exercise was that I did just before the start of the 100. She said it really psyched her out. Oh, I was bold that time.

On the victory stand I was thinking about my brothers, and all those years they got teased and people would say, "Your sister can beat you," and how they'd always let me play in their baseball games when we were kids.

More than seventy summers have passed since ABEL KIVIAT *finished second in the 1,500-meter run at the 1912 Games in Stockholm. In the years since, he worked as a court clerk in New York before retiring to Lakehurst, N.J. Most of the memories had faded when he was interviewed several months ago, but some did persist:*

I roomed with Jim Thorpe for one night. He was a wonderful chap—never a word to say, never had any money in his pocket. He walked on his heels, bent backward. They

separated us after one night because he came in feeling good, if you know what I mean. That Swedish punch would knock you off your feet worse than tequila.

We stayed on a ship, and we rode in horse carriages to the Olympic grounds. I thought my race was a dead heat, but they gave it to an Englishman, Arnold Jackson. After the Games they put tables full of food on the field and kegs full of that Swedish punch and we had a banquet. After dinner these big Swedes came out with blankets and picked up our big men and started tossing them in the air and catching them in the blankets. Not me, I was only 111 pounds. They said this was some kind of after-dinner Swedish custom.

DEBBIE MEYER-REYES *was America's aquatic heroine in the 1968 Games at Mexico City, a 16-year-old self-described water baby—"I never wanted to be away from the water, I was even born at the U.S. Naval Academy"—who glided to victories in the 200-, 400- and 800-meter freestyle events. Now married and living near Sacramento, Calif., Debbie recalls the Games with a clarity common to many Olympians:*

I didn't like the food at the Olympic Village, so I kind of existed on strawberry ice

continued

THE · FIT · FOR · THE · FIT

Gallery. Trim-fit fashion for today's body conscious man. Available at leading department and specialty stores.

GALLERY

BY · HAGGAR®

ABEL Kiviat, on the American team in Stockholm in 1912, stored up experiences that included a second place in the 1,500 meters and a brief, memorable role as Jim Thorpe's roommate.

cream and pound cake and peanut butter. My parents found a place where they could get peanut butter (imported from the United States) for something like $10 a jar, and one day my dad came to the pool and threw me this bag with two jars in it. I caught it and I was walking along beside the pool when the place became completely quiet because one of the finals was coming up, and then I dropped the bag and there was this *splat!* It was all you could hear and I saw my dad's face turning red.

I swam the 800 last and won by something like three-quarters of a lap. I just took the lead and held it. I can still feel the race. I can see the yellow tiles on the floor, the orange seats in the stands, the yellow timing system, the lane ropes. I can see the swimmers on benches on the side, and I can feel my arm strokes and the water. You hit the pain barrier at about 600 meters. It hurts to the point that you don't think you can lift your arms for another stroke, but then you get a second wind and it's like breaking through a sheet of butcher paper. You're like a submarine struggling to break the surface and all of a sudden you're hydroplaning and it's downhill. It's a neat feeling but it's murder getting to it.

After I got the third medal I remember climbing down from the victory stand and seeing my coach, Sherm Chavoor, smiling from side to side, with his arms open, ready to give me a hug. He was wearing a USA windbreaker and a blue-and-white shirt. He knew me so well, he was the reason I was there. If he said, "Jump," I'd say, "How high?" I can still see it so clearly, I put the medal around his neck and said,

"Here, Sherm, this one's for you." He said, "Thanks, honey." He called the other day and said he couldn't find the medal, but he didn't call back, so I guess he found it.

A 32-year-old wound to the ego can still fester, especially if it scars the memory of an Olympic triumph. LINDY REMIGINO, now a successful high school track coach in Hartford, Conn., wants it known that his victory in the 100-meter sprint in the Helsinki Games in 1952 was no fluke and he was no "Cinderella Kid," as the newspapers called him. "It bothers me because it sounds like I came out of the woodwork," he says. Here's the way Lindy remembers it:

Jim Golliday was our best American hope for a gold, but he got hurt. Andy Stanfield passed up the 100 for the 200; Barney Ewell and Mel Patton had retired; and Art Bragg broke down in a semifinal heat. I'm no dummy. I saw all this happening and I was gaining confidence. Herb McKenley from Jamaica and Emmanuel McDonald Bailey from Britain were the favorites, but I didn't feel like an underdog. In the first trial heat Remigino goes *biti-boom* and wins easily. Second one—*dit-dit-dit*, same thing.

Then I'm in the finals and I'm out in front at 80 meters and I want to win so much I do something strategically bad—I start leaning to the damn tape. I give it the Madison Square Garden lean like I'd done in all those 60-yard dashes at the Garden, and this shortens my stride. I hear McKenley coming up—*chuka-chuka-chuk*—and I felt the tape, but he went by me and I

thought he'd won and I go to congratulate him. Then the names go up on the board and—*bitiboom*—it says REMIGINO USA—*first*. And then I'm up on the victory stand. Here I am, the skinny, little guy from the Bronx with the meatball eyes, and they give me my medal.

They called me the Cinderella Kid, and it's stuck with me. But—and this is important—I ran against those guys in Europe after the Games and I beat them. I won everything. You know, I saw McKenley in Montreal in 1976 and we joked about it; we said we'd meet on the track at noon and have it out, once and for all. But I didn't show up and I found out later that he didn't show up either.

AL OERTER is an Olympic phenomenon. Four times the massive discus thrower from Long Island won gold medals in the Games—in 1956 at Melbourne, 1960 at Rome, 1964 at Tokyo and 1968 at Mexico City—each time setting an Olympic record. Olympic competition inspires and gratifies him in a way he finds difficult to explain. "It's being with the best of the best, it's seeing how well you can prepare and how good you really are"—and he cherishes it so that, at age 48, he trained for the 1984 Games. Oerter has experienced nearly every sensation an Olympic athlete knows:

In my first Olympics at Melbourne some of my competitors tried to play mental games. They'd say, "Look at the bottom of your shoe. See where it's wearing, it's on the wrong side, you're turning wrong." But what that means is that *they're* in trouble, they're worried. Most Russians don't know how to psych, they can't pull it off. But there was a weightlifter who tried to do it by picking up people, I mean heavy people, by putting his hands under their armpits at arm's length. Now that's almost impossible. There would always be a gaggle of Russians around, and what would happen is that one of the other Russians would get behind the guy where he couldn't be seen and push the weightlifter's hands up.

I went to Rome in 1960 very confident, but in the competition I just could not get it together. Then my teammate, Rink Babka—he was leading me by four or five feet—told me what I was doing wrong. It was something about my left arm. I corrected it and on the next throw I threw an Olympic record and Rink didn't get beyond me. That's what I think the Olympic spirit is—helping each other.

In 1964, I tore some cartilage in my rib

continued

*I*T'S

being with the best of the best that gratified discus champ Al Oerter during four Olympics—in each of which he won golds. Australian-born Michelle Ford, a USC student, "represented" her friends on the U.S. team in Moscow in 1980 by winning the 800-meter freestyle.

But, in the afternoon, she said, "Look, I'm sorry about this morning, but it was just such a blow that you're going and we're not." She said she hoped I'd represent them and that if they couldn't be there she was glad I would be.

Tracy gave me a letter to give to a guy on the British team, and the really weird thing was that his name was Jimmy Carter. It was so funny, I got to the Olympic Village in Moscow and they went through my bags and pulled out this letter and they took me aside. They said, "Who, who?" and I said, "Swimmer, swimmer." "Swimmer?" "Yes, yes." I was petrified, I couldn't believe it, but I finally convinced them that Jimmy Carter was a swimmer.

They called weightlifter PAUL AN-DERSON "the strongest man in the world," but on the day of the heavy-weight-lifting finals at the Melbourne Games in 1956 the stumpy giant from Toccoa, Georgia, wasn't so sure. He was ill and running a fever. Anderson and a lifter from Argentina, Humberto Selvetti, hoisted the same weight total, but the gold, under the rules, went to the lighter man, Anderson, at 304 pounds. Here is his recollection:

I had lost 25 or 30 pounds with this "bug" I had and I was feeling weak and feverish. I remember trying to get something for my cough at a drugstore on the day of the finals but I couldn't find a store open. The lifting competition started at 7 or 8 that night but the heavyweights had to wait for everyone else to finish. I was keyed up and I didn't want to watch the others lift, so I went to a movie by myself. It was called something like *Joe Macbeth.*

We didn't start lifting until about 1 a.m. I always had contempt for the weight. I didn't pace around and use up nervous energy worrying about it. My idea was to just jerk and lift it. But I felt so dizzy that when I got it over my head I didn't know where I was or which way I was facing. I wasn't sure if I could continue. Then a Hungarian woman athlete came up to me and said that the kids in her country admired me so much that they would lift broomsticks and pretend they were me. That helped me. I asked my coach how much I needed to lift to win—and I lifted just that much. When we finished it was 4 a.m. I went back to my room and painted my aching tonsils for the twentieth time.

cage during practice and the pain was awful. I couldn't rest, couldn't write, couldn't even eat without pain. I took about 12 gross of aspirin and the doctor said forget the competition, but I wanted to try it. I just wanted to see if I could get beyond the injury, to see if I could reach my capability. They shot me full of novocaine and taped me up and said I couldn't injure myself any further. On my fifth throw (of six) in the finals I hammered it as hard as I could with my arm and set another Olympic record. But I knew when the discus left my hand that I wasn't going to throw it again, I had reached some kind of barrier.

I carried the flag at the Closing Ceremonies in 1968 in Mexico City. It turned into a big party; the athletes were supposed to stay in the stands but they vaulted onto the field. Everybody meshed, people were singing and dancing arm in arm, and it was a true celebration and a thrill. It was like it's supposed to be. Since then it's been difficult to recapture that because the athletes have been more isolated.

MICHELLE FORD, *a swimmer from Australia, enjoyed an opportunity denied to athletes from the U.S. and many other nations—participation in the 1980 Games in Moscow. Michelle, a student at USC, who hopes to compete again in '84, trained with Tracy Caulkins and other U.S. swimmers. Then Michelle went to Moscow where she won the 800-meter freestyle. The Americans stayed home:*

When I found out I was going to Moscow, I couldn't tell Tracy. I knew she knew, but I didn't know what to say, and Tracy wouldn't talk to me that morning.

PAT McCORMICK's *goal was to become the first diver to achieve an Olym-*

continued

POLE-VAULTER *Don Bragg, on his land in the New Jersey Pine Barrens: "They say to me, 'Don, there's a lot more to life than the Olympics,' and I say, 'Oh, is there?'"*

pic "double double"—back-to-back gold medals in the springboard and platform competitions. The pretty blonde Californian pulled it off with brilliant performances in 1952 at Helsinki and in 1956 at Melbourne. Pat, whose daughter Kelly is a leading U.S. diving contender, may also hold the Olympic record for irreverence:

In 1952, I got an official to let me into Avery Brundage's room, and we took his underwear out of his dresser and ran it up the flagpole. If the officials ever knew that, they'd have died. We also moved all the furniture out of one of the chaperone's rooms and put it on the roof. Another time we decided to swipe an Olympic flag, and that was big fun. Six of us marched down together, lined up and took off our hats and lowered the flag and just walked off. Everybody thought it was part of the ceremonies. I still have it. Now they'll probably take my medals away.

When I was going for my fourth gold medal in 1956, I went into the final day in fourth place with only two dives left. I remember that on the bus back to the Olym- *continued*

PACIFIC BELL MEETS THE CHALLENGE OF THE 1984 OLYMPICS.

Next time you need help with your communications system, consider this: Pacific Bell was chosen over other major corporations to design and implement the network for the most complex communications event: the 1984 Olympics.

And we've met the challenge. Pacific Bell is providing the key telecommunications links between dozens of Olympic sites spread out over an area of 4,500 square miles. We're designing and implementing a complex network of tens of thousands of voice, video and data transmission circuits. We're creating, for the Olympics, a system that has the capacity and complexity to meet the communications needs of most FORTUNE 500 corporations.

The Pacific Bell Fiber Optics network will help give Los Angeles the most advanced metropolitan telecommunications system in the world. The key to the system is the

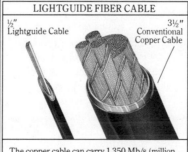

LIGHTGUIDE FIBER CABLE

½" Lightguide Cable

3½" Conventional Copper Cable

The copper cable can carry 1,350 Mb/s (million bits per second) of digital information. The fiber optics lightguide cable used for the Olympics can carry over 7 times as much or 9,720 Mb/s of encoded audio, video or data information.

fiber optics network: a light-wave voice, video and data transmission system that is a quantum improvement in the capacity, speed, accuracy and efficiency of information transmission. Fiber optics technology is revolutionizing information transmission in the same way that the integrated circuit revolutionized data processing. And our Los Angeles fiber optics network will become part of a statewide network that is already the largest and most advanced in the world.

In short: Next time you need help with your communications system, give us a call.

Official sponsor and supplier of the 1984 Olympic Games

PACIFIC ✕ BELL

*P*AUL *Anderson, "the world's strongest man" as an Olympic weightlifter in 1956, directs a rehab youth center in rural Georgia. Pat McCormick, who ruled both springboard and platform diving in two Olympiads, takes a daily beach workout with her retriever.*

pic Village the day before, I was really feeling sorry for myself. My roommate was in first and my husband—he was our coach—was talking to her. And then it was almost like I was touched by something. I started thinking that I'd been training for 15 years and it was going to come down to four seconds and two dives, and by the time I got off the bus I knew I would win. But my first dive wasn't perfect and now I had to do the best dive of my life to win. It was a two-and-a-half pike, and I just thought about the mechanics—my hips, and the long drop I had to make. I took off from the tower so hard I could feel it shake. I just hit it. I really nailed that dive and when I popped up in the water, I knew it, I knew that I'd won.

I think I can pretty well understand my daughter now. We never really discuss her diving. She'll sometimes ask me, but I have to be very, very careful. She's Kelly Mc-Cormick and I'm Pat McCormick and we have two different styles. But she is doing dives now that I don't think I could do. I'm proud of her as a diver, but I love her as my daughter more than anything.

DON BRAGG *is a big, beefy man with a laugh that fills a room, a pole vaulter who looks more like a weightlifter. He*

lives in a sprawling house beside a lake in the Pine Barrens of New Jersey, and like many Olympians he looks back on his performance in the Games—he won the pole vault at Rome in 1960—as the culmination of his life. "They say to me, 'Don, there's a lot more to life than the Olympics,' and I say, 'Oh, is there?'"

The U.S. track team took a train from Switzerland to Rome, and every time it stopped these wine vendors would come around. I wasn't going to drink, but it was hot and we finally got some. We started singing and dancing in the aisles, and there was a big window you could open, and about three feet out from the window there were telephone poles. So I picked up a distance runner—they told me I did this, I don't really remember—and stuck him out the train window to see how close I could get him to the poles without touching. The other guys were pulling at me; they were afraid I'd drop him. He didn't seem to mind; he was feeling good, too.

The main thing I remember about the Olympics is tension, pressure, nervousness, diarrhea, one meal a day to keep my weight down. The fear was in my mind all the time. When we were training, this German vaulter went over the bar using *one arm*—I'd never seen that in my life. A Finn

asked me what I thought of it, and I said, "He's probably one of the greatest one-armed pole vaulters in the world."

In the finals I wanted to quit a hundred times. You can just smell the tension of competition and I wanted to say, "Hey, I've had it, I'm a bum." Well, the bar was at about 14' 4" and I'm figuring I can tell everybody my leg was hurting and I couldn't do any better. I can say I was in the Olympics, tell my kids. But I got over, then I did the same thing at 14' 8", and I got over again. And now there are only four of us left, and I say to myself, "Wait a minute! Your whole life has been to be *here*, and here it *is*, so go get it, pick this apple and eat it." Then the bar went up to 15' 1", and I made it on the first try, and now it was just me and Ronnie Morris of USC.

I tried not to like my competitors. I tried to think up reasons to hate them. Ronnie had more misses than I did up to then, and if we didn't get any farther—I'm the champ, right? So what can I do here? We could go up to any height Ronnie and I agreed on, so I ran over and said, "Ronnie, you just cleared 15' 1⅛" by six or eight *inches*, that was *fantastic*." I said, "We've knocked off all the Europeans, it's just you and me, let's go for the world record—

continued

Shell introduces its new gold standard gasoline: SU 2000™ Super Unleaded

All gasolines are not alike. SU 2000's formula is so unique it's patented. And SU 2000 also has high octane. It's among the highest octane premium unleaded gasolines available. (Note: SU 2000 is never blended with methanol, a low-priced alcohol some suppliers use as an octane booster.)

- So unique it's patented
- High octane
- Reduces intake deposits
- Never blended with methanol

SU 2000 helps keep your engine clean mile after mile. It is designed to reduce critical intake deposits that

may be causing engine knock. In fact, the longer you use SU 2000, the better it can be for your engine.

For truly gold standard performance, get new SU 2000 Super Unleaded. In the black and gold pump at the Shell station nearest you.

The longer you use it, the better it can be for your engine.

U.S. *flagbearer in the 1968 Opening Ceremonies, Jan York Romary cherishes the honor that came after years of obscurity as an Olympic fencer. Australian swimming great Murray Rose, a television announcer, valued the letter from his coach "at a time when I was scared, when my legs felt like jelly."*

15' 10½"." And he said, "How about 15' 5⅛"?" I said, "O.K."

I figure if I make it on my first try it will blow his socks off. Half the stadium has emptied out, the lights are on and we've been at it seven or eight hours. I go down the runway—*perfect*—and I clear the crossbar by four or five inches. Now I go over to Ronnie and say, "Come on, Ronnie, it's just you and me, man"—I'm blowing smoke, you know—"just you and me. I just did it, *first try* I did it, you can do it, let's go, you can do it." He starts walking away, and I say, "I think." He stopped for a minute, like, did he hear me right? And he makes a nice jump, he almost made it, and my heart went pa-*wow*. He almost made that. But then his second jump wasn't too good, and on his third he almost went under the crossbar. So I've got it, but now I'm not satisfied. I want the world record and

so I put the bar up to the record and I'm damn near over and everybody's screaming and I swear their screaming knocks the bar off the pegs.

When I was on the victory stand I cut loose with my Tarzan yell. I always kind of believed I was Tarzan, you know. I was always swinging in the trees and I wanted to be like him. The yell was just a total physical release, really. The Olympics was not a great time. I was happy when I retired, I couldn't have handled the pressure much longer. The night after I won I kept waking up and asking my friend, "Chico, did I win or am I dreaming?" And he kept saying, "You won, you won, go back to sleep."

Olympic fencers enjoy a longer competitive life-span than many other athletes, but even by fencing standards JA-NICE YORK ROMARY's career has

been remarkable: She fenced in every Olympiad from 1948 to 1968, and in that year she carried the American flag in the Opening Ceremonies. Now the commissioner of fencing for the Los Angeles Olympic Organizing Committee, she has watched her sport struggle to emerge from the shadows of the more popular and glamorous Olympic events:

If your relatives back home wanted to know how you were doing, you had to call them. They couldn't find anything in the newspapers about fencing except perhaps a list of the first three finishers. Fencing was treated as a kind of stepchild. In 1948, for the London Games, we weren't even a part of the Olympic Village, but in 1956 in Melbourne we stayed at the Village and it made a tremendous difference. All the officiating used to be done by men, and the women were very aware that some judges liked tall blondes, some liked brunettes, some liked women rounder. You couldn't prove it, but some of the calls made you suspicious.

I couldn't believe it when I was chosen flag-bearer. No woman had ever done it before. I still get goopy when I talk about it. There were tears running down my face. I had never had that much attention in my life—and I liked it. If I had had any buttons they would have popped. But my arm got so tired I could hardly move it, and I felt it for three or four days afterward.

MURRAY ROSE *was one of the best of an extraordinary generation of Australian swimmers—Dawn Fraser, David Theile and John Konrads were others—who flourished in the late 1950s and early 1960s. A gold medalist in the 400-meter and 1,500-meter freestyle events before the home folks in Melbourne in 1956, Rose repeated in the 400 in 1960 at Rome and added a silver in the 1,500. An intense and incisive man, he is now a Los Angeles-based sports commentator for Australian television. His Olympic memories:*

When I was about to swim my first final in 1956 I found a letter in my locker, a la *Chariots of Fire*, from my coach, Sam Herford. He was always very emotional. He'd been like a second father to me since I was five, but he wasn't always good at verbal communication. He wrote this letter from his heart about how much our relationship had meant to him—cut it off right now, he was saying, and it's been the most meaningful event in my life—and how he knew I was ready and that I was the best-prepared athlete at the Olympic Games. It had a deep impact on me at a

continued

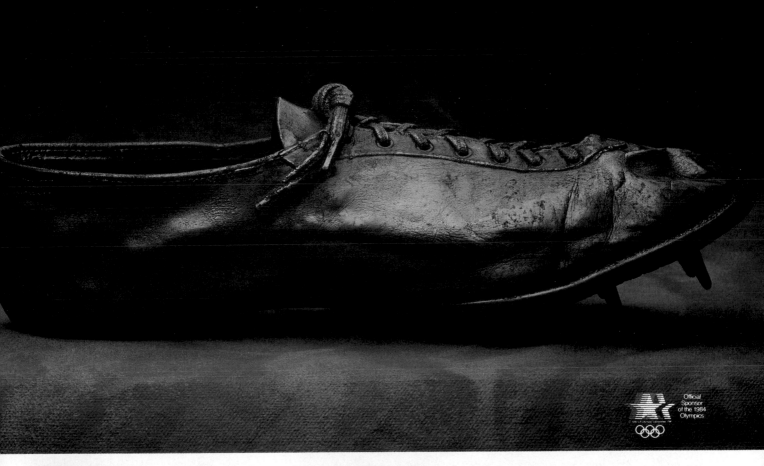

LEE   MILLS   RIGBY   MEYER   SPITZ

TYUS   REMIGINO   FORD   OERTER   KIVIAT

BRAGG   ANDERSON   McCORMICK   ROMARY   ROSE

HART   VON SALTZA   STONES   JOHNSON   DE VARONA

*T*HE *way they were: twenty athletes in their prime, eight decades of effort and excellence.*

time when I was scared, when my legs felt like jelly and my mouth was dry. I felt like I could hardly walk out on the deck, and I went out with a surge of emotion.

Every moment of the days of my Olympic finals seems to be indelibly printed on my mind. Every little detail becomes important. There's a heightened sense of awareness, you're more attentive to everything going on. I can remember getting on the bus at the Olympic Village and the sound of the bus doors and the dust on the bus window and the expressions on people's faces outside. I was thinking, "Lord, they're just walking around like it's a normal day. Don't they know what's going on?" Part of it was the adrenaline pumping. I suppose one could have the same experience walking to his execution.

In the 1,500 at Melbourne I wanted to go out apparently hard for the first few laps to show George Breen of the U.S., who was a front-runner, that he wouldn't have the race to himself. I then gradually slowed the pace down, and Breen came back to me. Tsuyoshi Yamanaka of Japan was on the other side of him. I took a little more off the pace each lap, but I knew Yamanaka would have a big finish, so I had to put some distance on him. About 300 yards from the finish I used Breen to shield me from Yamanaka and I made a big jump. By the time Yamanaka saw what was going on, it was too late. He'd let me get away. They ran a picture in the paper of the two of us embracing after the race, an Australian and a Japanese—and the date was December 7, 1956.

continued

BP-2000 HIGH SPEED BAND PRINTER

M-100L
MATRIX PRINTER

B-600 MEDIUM SPEED BAND PRINTER

P-80 MATRIX PRINTER

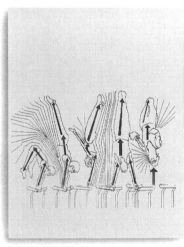

MODEL 480 MATRIX PRINTER

DP-55 DAISYWHEEL PRINTER

DP-35 DAISYWHEEL PRINTER

P-80 MATRIX PRINTER

P-132 MATRIX PRINTER

M-120 MATRIX PRINTER

...and so on.

Dataproducts printers.
Nobody puts ideas on paper so many ways.

DATAPRODUCTS CORP., 6200 CANOGA AVE., WOODLAND HILLS, CA 91365. (818) 887-3924. IN EUROPE, 136-138 HIGH ST., EGHAM, SURREY, TW 20 9HL ENGLAND.

*E*DDIE
Hart teaches at a college 12 years after a coach's error cost him a run for a sprinter's gold. Business executive Chris von Saltza realizes her life was dramatically changed within minutes in an Olympic pool.

The story of EDDIE HART *and* REY ROBINSON *is a sad footnote in the Olympic history books, a pocket drama lost amid the heroic sagas of the Nurmis and Owenses and Oerters. Hart and Robinson were the sprinters who failed to show up for their quarterfinal 100-meter heats in 1972 at Munich and were disqualified as a result. It was a simple mistake—their coach had the wrong schedule—but its consequences were irrevocable: They were out. Hart, who had tied the world record for the 100 in the Olympic Trials, could salvage some satisfaction as a member of the winning 400-meter relay team, but not much:*

We ran our first heats in the morning and Coach Stan Wright's schedule said we didn't run again for something like five or six hours. He suggested that we all go back to the Olympic Village and relax for a couple of hours and then come back. I had some literature that had been given to us, and I was going through it in my room when I noticed that there was a discrepancy between the time it said and the time the coach had given us. We weren't really alarmed, but we decided to go back to the stadium anyway. We got to the gate of the Village and ABC had a television setup there and they were showing a 100-meter race. We asked if it was a replay and they said, "No, it's live," and just then the race went off with an empty lane and we found out later that was Rey Robinson's race.

We jumped in an ABC car and went to the stadium. We went down one-way streets the wrong way and when a policeman tried to stop us we just went around him. We got to the stadium and ran into a tunnel and I was about a quarter of the way through it when another race went off

and that was my race. I was that close.

After that it was like I was in the clouds for a while. Stan took it very hard; he took the blame. I wanted to be alone, I had some crying to do, but Stan didn't want us to be alone. I wasn't going to say the heck with the whole deal and go home, and I wasn't the kind of person who would commit suicide. But I'd been training and pointing for these Games for 10 years and now it all kind of crumbled. Your perspective changes—I'm a husband and a father now and those things are more important than a medal. It would have been tougher if I didn't have the relay, and Rey didn't. But I'm not going to lie. I simplify it sometimes, but it wasn't simple and it wasn't easy to get over it.

CHRIS VON SALTZA's *Olympics were the 1960 Games in Rome, where she swam on two winning relay teams and captured an individual gold in the 400-meter freestyle and a silver in the 100-meter freestyle. Now a systems engineer for IBM and the mother of two sons, Chris is a thoughtful and perceptive woman who bears a resemblance to actress Mariette Hartley. For Chris, as for many other Olympians, the real struggle began when the Games ended:*

I remember standing on my blocks before diving in and looking at the 24-hour clock at the end of the pool. It said 21:35 or something like that and I was thinking, "Wow, in five minutes it's all going to be over"—it was terrifying in a way. This was it! It was like "Hey, lady, you don't get another shot at this." I knew my life would be permanently changed one way or the other after those five minutes.

Winning made me special, unique, the

best in the world at one time. It made me a part of history. I think I would have been a different person if I didn't win. It wouldn't have devastated me, but it would have changed the choices and opportunities I had later. But then I had to accept the idea that because I was the best at something once didn't mean I had to be the best at everything always. Some people expect that level of excellence from you at everything. You have to come to terms with that. I think a study of the reentry problems of Olympic gold medalists would be a wonderful subject for a Ph.D. paper.

High jumper DWIGHT STONES *won his first bronze medal as an 18-year-old long shot in 1972 in Munich and his second when he was the odds-on choice for a gold in 1976 in Montreal. Now 30 years old and a father, Stones began 1984 with hopes of trying for gold in Los Angeles, confident that he had grown beyond the adolescent gaffes he blames for his Olympic disappointments:*

When I realized I was a medalist in 1972 I felt like I'd reached my goal, and that was my mistake. I relaxed, I was so pleased that it was like I didn't care if I jumped any higher. I was thinking, "I'm gonna be on that podium, it doesn't matter what I do now—I can go under the bar three times, I can *break* the bar and I'm still a medalist. Hey, the competition's over!"

Going into Montreal in '76 I thought it would be a piece of cake. No problem. I had the world record, I'd dominated the event for four years, I mean *give me the gold.* I was at the absolute height of belligerency and obnoxiousness—I was the worst. You couldn't tell me anything, I'm

continued

*D*WIGHT *Stones trains for another Olympic high jump and looks back at his erratic behavior as "undeserving" of a gold medal. Rafer Johnson, surrounded by some of his playground protégés, can still feel the pain that he bore throughout his 1956 decathlon.*

number one, so get out of my sight. I went to Montreal and then decided to go home to train. I had had a room with 13 roommates, one bathroom. I didn't like the training field, I couldn't stand it there. I just cut out. I was bad. I think what a jerk I was and I don't know why somebody didn't punch me out.

On the morning of the qualifying jumps there was a story in a newspaper that quoted me as saying, "I hate French Canadians." Oh, man, I mean I said a lot of things, but I didn't say that—give me a *break*. People were cheering when I missed, and I blew kisses to the crowd, thankyou thankyou thankyouverymuch. I mean I was out of *control*. I wore my Mickey Mouse shirt, I was into wearing the wrong stuff on purpose and breaking all the stupid little rules.

I made a good jump at 7′ 3″ in the finals—I mean I *screamed* it, cleared it by four inches. But then it started raining hard. I can't accelerate into my turns in the rain, it's like driving a car at the Indianapolis 500. I'm talking hydroplaning. I didn't get higher than 7′ 3″. The guys that beat me were power jumpers who relied on strength rather than technique like I did. If one of the Russians didn't make a giant *bozo* and pass twice at 7′ 3¾″, he would have got the bronze instead of me. Some-

body had threatened to shoot me, which is why I moved around a lot on the victory stand. I figured if I kept moving maybe they'd just wing me.

It took the Olympic Games to wake me up to what a jerk I was. Maybe it rained for a reason. I had a lot of soul-searching to do. I realized that I really wasn't a very nice person. I'd do anything for a laugh and I didn't mind embarrassing people. I didn't deserve to win the gold medal, the honor and dignity and integrity that go with it. Maybe I'll never deserve it, but I decided to work on deserving it more than I did then. That was just the year I picked to be a jerk.

RAFER JOHNSON *rebounded from an injury-shadowed, silver-medal performance in the 1956 Olympic decathlon at Melbourne to edge out his UCLA teammate and friend, C. K. Yang of Taiwan, in the 1960 Games at Rome. Johnson remembers both the travail and the triumph:*

I had a serious knee injury in 1956. There was no time during the competition when I wasn't in pain. It was the most disappointing time of my athletic career, to be at the threshold like that and then fall short. I think I cried for like an hour. I couldn't stop. I've seen films of the medal ceremony and I actually had trouble get-

ting up into position on the victory stand because I was still in pain.

When I won in 1960 I felt disappointed for C. K.—he was my best friend—but I'll be honest, I wasn't there for a tie. He had to beat me by something like 50 or 60 yards in the 1,500-meter run to wipe out my lead, and I finished a stride behind. That night I was so pumped up and sore that I couldn't sleep, so I got up and walked around Rome for hours. Nobody recognized me—I didn't see many people—but then an American medical student who'd seen the Games asked me if I wanted to take a ride to Tivoli. We spent a few hours there and I got back to the Olympic Village at about noon the next day.

Her stunning looks and confident on-camera style have made DONNA DE VARONA *a successful sports commentator on major networks, but in 1964 in Tokyo she was a muscular 17-year-old swimmer at the zenith of her athletic career—and apprehensive about the world beyond the pool. Here she recalls the year she won the 400-meter individual medley:*

My most vivid memory is that I forgot my pass on the day of the trial heats for my race and the guard wouldn't let me in. There were three Russians there and they
continued

*T*V *personality Donna de Varona, on a day of sparkling snow in New York's Central Park, is happily haunted by the Olympic triumph which, she realized, ended her dream.*

told the guard to let me in. They said, "She's Donna de Varona, number one," and even though they were the other side, they got me in.

I'd been having respiratory problems and so I wasn't at that peak where you fly and the pain feels good. I'd been at that point about eight times in my career and I wanted the ninth time to be at Tokyo—where everything comes together and you put the pain outside of yourself. I still felt I would win. In the Olympics you have to

think that way. I wanted to get the feel of the water before the race but we didn't get a chance to, so when we were in the ready room I just sort of announced to everybody else in the race that I was going to false-start. Can you imagine the audacity of it? They were all sitting there wondering if I meant it. It totally put them in my race, like I was saying, "You can swim in my race if you want to come along for the ride, but. . . ." If somebody had done that to me, I would have said, "Who does she think she

is?" But I considered that race mine. After the false start, I got in front and stayed there and won by six or seven seconds.

When it was all over I remember going back to the pool and standing in the empty stands by myself for a long time, just letting my emotions fill me up. I was thinking that this was the place of my triumph, but the triumph was death, in a way. It's like when you give up your dream you die, and I had realized my dream, I'd reached the top of the mountain—so what's next? ∎

The Perfect Take-Home Gifts For Everyone On Your List

(and make sure you don't forget yourself!)

THE OFFICIAL
LICENSED
PEN and PENCIL
of the Los Angeles
1984 OLYMPICS

These are the most collectable of the collectables!

Fine Pentel® writing instruments in a very limited-edition collection that are certain to be amongst the most sought-after treasured gifts. In limited-edition chalk-white is the internationally famous Rolling Writer® roller pen & the exciting new Sharplet-2™ fully automatic pencils. In glistening gold-tone color (packaged in handsome velour presentation cases), your limited-edition collectables offer the magnificent Slim Excalibur® executive roller pen in brushed gold finish or the classic Excalibur pen & automatic pencil set. All in this limited collection are, of course, emblazoned with the 1984 Olympic emblem.

Find them at better stores & souvenir stands throughout the Los Angeles area. To insure the value of these limited-edition collectables, once the existing supply has been exhausted no more will be produced. Don't be disappointed, get yours today!

Pentel®
PENTEL OF AMERICA, LTD.

BEING BETTER IS WHAT WE'RE ALL ABOUT™

"After a workout you really build up a big hunger."

John Siman, 1980 Olympic Water Polo Team.

"As a water polo player we have these marathon workouts on the weekend. We go 4 and 5 hours a day. And usually when you're done with that you're pretty hungry. You want a snack that's going to hold you over till your next meal. For me it's a SNICKERS® Bar.

It's got some good ingredients in it ... peanuts, milk chocolate, caramel and peanut butter nougat.

SNICKERS gets rid of that hollow feeling in my stomach and just seems to satisfy me."

Packed with peanuts SNICKERS really satisfies.™

© 1980 L.A. Olympic Committee

Official Snack Food 1984 Olympics

© Mars Inc. 1984

Approved by FINA, USAS, Inc. and USWP, Inc.

Authors' GALLERY

In the world of the Ancient Greeks, Pindar composed odes to Olympic heroes. In the wake of Victorian England, Sherlock Holmes' creator wrote with awe of the Olympic spirit. From Antiquity to today, excellence in athletics has inspired excellence in poetry and prose. Olympic effort has enriched literature with drama, with humor and—as happened when Holmes' creator, Sir Arthur Conan Doyle, reacted to the 1908 marathon race—with celebration of the competitive soul. "It is horrible, yet fascinating," he wrote, "this struggle between a set purpose and an utterly exhausted frame."

*Memorable
writing about
the Games by
Ring Lardner
Thomas Wolfe
Red Smith
Melvin Durslag
A. J. Liebling
Jim Murray
John Lardner*

Authors' Gallery offers a sample of notable writing from the Olympic past—observations and insights that bring alive the events pictured

here and identified on the following pages. Ring Lardner engages social attitudes of the 1920s and, with his special vernacular, conceives a "modest proposal" to make the Games more relevant. Thirty years later, Ring's son, John Lardner, likewise extracts amusement from the Games while, in turn, Thomas Wolfe, Red Smith, Melvin Durslag, A. J. Liebling and Jim Murray illuminate other aspects of the Olympic experience.

Ring Lardner is best known for *You Know Me Al, Alibi Ike* and stories that have become American humor landmarks. Thomas Wolfe wrote the literary classics, *Look Homeward Angel* and *You Can't Go Home Again*. Red Smith, a Pulitzer Prizewinner, was for

nearly five decades the writer colleagues on the sports beat respected most. A. J. Liebling and John Lardner wrote regularly on a range of subjects for *The New Yorker* and other prominent outlets. Melvin Durslag and Jim Murray are award-winning Los Angeles columnists.

IN LESS THAN HALF THE TIME IT'LL TAKE TO WIN THE OLYMPIC MARATHON, YOU COULD BE WINNING IN NEVADA.

In about an hour, you can fly to fabulous Las Vegas and take a cab to your hotel.
In just over an hour you can fly to Reno, or even Lake Tahoe.

Wherever you land in Nevada, you'll find a kind of fun and excitement available no where else on earth. Glittering 24-hour casino action. Superstars and stage extravaganzas. Top notch restaurants. And more than 81,000 hotel and motel rooms in Las Vegas, Reno and Lake Tahoe alone.

You'll be minutes from towering mountains, dazzling lakes and quiet deserts. You can discover lively small towns and historic ghost towns.

Nevada's got it. All of it.

Right next door.

Yet maybe the most surprising thing about visiting Nevada is how little it costs. No other place offers so much fun for so little.

So come and get it.

While you're here, call any Los Angeles travel agent and ask about air and bus schedules and fares to Nevada, and accommodations.

You're so close. Why not go all the way?

NEVADA
NEVADA'S GOT IT

Nevada Commission on Tourism • Capitol Complex • Carson City, NV 89710 • (702) 885-3636

High Time For Reform

BY RING LARDNER

THE EYES OF the athaletic world is centered every four years in the place where ladies and gents from all the countries that is left are participating in what is aptly termed the Olympic games. These games was began pretty near 800 years B.C. . . . at a place called Olympia and consisted of one event which was a footrace. The encyclopaedia says it was win by a athalete named Coroebus in 776 B.C. but they's no way of telling if that was good time or not as the distance ain't stated. In later years they kept adding other events till they had a long run, a footrace for men in armor, a four horse chariot race and a contest for trumpeters and heralds, to say nothing about a combination boxing and wrestling match in which the contestants was allowed to tape their hands with andirons. It was understood that after a guy had win the all around championship he should live at public expense like one of our present day congressmen.

This all around championship was awarded to the party that got the most points in what they called the pentathlon from the Greek words pen meaning five and athlon meaning oof. The five events in the pentathlon or five-oof was running, jumping, discus and javelin throwing and wrestling.

Well finely people begun to realize that the most of the contests was not only silly but it was almost impossible to stage them, like for inst. the four horse chariot race, even if you did happen to have a chariot around the house where was you going to get a hold of four horses. . . .

So one by one they weeded out what they considered obsolete and substituted contests which was considered up to date and are still clinging to same, which is the reason why I am writing this little article, namely to try and show that it is high time for another general reform. If the purpose of athaletics and especially the Olympic games is to benefit the contestants and make them more valuable citizens and better boys and gals, and husbands and wifes, then why not arrange a programme of events that will tend to same instead of running off a serious of contests that don't get nobody nowheres or prove nothing except that the entrants has wasted a lot of time practising?

For example suppose a man gets so as he throw a javelin 189 ft. 4¼ inches, will somebody kindly tell me how that is going to buy spare tires for his first baby's go-cart? And did you ever hear of a gal's mother saying to her suitor, "Why, certainly you can have Kate. I know you will make her a good husband because you have did 57 ft. 11½ inches in the running hop, step and jump." And in these days of the long distance telephone to say nothing of motorcycles, how many men is going to get a job as a Western Union messenger boy because they can run 26 miles in 2 hrs. 55 min. 20 sec. Even a man that can clear 6 ft. 5 in the running high jump ain't going to be no use hanging pictures because he don't stay up there long enough to be sure he is getting them straight.

I will leave it to the Olympic committees to figure out decent substitutes for the silly events now on the regular programme and will content myself with suggesting a new pentathlon consisting of contests which will show if a man . . . will make a good or a bad husband . . . and when I say good I mean the kind that can sail the matrimonial seas without stubbing their toe on the rocks of petty annoyance.

1. *Appreciation.* For this event they must be provided a house and a woman which the contestants pretends is their house and their wife. The contestants examine the house and then leave. During their absence, the pseudo-wife changes the furniture all around and hangs new curtains in all the windows. The contestants return and each enters the home separately. First prize goes to the contestant noticing the most improvements and making the most laudatory comments in regards to same. Booby prize to the contestant that don't know they's been any improvements.

2. *Punctuality.* This contest should take place on a Saturday or Sunday noon. The contestants each calls up the pseudo-wife and tells her they are going to play golf but will be home at 6:30. The winner is the one that gets there on or before eight o'clock.

3. *Immutability.* The pseudo-wife appears in a new hat or new dress. The contestants all tell her it looks great. The winner is the one that don't change his mind the second or third time she wears it and tell her it looks terrible.

4. *Tolerance.* The contestants and the mock wife go out on a drinking party. The contestants drink 20 cocktails apiece and get pie eyed. The winner is the contestant that lets the wife finish her 2d cocktail without telling her she has had enough.

5. *Versatility.* This event will require some time. Each contestant, in conjunction with the mock wife, entertains different friends at dinner every evening for a week. During every evening, the contestants must tell three anecdotes, personal experiences. The winner is the contestant that don't tell the same anecdote more than five times during the week. . . .

In ancient times the Games offered footraces, a chariot race and a contest for heralds and trumpeters.

BUD LIGHT ®
BEER

*Official sponsor of the
U.S. Olympic Team.*

The best in all of us.
It's a torch lit briefly.
A small moment compared to the centuries
through which it comes to us.
So we can simply witness. Or we can truly share.
Share in what the Greeks knew long ago…
that the true measure of the Olympics is not in the
winning, but discovering the best in all of us.

Symbol Of The New Collective Might

BY THOMAS WOLFE

BERLIN 1936—It is said that Byron awoke one morning at the age of 24 to find himself famous. George Webber had to wait 11 years longer. He was 35 when he reached Berlin, but it was magic just the same. Perhaps he was not really very famous, but that didn't matter, because for the first and last time in his life he felt as if he were. Just before he left Paris a letter had reached him from Fox Edwards, telling him that his new book was having a great success in America. Then, too, his first book had been translated and published in Germany the year before. The German critics had said tremendous things about it, it had had a very good sale, and his name was known. When he got to Berlin the people were waiting for him. . . .

The German critics outdid each other in singing his praises. If one called him "the great American epic writer," the next seemed to feel he had to improve on that and called him "the American Homer." So now everywhere he went there were people who knew his work. His name flashed and shone. He was a famous man.

Fame shed a portion of her loveliness on everything about him. Life took on an added radiance. The look, feel, taste, smell, and sound of everything had gained a tremendous and exciting enhancement, and all because Fame was at his side. He saw the world with a sharper relish of perception than he had ever known before. All the confusion, fatigue, dark doubt, and bitter hopelessness that had afflicted him in times past had gone, and no shadow of any kind remained. It seemed to him that he had won a final and utterly triumphant victory over all the million forms of life. His spirit was no longer tormented, exhausted, and weighted down with the ceaseless effort of his former struggles with Amount and Number. He was wonderfully aware of everything, alive in every pore. . . .

It was the season of the great Olympic Games, and almost every day George and Else went to the stadium in Berlin. George observed that the organizing genius of the German people, which has been used so often to such noble purpose, was now more thrillingly displayed than he had ever seen it before. The sheer pageantry of the occasion was overwhelming, so much so that he began to feel oppressed by it. There seemed to be something ominous in it. One sensed a stupendous concentration of effort, a tremendous drawing together and ordering in the vast collective power of the whole land. And the thing that made it seem ominous was that it so evidently went beyond what the Games themselves demanded. The Games were overshadowed, and were no longer merely sporting competitions to which other nations had sent their chosen teams. They became, day after day, an orderly and overwhelming demonstration in which the whole of Germany had been schooled and disciplined. It was as if the Games had been chosen as a symbol of the new collective might, a means of showing to the world in concrete terms what this new power had come to be.

With no past experience in such affairs, the Germans had constructed a mighty stadium which was the most beautiful and most perfect in its design that had ever been built. And all the accessories of this monstrous plant—the swimming pools, the enormous halls, the lesser stadia—had been laid out and designed with this same cohesion of beauty and of use. The organization was superb. Not only were the events themselves, down to the minutest detail of each competition, staged and run off like clockwork, but the crowds—such crowds as no other great city has ever had to cope with, and the like of which would certainly have snarled and maddened the traffic of New York beyond hope of untangling— were handled with a quietness, order, and speed that was astounding.

The daily spectacle was breathtaking in its beauty and magnificence. The stadium was a tournament of

continued

As reflected in this opening day march, "the sheer pageantry of the occasion was," in the author's words, "overwhelming, so much so that" one could "feel oppressed by it."

continued

Relaxing here with Germany's Luz Long (left), Jesse Owens of the "Oo Ess Ah" was the athletic star of the '36 Berlin Games.

color that caught the throat; the massed splendor of the banners made the gaudy decorations of America's great parades, presidential inaugurations, and World's Fairs seem like shoddy carnivals in comparison. And for the duration of the Olympics, Berlin itself was transformed into a kind of annex to the stadium. From one end of the city to the other, from the Lustgarten to the Brandenburger Tor, along the whole sweep of Unter den Linden, through the vast avenues of the faery Tiergarten, and out through the western part of Berlin to the very portals of the stadium, the whole town was a thrilling pageantry of royal banners—not merely endless miles of looped-up bunting, but banners fifty feet in height, such as might have graced the battle tent of some great emperor.

And all through the day, from morning on, Berlin became a mighty Ear, attuned, attentive, focused on the stadium. Everywhere the air was filled with a single voice. The green trees along the Kurfürstendamm began to talk: from loud-speakers concealed in their branches an announcer in the stadium spoke to the whole city—and for George Webber it was a strange experience to hear the familiar terms of track and field translated into the tongue that Goethe used. He would be informed now that the *Vorlauf* was about to be run—and then the *Zwischenlauf*—and at length the *Endlauf*—and the winner:

"Owens—Oo Ess Ah!"

Meanwhile, through those tremendous banner-laden ways, the crowds thronged ceaselessly all day long. The wide promenade of Unter den Linden was solid with patient, tramping German feet. Fathers, mothers, children, young folks, old—the whole material of the nation was there, from every corner of the land. From morn to night they trudged, wide-eyed, full of wonder, past the marvel of those banner-laden ways. And among them one saw the bright stabs of color of Olympic jackets and the glint of foreign faces: the dark features of Frenchmen and Italians, the ivory grimace of the Japanese, the straw hair and blue eyes of the Swedes, and the big Americans, natty in straw hats, white flannels,

and blue coats crested with the Olympic seal.

And there were great displays of marching men, sometimes ungunned but rhythmic as regiments of brown shirts went swinging through the streets. By noon each day all the main approaches to the Games, the embannered streets and the avenues of the route which the Leader would take to the stadium, miles away, were walled in by the troops. They stood at ease, young men, laughing and talking with each other—the Leader's bodyguards, the Schutz Staffel units, the Storm Troopers, all the ranks and divisions in their different uniforms—and they stretched in two unbroken lines from the Wilhelmstrasse up to the arches of the Brandenburger Tor. Then, suddenly, the sharp command, and instantly there would be the solid smack of 10,000 leather boots as they came together with the sound of war.

It seemed as if everything had been planned for this moment, shaped to this triumphant purpose. But the people—they had not been planned. Day after day, behind the unbroken wall of soldiers, they stood and waited in a dense and patient throng. These were the masses of the nations, the poor ones of the earth, the humble ones of life, the workers and the wives, the mothers and the children—and day after day they came and stood and waited. They were there because they did not have money enough to buy the little cardboard squares that would have given them places within the magic ring. From noon till night they waited for just two brief and golden moments of the day: the moment when the Leader went out to the stadium, and the moment when he returned.

At last he came—and something like a wind across a field of grass was shaken through that crowd, and from afar the tide rolled up with him, and in it was the voice, the hope, the prayer of the land. The Leader came by slowly in a shining car, a little dark man with a comic-opera mustache, erect and standing, moveless and unsmiling, with his hand upraised, palm outward, not in Nazi-wise salute, but straight up, in a gesture of blessing such as the Buddha or Messiahs use.

"I've had many fine experiences.
But the Olympics was the best."

Muhammad Ali

FASTER, HIGHER, STRONGER: SANYO HELPS IT HAPPEN.

Sanyo video products are being used in the training of athletes of the 1984 U.S. Olympic Team,
helping them make their best better, and their better the best in the world.

Official Video Products of the 1984 L.A. Olympics

He Ran Like A Man With A Noose About His Neck

BY RED SMITH

HELSINKI 1952—In the morning there was a headline in a paper from Paris reading: LA FINALE DU 5,000 METRES? CE SERA LA BOMBE ATOMIQUE DES JEUX! (This will be the atomic bomb of the Games!) In the afternoon there was thin sunshine, turned on specially for the occasion by the Finns, to whom nothing is impossible when it involves entertaining the thieves of time and destroyers of distance in congress here from all the nations of the world.

Thousands of athletes not engaged on the day's card sat among the cash customers, taking time off from their rehearsals to see the *bombe atomique* go off. Even on the field there was uncommon congestion. On the fifth day of boisterous combat, this conclave of gristle had achieved a climax with the second bid for a gold medal by the comical contortionist Emil Zatopek. Four years ago, this gaunt and grimacing Czech with the running form of a zombie had made himself the pinup boy of the London Games. Witnesses who have long since forgotten the other events will wake up screaming in the dark when Emil the Terrible goes writhing through their dreams, gasping, groaning, clawing at his abdomen in horrible extremities of pain. In the most frightful horror spectacle since *Frankenstein*, Zatopek set an Olympic record for 10,000 meters in London in '48 and barely failed to win the 5,000 from Belgium's Gaston Reiff. This year he broke his own records for both speed and human suffering at 10,000, and now he was back in the 5,000 final, trying for a distance double that had defied every mortal save Finland's Hannes Kolehmainen, who won these two tests in 1912. To the Finns, these are the races that count; anything shorter is for children.

For example, an old gaffer around here overheard mention of Andy Stanfield, the Jersey City sprinter, and asked: "Stanfield? Who is he?"

"The American champion," the old man was told. He blinked.

"How can he be champion to run two hundred meters?" the old guy said. "He should run anyway five kilometers."

That's what Zatopek was doing, along with Reiff; Alain Mimoun, the French Algerian schoolmaster; Herbert Schade, the German favorite; and Chris Chataway, the Oxford blue. These five were the leaders from the start, and they made up a sort of gentlemen's club on the front end, some distance removed from the ten other starters. Then Reiff quit the lodge, giving up on the eleventh turn.

All through the race, Zatopek had commanded the rapt attention of spectators, and with every agonized step he had rewarded them. Bobbing, weaving, staggering, gyrating, clutching his torso, flinging supplicating glances towards the heavens, he ran like a man with a noose about his neck. With half a mile to go, Schade and Chataway passed him. He seemed on the verge of strangulation; his hatchet face was crimson, his tongue lolled out. A quarter-mile left, and he went threshing to the front again, but as they turned into the backstretch for the last time, he was passed by Schade, then Chataway, then Mimoun.

Now he was surely finished, a tortured wreck three yards back of the three leaders who ran in a tight little cluster into the last turn.

Suddenly, midway in the turn, there was a flash of red on the outside. Four times in front and four times overtaken, that madman was rushing into the lead with his fifth and final spurt. He went barreling past the rest in an unbelievable charge. There was a jam on the inside, and Chataway sprawled over the curb into the infield. Mimoun took out after Zatopek. The little Algerian made a fine run, as fruitless as it was game. He tailed Zatopek home. Even Schade, who finished in third place, broke Reiff's Olympic record.

A little later in the day, Mrs. Zatopek (Dana Zatopkova) won the javelin throw in the women's department. Czech and double Czech.

With every agonized step Zatopek commanded the rapt attention of spectators at Helsinki as he won the 5,000 meters. Later, shown here, he grimaced to victory in his first Olympic marathon.

"I'll never forget that feeling of exultation. The Olympics are the world's greatest sporting event!"

Frank Shorter

FASTER, HIGHER, STRONGER: SANYO HELPS IT HAPPEN.

Sanyo video products are being used in the training of athletes of the 1984 U.S. Olympic Team, helping them make their best better, and their better the best in the world.

©1980 L.A. Olympic Committee TM

Official Video Products of the 1984 L.A. Olympics

JCPenney

Salutes
The 1984
Games

The Lee Wright Collection

An Inch Away… Again

BY MELVIN DURSLAG

MELBOURNE 1956—The natural drama that unravels in a dressing room at any Olympic Games is something quite unmatched in sports. The international flavor of the event is probably one reason, but more important is the hopeless despair created by time.

A guy who loses can't square himself next month or even next year. He must look bleakly to four years in the future, which, in his dejected state, can take on proportions of several lifetimes.

We had a pretty good sample of this yesterday following the 110-meter high hurdles. The favorite, Jack Davis, former USC star, was beaten by only an inch by Lee Calhoun, the fine young runner from North Carolina College.

Davis had faced the wretched future one day in Helsinki four years ago. He was beaten there, also by an inch, by Harrison Dillard.

Davis resolved to get even. He dedicated himself for four years to the only race that held any further interest for him—the one he lost yesterday.

Curiously, Davis was beaten here under the identical circumstances under which he was beaten at Helsinki. Dillard had stolen a quick lead from the holes and it was Davis' job to catch him.

Davis never did. He lost in the Olympic record time of 13.7 seconds, the same clocking given to Dillard, the winner.

Nor did Davis catch Calhoun yesterday. It was a chase all the way with Davis drawing up just a fraction short in Olympic record time of 13.5, the same as Calhoun.

A photo finish was called on yesterday's race and studied for 15 minutes before officials could finally pick the winner.

Davis and Calhoun sat on the grass in agonizing suspense, watching the electric scoreboard which would soon reveal the placings. When Calhoun's name was flashed on top, Davis shook his hand and walked hurriedly to the dressing room.

Davis isn't an emotional boy and he tried hard not to be yesterday, but he was heavy in the chest and he fought desperately to hold back the tears. He didn't altogether. His words seemed to flutter out and he was as overcome with misery as one can be.

Davis took a deep breath and said shakily, "I wanted to win that race more than anything else in my life."

He began to cry, and feeling a little ashamed, caught himself and tried to rationalize.

"I'm no better than the rest," he said. "I have to take it as all the others do. A lot of good ones have gone down here."

Asked if he would try again in the 1960 Olympics, Davis replied firmly, "No I won't. I'm quitting. I really couldn't take four more years of waiting."

In another room, meanwhile, Calhoun was surprisingly calm for one who had scored such an upset.

"I had a feeling all along that the race would be decided by the final lunge," said Calhoun, a veteran of the Korean War. "And that's just the way it happened. I had a feeling I had won when we hit the tape, but I didn't take any chances—I prayed all the time the photo was being developed."

Calhoun is a minister's son from Gary, Indiana, who happened to go to North Carolina College, a small black school in Durham, when offered a scholarship as a high jumper.

A failure as a high jumper, Calhoun switched, at his coach's request, to the high hurdles and knocked over six hurdles in his first race.

But he's come a considerable way since then. He ran beautifully yesterday—just about one inch more beautifully than Davis.

In the 110-meter hurdles at Melbourne it was a chase all the way with Jack Davis (left) *a fraction short—but in Olympic record time of 13.5, the same as winner Lee Calhoun* (right).

UPI

You may never need a tire this good.

Tiger Paw Plus with Royal Seal. Just one nail through the tread in the middle of nowhere is enough to make you wish you had a tire this good.

It's Uniroyal's Tiger Paw Plus with Royal Seal. An excellent example of high technology protecting you from the harsh realities of the real world.

For this tire has two steel belts as a formidable barrier against tread punctures. And it also has something more. A patented substance that automatically and permanently seals most tread punctures up to 3/16 of an inch in diameter. That alone is probably

enough to make you want it. Even if it didn't have a projected tread life 20% greater than Michelin X. Which it does. And even if it weren't an excellent all-weather tire. Which it is.

In fact, we're now backing it with a unique, industry-leading limited warranty covering the whole tire—both tread and sidewall.

If any road hazard makes it unserviceable during the first 2 years or 30% of tread depth (whichever comes first), we will replace it. Free.

You may never need a tire this good. But it's nice to know you've got it.

U.S. Olympic Committee contributor.

Tiger Paw Plus with Royal Seal.

Arrivederci, Abebe

BY A. J. LIEBLING

ROME 1960—There is a childish sadness about departing from an Olympic stadium after the last day of the Games. It is like leaving a school where one has been happy, and knowing that the school will never reopen. A world has fused, existed and dissolved. Here in Rome, the first day of the Games, when nobody knew his way about, has receded into the distant past, although it was only two weeks ago. Actually, there were only eight days of competition in this particular stadium—the Opening Ceremony having preceded the starters' guns by a week—but so many exciting things happened in those eight days that they seem a long time.

At the opening, the blue-smocked girl ushers huddled, intimidated, in the runways, sure that they would never be able to make themselves understood by the *forestieri* (foreigners), and accepted your ticket only when you forced it upon them; then they led you to someone else's place and abandoned you. And the boy vendors, crying "*Aranciata! Coca! Birra! Limonata!*" walked on your feet and spilled the drinks down your neck. But by the last day the girls had become helpful and authoritative, bouncing deadheads with a wave of a girlish hand, like an umpire calling an out, and the boys had become nimble as chamois, threading their way between bony English knees and vast German paunches without touching a marker, and making change for a thousand-lira note with one hand while pouring a soda with the other.

These talents, laboriously acquired, have now become useless. Once the seats seemed hard and narrow; at the end, *we* had become hardened and narrowed to them. Seats that commanded a good view of the finish were in a category marked "extra"—pronounced by the ushers "ek-ke-stra"—and were priced higher than mere first-class. They were also ek-ke-stra narrow, because our thrifty Olympic hosts wanted to fit in as many of them as possible. (A seat was the space between two lines on a bench; they were drawn by a man whose regular job was cutting diamonds.) But by the last day these hardships seemed jokes, for we—*forestieri* and *Italiani* alike—had shared emotions that men experience only at Olympia; elation that was not based on doing somebody in the eye, despair that washed away at

continued

Ethiopian Abebe Bikila ran barefoot all over Rome to win the marathon, leading Morocco's Abdeslam Rhadi across the finish line at the Arch of Constantine.

From an article in *The New Yorker;* © Copyright 1960 The New Yorker Magazine, Inc.

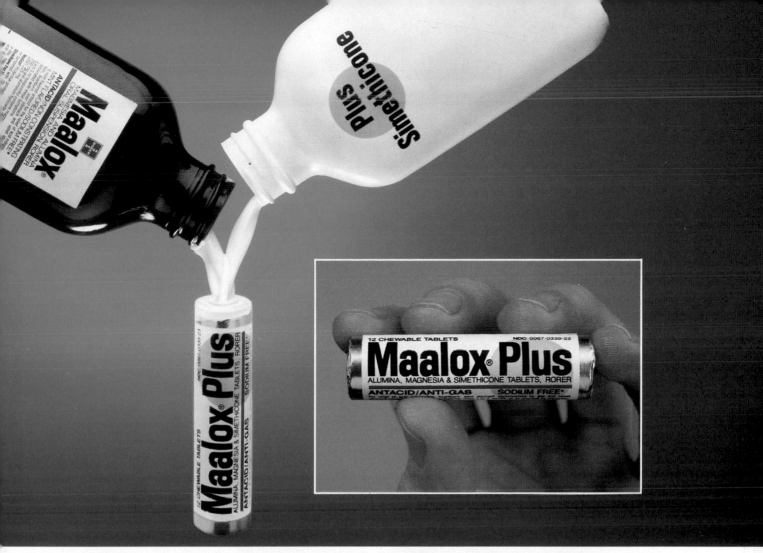

Announcing...Maalox®Plus Tablets in New Handy Roll Packs!

Maalox®, America's number one antacid for relief of excess acid and heartburn, plus the number one reliever of painful gas are now combined in new, handy roll packs of Maalox® Plus Tablets...

- **Relieves excess acid and heartburn with Maalox®.**
- **Relieves painful gas pressure with simethicone.**
- **Has a great swiss-creme flavor.**
- **Is sodium-free*.**

Discover the one-two acid-gas relief of Maalox® Plus Tablets... use one of the coupons!

*Dietetically sodium-free. Contains approximately 0.03 mEq sodium per tablet.

After his unshod Olympic victory Bikila returned to his uniformed job as guard at the royal palace in Addis Ababa.

continued

the stadium gate on the way home. And now it was done. For the last time we heard the loudspeakers of the police announcing, in three languages, one after another, the loss of some wretched child by its parents, who had not had the sense to hold onto it. (And if they had had more sense, they would have left it at home in England or Milwaukee.) For the last time, in the gathering dark, we walked over the bronze letters, spelling DUCE DUCE DUCE, that were set in the pavement.

I noted two weeks ago that when the Ethiopian athletes marched past the president's tribune in the *Cerimonia di Apertura*, I wondered what they were thinking about. They were next door to a stadium begun by a man (*Il Duce:* Benito Mussolini) who had suppressed their country. The inscriptions commemorating the fall of Addis Ababa still deface marble blocks in the stadium approach. There is a highly vocal Neo-Mussolinian group here that opposes all attempts to erase the words of the great maker of hollow phrases; for example, the editorialist of *Il Tempo* suggested in a front-page piece this morning that all the troubles of the Western world had started with Italy's expulsion from Africa. What at least one Ethiopian had been thinking at the *Cerimonia* became apparent yesterday evening. He was a man named Abebe Bikila, and he had been thinking, correctly, that it would be a fine thing for the home folks if he could run barefoot all over Rome and win the marathon. So he did. It wasn't even a race; he just ran away from the field, accompanied most of the way by a Moroccan, Abdeslam Rhadi, who had used the 10,000 meters as a tune-up for the marathon. I had rooted for Rhadi, first, because I have

had a sentimental interest in North Africa ever since I took Carthage's side against Rome, and, second, because I wanted to see one of the new nations win a big event, to encourage the others.

Now the two Africans, symbolizing the escape of their continent from people like the editorialist for *Il Tempo*, fled through the night, leaving behind the representatives of the colonial powers. They moved so unobtrusively that half the people in the streets didn't know that the business end of the marathon had passed by. They did not stop even for an *espresso*. Whether they spoke to each other, or what they said, is not on record in the public press, but all agree that they appeared in good spirits. Half a mile or so from the Arch of Constantine (the finish line), the Ethiop left the Moor. He ran on alone, no doubt thinking how kind the ancient Romans were to have spread soft cobblestones for his feet; it was about the best break they ever gave anybody. Arriving at the Arch, he inclined his head and waved his hands in greeting. He was polite; clearly, he hoped that the people were glad to see him. He had had a nice lope, and in his inner Amharic mind perhaps he attributed Rhadi's defeat to the Moroccan's addiction to shoes. He walked about to keep warm until the Olympic victory ceremonial, which could not be consummated until the appearance of the third man, a New Zealander, who did not arrive for a considerable time. After him, the other representatives of the higher cultures arrived, at intervals of from three minutes to half an hour, and fell on their faces. It was a glorious ending to the Olympic Games that Benito Mussolini had planned to hold, and should teach *Il Tempo* that a man's a man for all that. *Evviva l'Etiopia!*

Proud suppliers to the 1984 U.S. Olympic Team.

Best of Luck to the 1984 U.S. Olympic Team.
From Hostess® Cake and Wonder® Bread.
Proud suppliers and official sponsors of
the 1984 U.S. Olympic Team.

From the Bakery People of ITT

The Challenger Who Wasn't There

BY JIM MURRAY

MONTREAL 1976—It was the night before the 800-meter final, and the world's early favorite to win this event briefly weighed whether to have another beer or go for some more of the white wine. Service had been slow in the Café Martin, one of the plush Frenchtown restaurants, but it was still well before midnight—at least 40 minutes, in fact.

The onion soup was resting easy in his stomach, the rib steak was smothered in french fries, each of which he dipped in the gravy before eating. He eyed the dessert table with its mounds of whipped cream.

To be sure, there were still 15 hours before his event, but any coach would have fainted dead away at the sight and, upon being revived, would have fired him off the team and out of the Olympics.

The trouble was, somebody already had. This was Mike Boit, one of those marvelous Kenyans who have stormed the Olympics these past eight years like a flight of wildebeest over the veldt. This was to have been Mike's gold-medal year. He won the bronze at Munich. He ran the second-fastest 800 meters (1:43.8) ever. He was no worse than even money in this year's Olympic 800.

But an unfunny thing happened to Mike on his way to the victory stand. He got caught in the political squeeze which removed the African ring from the five-continents Olympic flag. No one cared this night if Mike Boit drank champagne out of a slipper, ate oysters and got the gout.

If Mike Boit fully comprehends what has happened to his four years of hard work, sacrifice, pain and dedication, it shows only in his diet. His conversation eerily dwelt on strategy he would employ in the race, pique at the prerace quotes of Rick Wohlhuter, his principal competitor, a grand overview of what the race would mean in history. Like Gloria Swanson in *Sunset Boulevard*, Mike thinks he is still a star and not yesterday's news.

"Tomorrow," said Boit, flashing an amiable gold-toothed smile, "I would have taken the race out slowly with a slow 200, then I would have turned it on with the third 200. Wohlhuter will miss me. He will not know how to race as well with me not there. How can he say I am not a good tactician when I

have beaten him six times out of eight last year?"

The subject was changed. It is not good to see a man in pain. Mike Boit with his pathetic little relics of his Olympics—buttons he exchanged with other athletes before he left the Olympic Village—was a man in torment.

For him, the 800 meters was like attending the wedding of your very best girl, watching somebody else raise your child, steal your birthright. Athletics took Mike Boit from a thatched hut and a hardpan-floor life to a red velvet restaurant in Montreal, where one bottle on the wine list could have supported his family of a widowed mother and eight children for a month a few years ago.

For the athletes on the track, the 800 was a one-minute-and-43-second lungache. For the wistful young African in Section D, Row 5, Seat 22, it was a four-year heartache.

It was won by a powerful runner from Cuba. Alberto Juantorena did not bother with style, strategies or blueprints. He just ran as fast as he could for as long as he could—a strategy which has sustained generations of runners whether they are running from a lion, the secret police or for a medal.

It was lost by Rick Wohlhuter, who had almost as much trouble staying in this race as Mike Boit. Wohlhuter ran an uncertain race, rather like a guy with a hunt-and-peck system on the typewriter or a guy trying to learn the samba.

Kenya's boycott may have cost more than Mike Boit a medal. It may have cost Rick Wohlhuter a gold. Rick ran a bewildered third, looking for all the world like a guy on the Santa Monica Freeway looking for the downtown exit. He had no more idea how to run against Juantorena than he would a zebra.

Asked in the postrace interview whether he had missed the presence of Mike Boit in the final, Wohlhuter admitted that he did. "All my training and planning was based on the fact that Mike would certainly be in the race and the main threat."

The little man who wasn't there, who sat in the stands with the french fries resting uneasily in his stomach, may have had more to do with the Juantorena runaway than the little men who were there. "I thought the pace was right. I thought the 400 was right and at 600, I felt in good position to attack," sadly admitted Wohlhuter.

By 600 meters, Juantorena had already stolen the race. A runner from India burst out in 50.85 for the first 400 with Juantorena right behind. The third 200, where Boit would have kicked in the afterburner for his medal, was almost a breather for the Cuban. He won by five yards.

Walking out of the stadium, Alberto Juantorena was on his way to a hero's reception in Havana.

Walking the same route was a lonely little man in a bush jacket with all the pins on it and a sad smile. Mike Boit was on his way to his room in the Ramada Inn. To watch the television and the cheers for other men appearing on the screen with his medal around their necks.

Mike Boit (573) took a bronze medal for Kenya in the 800 meters won by Dave Wottle (1033) at Munich in '72. But politics prevented Boit from racing for a gold in '76 at Montreal.

You're right next door to Mexico.

Palenque

Guadalajara

Taxco

Cabo San Lucas

©1984 Mexico Ministry of Tourism

Wouldn't it be a shame to miss it?

Imagine. In about the time it takes you to drive to the Coliseum, you could be in Mexico.

Exploring ancient Mayan ruins.

Sun worshiping on over 6,000 miles of uncrowded beaches.

Or spending nights in a hacienda that was once the home of Cortez.

In Mexico, you'll discover sights and experiences unlike any others

in all of the Americas.

Come climb the magnificent Pyramid of the Sun at Teotihuacan, the site of Aztec rituals. Shop our markets for handcrafts rich with tradition. Stroll the streets of beautiful colonial cities unchanged since the days of the conquistadors. Enjoy the world's finest marlin fishing at Los Cabos in the Baja. Or take the sun at famous beach

resorts like Puerto Vallarta, Ixtapa, Mazatlan and Acapulco.

It's all ready for you now, in Mexico. And it's all so close, you're practically there.

For more information, call our Mexican Government Tourism Office in Los Angeles at 213-274-6315 and ask about special package plans now available. Or contact your travel agent.

MÉXICO IS READY...
to show you a world of vacation pleasure.

© 1980 L.A. Olympic Committee ™

The Official 35mm Camera of the 1984 Olympic Games

Go for the Gold,™
Official 35mm Camera of the

Perhaps more so than all other human endeavors, the energy and enthusiasm of Olympic competition produces an extra dimension of excitement for athlete and spectator alike. Every Olympian is already a champion, but their former successes only heighten their desire to win it all. To go for the gold.

As the Official 35mm Camera of the 1984 Olympic Games, we know that the only people who will be called upon to perform as consistently as the athletes, with equal precision and dedication to excellence—day in and day out at the peak of their performance—are the professional sports photographers whose job it is to capture the spirit of the games on film. They, too, are

judged by their performance at the finish line. And they often only get one shot.

Canon is the world's leader in 35mm photography, with a wide variety of SLR models and over fifty interchangeable wide-angle, telephoto, zoom and macro lenses that can be used with them.

The New F-1 is the Canon choice for professionals, featuring an incredible system of interchangeable components that allow the photographer to custom-tailor the camera to meet his needs.

The A-1 is the most advanced Canon automatic SLR camera, featuring six exposure control modes including programmed automation for focus-and-shoot

Canon T50
Our simplest SLR ever—just focus and shoot for automatic pictures indoors or out, day or night! A built-in Power Winder even provides automatic loading!

Canon A-1
Six exposure control modes— including programmed automation, electronic digital readout in viewfinder, up to 5 fps. shooting with Motor Drive MA.

with Canon.
1984 Olympic Games

convenience, shutter-priority, aperture-priority and stopped-down automation for creative control, auto flash and manual.

The AE-1 PROGRAM is so advanced, it's simple, providing both programmed and shutter-priority automation, plus auto flash and manual.

The new Canon T-50 provides all the sophistication of other Canon SLR's in an incredibly compact, affordable package complete with built-in Power Winder. Like all Canon 35mm SLR cameras, it accepts the entire line of over fifty interchangeable Canon FD lenses.

Whether you shoot sports, vacation or just fun family photos, do the very best you can. Go for the gold,™ with Canon.

Canon®

Contributor to the U.S. Olympic Team

Canon USA, Inc., One Canon Plaza, Lake Success, New York 11042
Canon USA, Inc., 140 Industrial Drive, Elmhurst, Illinois 60126
Canon USA, Inc., 6380 Peachtree Industrial Blvd., Norcross, Georgia 30071
Canon USA, Inc., 123 Paularino Avenue East, Costa Mesa, California 92626
Canon USA, Inc., 2035 Royal Lane, Suite 290, Dallas, Texas 75229
Canon USA, Inc., Bldg. B-2, 1050 Ala Moana Blvd., Honolulu, Hawaii 96814
Canon Canada, Inc., Ontario

Canon New F-1
For professionals and advanced amateurs, w/speeds from 8 seconds to 1/2000th sec., 32 interchangeable focusing screens, 5 viewfinders, 3 metering patterns, choice of backs and motorized transport systems. And more.

Canon AE-1 PROGRAM
Programmed automation plus Shutter-Priority automation, 8 user-interchangeable focusing screens, choice of Power Winders or the Motor Drive MA for up to 4 fps. action shooting.

© 1983 Canon U.S.A., Inc.

THERE'S STRENGTH IN NUMBERS.

Some people seem to think that beef is just too good tasting to be good for you.
But the new numbers are in.* And they are impressive.

76%	35%	51%	19%	100%	13%
PROTEIN	NIACIN	ZINC	IRON	VITAMIN B-12	CALORIES
Beef is a super source of complete, high-quality protein.	Needed to produce energy within cells.	A component of many vital enzymes.	A great source of the iron you most easily absorb.	Essential in making new red blood cells.	You get all the bigger numbers for just 250 calories, 13% of a day's intake.**

BEEF GIVES STRENGTH.

*1983 Beef Nutrient Composition Study coordinated by the Meat Board with the USDA, Michigan State University, and University of Kentucky
**All percentages are based on a 4 oz. serving and recommended dietary allowances, women 23 to 50 years.

He Started The Race Alone But Finished As A Group

BY JOHN LARDNER

MELBOURNE 1956—Unofficial statistics show that good will prevails over bad will in the Olympic Games by a ratio of about nine to one, which is why the Games are still in business—and a fine thing, too.

Nonetheless, the mind of a man (a trouble-loving organ, at best) turns back with relish to such dates as the 1904 Olympics, when Fred Lorz tried to revolutionize marathon running. With most connoisseurs this is the favorite Olympic rhubarb. Boiled down, it appears that Lorz, representing the Mohawk Athletic Club and America in the Games at St. Louis, developed cramps while he was still 17 miles from the finish. The motor-car had just been invented. A motor-car was going Lorz's way. He climbed aboard, and soon outdistanced the field, to which he waved as he passed it. Five miles from home, the car took a tip from Lorz and broke down. Fred did the last five miles on foot, breezing. He breezed into the stadium, and was about to accept his prize from the President's daughter, Alice Roosevelt, when word got out that he owed his long lead to the internal combustion engine.

Lorz was not lynched by the crowd. However, he was barred by the AAU (only to be later reinstated). Lorz became as popular in amateur sports as Benedict Arnold is with U.S. history students. There seems to be no doubt that Lorz was joking. There seems to be no doubt, either, that he had the narrowest escape from death of any Olympic counterfeiter since Pisidorus' mother.

Pisidorus was a runner in the Ancient Greek Games at Olympia. His mother was also his trainer. Women were not permitted in the stands in those days. The mother of Pisidorus disguised herself as a man, took a seat, saw her boy win, and expressed her satisfaction with tribal yells. It was this that tipped off the law. "That fellow is getting quite a bang out of the race," said one badger to another. (Badgers, or badge-wearers, or officials, are as old as Olympic history.) "True," said the other badger, looking closely at the noisy fan, "and she is a dame." The boys studied the rules and found that the penalty was death. Eventually, however, this was commuted to a handshake and a season's pass to the Games, for the public was on the lady's side. The heat was removed from Pisidorus' mother by another rhubarb, when a boxer named Eupolus was convicted of bribing three of his Olympic opponents to take it easy.

Centuries passed, the old Olympics died, the modern Olympics were born, and we find the badgers still at work. Prince George of Greece, who stood 6′ 5″ tall, was officiating in the 1,500-meter walk at Athens in 1896. Wilkinson, of England, was a great walker, as walkers go—but few walkers go very far without cheating. Like trotting horses, they tend to "break" into a run. The Prince noticed that Wilkinson had begun to run like a cheap silk stocking. He stepped out on the track and waved the Englishman off. "You are all through," he said, except that he said it in Greek. Wilkinson went right on going, but, as he came around on the next lap, Prince George struck a blow for badgers everywhere by blocking him and knocking him off the track.

"Why didn't you stop the first time?" Wilkinson was asked later. "I don't speak Greek. I thought he wanted my autograph," said Wilkinson, as cool a walker as ever broke into a gallop.

continued

Dorando Pietri of Italy reeled into the stadium as front-runner at London in 1908—and was hauled to the finish line by loving arms.

continued

At London, in 1908, Dorando Pietri of Italy reeled into the stadium ahead of the rest of the field in the marathon, looked wistfully around him and fell on his face, through for the day. He was hauled the rest of the way to the finish line by loving arms. With Dorando still unconscious, or thereabouts, there came into view a New York store clerk named Johnny Hayes, just running out his race. Hayes crossed the line and became the startled winner of the 1908 Olympic marathon. Dorando was disqualified for starting the race alone but finishing as a group. ROBBERY! yelled the headlines in Italy. The howling continued until Thanksgiving night of the same year, when someone thought to sell tickets to a Hayes-Pietri rematch in Madison Square Garden.

Virtually every Irish-American and Italian-American in New York bought a seat in the Garden, or tried to break down the doors to get in. Bands played, and the customers beat time to the music on one another's jaws. Dorando—and his fans—went home early. Not even all the Irishmen in the house waited for Johnny Hayes to finish that night, since they had breakfast to eat.

En route to Antwerp, in 1920, the American Olympic team mutinied against its keepers because—the boys said—the beds aboard the transport *Princess Matoika* were for horses, and the meals were for dogs. "All right, so go home," said the Olympic Committee. The boys looked around at the Atlantic Ocean, and saw that this was not the place for it. The mutiny was adjourned to Antwerp, where the team lived in barracks. The Committee fired a hop-step-and-jumper named Dan Ahearn for decamping to a hotel, an unheard-of move for a hop-step-and-jumper. After the whole team went on strike, Ahearn was reinstated—and finished sixth in the hop-step-and-jump.

For the Summer Games of 1932, in Los Angeles, the Brazilian team had no money, so its government put the boys on a ship with 50,000 sacks of coffee and told them to beat their way north by selling the stuff en route. Coffee sales were so poor that when the athletes docked in California, 45 of them couldn't afford the $1 landing charge. The rest went ashore, and the ragged 45 sailed up and down the West Coast peddling coffee until the Games were over.

In 1936, on the ocean voyage to Berlin, Eleanor Holm, the backstroke swimmer, wet her lovely whistle with a champagne cocktail or two, and was detached from the U.S. Olympic team by Mr. Avery Brundage, the noblest badger of them all. "The athletes rode in steerage, dry," reports Miss Holm. "The sportswriters rode first class, which was wet. The sportswriters invited me up, and I went." Miss Holm adds that, dry or fueled, she could have won her event with one hand.

British-American war broke out again, on a small scale, in the Games in London in 1948. The U.S. 400-meter relay team of Barney Ewell, Lorenzo Wright, Harrison Dillard and Mel Patton won clearly from the British team in the final. But the judges ruled that England had won, because the Americans had committed a foul in passing the baton outside the legal zone. The winning medals went to the British runners. Then someone thought of consulting J. Arthur Rank's motion pictures of the race. The films showed that America's baton-passing had been as clean as a baby's mind—and the medals were pried loose from the British just in time to save the English-Speaking Union.

There is a moral in this: Films can prevent rhubarbs, and restore peace to the Olympic Games. That leaves one burning question: Who gets the film rights? As 1956 began, they were having a rhubarb about it. ∎

ESPRIT

THE ESPRIT STORE
Santa Monica at La Cienega
Opening Summer '84

HOW TO PLUG YOUR FAMILY INTO MODERN TIMES.

Hooking up the new IBM® PC*jr* isn't much harder than plugging in a lamp. But you should find it much more enlightening.

"Junior" is IBM's new personal computer and it's full of bright ideas.

THE LIVING ROOM REVOLUTION

PC*jr* is a tool for modern times that works with the family TV set.

It will open up new channels of information for you. New avenues of education for your child. And new experiences for all. Many of the things you now do with words, numbers, pictures or music, you may soon find yourself doing faster, easier and more accurately with the IBM PC*jr*.

FAMILY COMPUTING MADE EASY

IBM designed PC*jr* with first-time users in mind. An instructional exercise built into the machine lets the learning begin immediately. A program included with diskette-drive systems lets you explore computer fundamentals at your own pace. And to get you off and running from the very first day, a sample diskette with eleven useful mini-programs is also included.

Junior's keyboard doesn't need a cord, so you're free to get comfortable with it. (Which is why we call it the IBM "Freeboard.")

The keys are color-coded to make hitting the right ones easy.

New software programs for PC*jr* are easy, too. A diskette word processing program, for example, uses pictures as well as words to guide you along.

GROWING UP WITH JUNIOR

PC*jr* is simple to use. But it's powerful enough to perform complex tasks. And as your needs become more sophisticated, you'll find that Junior is ready to grow up with you.

The lowest-priced PC*jr* has a 64KB user memory that can be expanded to 128KB.

It will work with an IBM Personal Computer Color Display, as well as a TV set. There's room to add a diskette drive and an internal modem for telecommunications. There's even a choice of printers.

Best of all, PC*jr* is compatible with many existing IBM software programs for other IBM personal computers.

HOME ECONOMICS FROM IBM

The IBM PC*jr* holds lots of surprises. But perhaps most surprising is the price.

The starting model includes a 64KB cassette/cartridge unit and Freeboard for about $700. An enhanced model with 128KB and diskette drive is about $1300. (Prices apply at IBM Product Centers. Prices may vary at other stores.)

Take modern times into your own hands at your local authorized IBM PC*jr* dealer. For the store nearest you, just dial 1-800-IBM-PCJR. In Alaska and Hawaii, 1-800-447-0890.

L.A. '32:
Good Times and Hard Times in Fantasyland

By Michael Leahy

At the last Los Angeles Olympics, the city had nickel hamburgers, lush orange groves and thousands of acres of virgin land. The nation was beset by the Depression, but here— for a moment—the Games helped people forget.

"During the winter before, I scraped snow off the ground in Massachusetts to work out.... We had the worst facilities, and not very good shoes. We had no money. They gave us free shoes in Los Angeles to run in. I think I remember those shoes as much as anything."

—Mary Carew, 18, sprinter

"I was this little kid, and they flew me in this old trimotor from Dallas to Los Angeles.... At the Olympic Village, women were trying to get over the barbed wire to see us. They were quite mad, really. We had a great time. You didn't think at all about being poor in those couple of weeks."

—Rowland Wolfe, 17, gymnast

"After the Games, there was post-Olympic competition in different parts of the country.... It had been a marvelous two weeks, and an escape from all the problems. In Cleveland, we went to a speakeasy. It was during Prohibition, you understand.... Everyone drank. No one wanted the fun to stop. No one wanted to go back home to all the problems."

—Evelyne Hall, 22, hurdler

IT WAS THE WORST OF TIMES, it was the worst of times. When high jumper Jean Shiley of Philadelphia made the 1932 United States Olympic team, she boarded the team train leaving Chicago for Los Angeles with $5 in her pocket. Years before, business at her father's automobile garage had suddenly died, and slowly, inexorably, the family had lost first the garage, then their home and then all the money they had in the bank. After that, $5 was a lot for Shiley to be carrying. Sometimes people would ask her how she was faring, and she would pause, not knowing how to describe her financial condition. The word "Depression" was not part of her vocabulary. She only knew that she was happy to ride the Olympic train because, among other things, it meant that she would get free meals. For a couple of weeks there would be a reprieve from the potato-salad sandwiches that she subsisted on as a student at Temple University. "I didn't think anything of it," Shiley said. "So many people were in the same boat. Really, everything was fine."

The Depression encouraged an acceptance of fate that bordered on self-delusion. Fortunes had been lost, lives had been torn, and yet people moved eerily through the days as if not all that much had really changed. Newspapers fostered the delusion, too, keeping news about the stagnant economy to a minimum. As the Olympic Games approached, the *Los Angeles Times* offered readers stories of how the town's citizenry were enjoying July

THE MYSTIQUE OF THE MOVIES PLAYED A ROLE IN BRINGING THE GAMES TO THE CITY

Oil wells rose above La Cienega Boulevard at present site of Restaurant Row. Inset: Mary Pickford deplaned to an Olympic salute from competitors and, from left, Charlie Chaplin, a Prince of Siam, Douglas Fairbanks.

Fourth; of a fireworks display and grand party at the Bel-Air Bay Club; of Eileen MacDonald looking "perfectly ravishing in summer's loveliest printed chiffon at the club's supper"; of the Richard Schweppeses hosting an all-day tennis party at their Santa Monica manor; of young Van Niven, he of Yale, playing tennis with the pretty Jacqueline Smith, she of Radcliffe, on the court of Mr. and Mrs. Bertward Smith, who were on their annual summer holiday in Europe. The images radiating from the stories were of an Olympic city basking in bliss and wealth. The images did not include the soup-kitchen lines, shut-down factories, foreclosed homes or morose men riding the rails. It was as if millions of unemployed people were invisible.

In a milieu where the promulgation of happy news is a good thing, there could be no better dream, no bigger fantasy than an Olympic Games. "It was like a fantasyland," recalled Chicago hurdler Evelyne Hall. "It was the land of plenty. Nobody thought about their problems."

The Los Angeles of 1932 had a look strikingly different from its present shape.

Michael Leahy is a writer living in Santa Monica, California. He writes frequently about television and is working on a book about the current movie industry.

The city population of 1.3 million had not yet seen a freeway; "smog-alert" was not a part of the lexicon; everyone welcomed growth; no one could imagine that the San Fernando Valley, thousands of acres of orange groves and virgin land, would one day be overrun by housing tracts, fast-food stands and shopping malls.

For 25¢, people could ride all the way from Long Beach to downtown Los Angeles on the Red Cars, the nickname given to the Pacific Electric trains. The trains ran with large passenger loads and government officials spoke of the wonders of mass transportation. Yet, even as the politicians pontificated, great change was there awaiting recognition. Los Angeles already possessed more motor vehicles per capita than any other American city. The automobile was swiftly becoming the status symbol, connoting wealth and prestige in difficult times. The first drive-in movie theatre was soon to open on Pico Boulevard.

While the poor struggled and dreamed of being car owners, the rich lived in Beverly Hills or in Hancock Park and Pasadena. A manor in Hancock Park sold for $22,000; a middle-class home in Westwood for $4,000. A hamburger cost 5¢, a gallon of gas 12¢, a movie ticket 25¢ or less.

The mystique of the movies, the area's fast-growing industry, had played a role in

the choice of Los Angeles as site for the Olympic Games. "Is Los Angeles near Hollywood?" a delegate of the International Olympic Committee had asked William Garland, Los Angeles' representative during discussions about the '32 host city. When given an affirmative reply, the delegate said, "Then I'll vote for your city. I want to see how they make movies."

Movie glamour and the majesty of the Olympic Games, with about 1,500 athletes from all over the world, obscured the reality of widespread hard times. And today, when the 1932 Olympic athletes reread old clippings of their exploits, many confess to wishing they could relive the experience. The memories become so immediate for them; it is almost as if they are still there. . . .

Twenty-one-year-old Mildred "Babe" Didrikson, a typist for the Employers Casualty Company in Dallas, Texas, took five firsts in the 1932 AAU championships and tied for another. Now, as the Olympics are about to begin, she is generally acclaimed as the world's greatest female athlete, with most sportswriters making her the heavy favorite to win the javelin, 80-meter hurdles and the high jump. "I am here to win all three," she says, matter-of-factly.

Babe Didrikson likes challenges. "She

continued

The 1984 Olympic Games will be judged by a very select group.

Many products have been designated to display the symbol of the 1984 Olympic Games. But very few will actually participate in the Games. Bushnell sports optics are among the proud few.

Bushnell binoculars and spotting scopes will be used by the judges of the 1984 Olympic events requiring precision sports optics. This is one more measure of the international respect Bushnell has earned for the high quality and reliability of its optical products.

Announcing Medalist. A limited edition sport binocular of the 1984 Olympics.

To commemorate the XXIIIrd Olympiad and our part in it, we have issued a special limited edition Medalist binocular. The Medalist 7x35 sports binocular is ideal for viewing a broad range of sporting events. Its 7 times magnification and crisp, bright image will put you on the field or in the ring from any seat in the house. Look for the popularly-priced Medalist binocular wherever Bushnell quality optics are sold.

There's a Bushnell binocular or scope exactly right for your sports requirements, priced from $49.95 to $1,100.

BUSHNELL
DIVISION OF BAUSCH & LOMB
All products backed by limited lifetime warranty.

© 1980 L.A. Olympic Committee
Official Supplier

ATHLETES WANDERED THROUGH THE ALL-MALE OLYMPIC VILLAGE EXCHANGING GIFTS, SHARING WINE AND BEER

Sights of the city: The UCLA campus had acres of empty space when India's field hockey team practiced there for the Games. Early photo of Hollywood Bowl site caught musicians during an acoustical test. The city's first drive-in theatre was ready for filmgoers in '33. Inset: A delivery truck bore endorsement proclaiming Helms Bakeries the "official" Olympic breadmakers.

would hear a girl's time in a race," Paul Zimmerman, a sportswriter for the *Los Angeles Times*, recalls later, "and she would say, 'I can beat that.' She said what was on her mind, which was pretty unusual back then. And she could back it up; she was simply a fantastic athlete. She went bowling with a bunch of sportswriters, and she said it was the first time she had ever tried the sport. She rolled strike after strike. Nothing to it."

While other athletes concentrate upon preparing for their events, Babe thinks of other things. "Say, do you know if Douglas Fairbanks plays golf?" she asks a writer one day.

"I think so. Why?"

"Well, I just thought I'd like to shoot a few balls with him. If he's *good*, that is. I've only played ten times or so, but I shoot around 82 or 83."

Amateur athletics are different in 1932. Runners take time out for a few rounds of golf. Swimmers go dancing. Most youngsters do not get involved in competitive athletics and fall under the influence of coaches until their late teens. Eighteen-year-old Herbert Barthels had been taking boxing lessons at the Los Angeles Athletic Club in 1928 when, after a workout, he jumped into the club's pool to unwind. A coach noticed him flying past the club's top swimmers.

"You like to swim, boy?" asked the coach.

"I like it real fine," Barthels said.

"What are you doing here?"

"Boxing."

"Boxing? You're not boxing anymore! You're going to be swimming."

And so the next day Barthels reluctantly traded in his boxing gloves for a swimsuit. Four years later, in '32, he makes the Olympic team in the 400-meter freestyle.

There are a lot of stories like Herb Barthels'. Pete Mehringer, who will be a wrestling gold medalist in the light-heavyweight division in '32, does not have a coach at all. Living in the tiny town of Kinsley, Kansas, he learned how to wrestle from a correspondence course, looked at the pictures, emulated the moves. "Lots of good times," he remembers, "and I didn't do a lot of groaning and sweating either."

Good times. That seems to be the paramount concern of the male athletes inside the '32 Olympic Village, a complex of 500 cottages on more than 300 landscaped acres in Baldwin Hills. The women competitors are miles away at the Chapman Park Hotel in the Wilshire district. The

continued

From top: Delmar Watson Los Angeles Archives; California Historical Society/Ticor Title Insurance (L.A.); Whittington Collection Huntington Library / San Marino; inset: "Dick" Whittington Photography

AT&T IS PROUD TO HAVE MADE POSSIBLE THIS VERY SPECIAL LONG DISTANCE CONNECTION.

We're proud to sponsor the running of the Olympic Torch to Los Angeles. After 100 years of making long distance connections, we recognize that the greater the distance, the more vital the connection.

THE GAMES BEGAN IN PROMISED SUNSHINE WITH THE RELEASE OF 4,000 DOVES

Schoolchildren boosted the Olympics with a parade in the costumes of competing nations. Inset: Flier Amelia Earhart received celebrity attention at the Coliseum.

American men wander through the Village from cottage to cottage, meeting Germans here, French there, exchanging gifts, happy to learn that the Italians have brought wine and beer—precious commodities during Prohibition in the U.S.

On the eve of the Games, the Village screens a movie, *Strange Interlude*, starring Clark Gable and Norma Shearer. American athletes find themselves sitting among Argentinians. The Argentinians stare at them. The Americans stare back. Most of the Americans have never before met a foreigner, so everyone mostly nods and smiles.

For the first time, black runners lead the American track team in the sprints. The dominance of Ralph Metcalfe and Eddie Tolan at the U.S. Olympic Trials in Palo Alto surprised sportswriters who had expected victories from highly publicized white athletes attending major track powers such as the University of Southern California.

The emergence of the black athletes is a phenomenon to the public and the press. Reporters write about a "sleepy-eyed" Metcalfe, a "mumbling" Tolan, and the emerging portraits are of two young men bearing a distinct resemblance to caricatures from *Amos 'n' Andy*, a popular radio comedy series about stereotypical blacks. Actually, Tolan is a recent graduate of the University of Michigan. Metcalfe of Marquette University will one day become a

United States Congressman from Chicago.

U.S. Vice President Charles Curtis arrives in Los Angeles as a stand-in for President Herbert Hoover at the Opening Ceremonies. Hoover is busy preparing for his fall reelection campaign against New York Governor Franklin D. Roosevelt, and the Vice President neither boosts the President's cause nor charms the Olympic organizers with his explanation of Hoover's absence: "There are just 27 words in the official opening statement," says Curtis. "It really wasn't worthwhile for the President to come here from so far away."

Back in Washington, D.C., during the 1932 summer, federal troops drive out a band of disgruntled World War I veterans known as the bonus army. Out of work and hungry, these men had come to the capital to ask that the government give them their veteran's bonuses as soon as possible, rather than wait until 1945, as originally scheduled. "They are an army where each soldier represents ten thousand Americans out of work," says Roosevelt.

They aren't an army at all. They are farmers without farms. They are workers without assembly lines. They are men who have been reduced to panhandling on Washington's streets. In their confrontation with the Administration of 1932, they are teargassed and driven out of town. "A challenge to the authority of the United States Government has been met swiftly and firmly," says Hoover.

In the promised L.A. sunshine on Saturday, July 30, 1932, before nearly 100,000 people in the newly refurbished Coliseum, organizers release 4,000 doves into the air, and athletes from about 40 nations take the Olympic oath. Jim Thorpe, star of the 1912 Olympics, whose medals were taken from him when it was discovered he had played professional minor-league baseball, watches from the press section. Earlier that day he suffered the indignity of being turned away from a VIP ticket window, and now is a spectator in the stadium only because the Vice President interceded on his behalf. The greatest athlete America has ever produced, Thorpe knows that nothing is so passé as a former idol.

On the first day of competition, Leo Sexton of the United States wins the shotput, and Didrikson, at 5' 6" and 128 pounds, breaks by 11 feet the world record in the javelin with a throw of 143' 4". She is swiftly becoming the star of the 1932 Games. Photographers pose her next to an oversized phonograph record for a picture with a caption reading, ONE RECORD BABE

continued

Computer-controlled ATZ receivers put sensational sound at your fingertips.

Our new line-up of ATZ™ car stereo receivers looks terrific and sounds phenomenal. Every one has been engineered with pure audio performance and ease of operation in mind. That's why an exclusive Jensen® designed and developed computer is built right in the ATZ. It controls all the major functions of the AM/FM tuner and full logic tape deck for you. So you can just sit back and enjoy the smooth sounds. And all ATZ receivers fit the standard dashboard installation openings available in virtually all of today's domestic and import cars. So when it's the sound that moves you, let Jensen ATZ receivers point the way.

JENSEN
CAR AUDIO

When it's the sound that moves you.

Quick, name an airline!

We're not surprised that you got it right. British Airways flies more people to more countries than anyone else. In fact, it's the world's favourite airline. But, do you know why?

Flights from more U.S. gateway cities to London than any other airline.
British Airways has convenient departures from Anchorage, Boston, Chicago, Detroit, Los Angeles, Miami, New York, Philadelphia, San Francisco, Seattle, Baltimore and Washington, D.C.

Flights from London to more countries than any other airline.
When you fly British Airways, London is the departure point to more than 58 European cities, not to mention Africa, the Middle East, the Orient and the South Pacific.

The only foreign airline with their own terminal.
Why end up in Kennedy's crowded International Arrivals Building. On British Airways, you won't. You'll clear customs in the comfort of our own terminal.

The only Concorde flights to London.
Leave New York City, Washington, D.C. or Miami. Arrive in London in virtually half the usual time.

The widest business class seat.
Our Super Club® seat is wider than any other business class seat, and always on a window or an aisle, for additional comfort and convenience.

American Airlines AAdvantage® Program
Your flight miles on British Airways between the U.S. and London will count towards your AAdvantage travel award plan. And when you fly Concorde or First Class, you get credited 150%.

See your travel agent or British Airways for details and make your next flight on

British airways
The World's Favourite Airline™

DIDRIKSON HASN'T BROKEN. Grantland Rice, the great sportswriter, proclaims, "Babe breaks records easier than dishes." Yet, she is not readily accepted as America's darling. Other women athletes look at the powerful arms and legs and whisper that she looks like a man. The beautiful 18-year-old Eleanor Holm, soon to win a gold medal in the 100-meter backstroke, does not try to hide her disdain for bodies like Didrikson's. "If I had to choose between winning swimming championships and losing my looks because of big muscles, I'd give up the championships," says Holm. "The moment swimming makes me look like an Amazon, I'll quit."

Hiding her hurt, a wounded Babe waves her gangly arms and responds to the sniping. "I do things that other girls do," she says. "I cook, I sew. . . ." But she never sounds convinced herself that she is like everyone else, or that she even wants to be.

At the Chapman Park Hotel a U.S. team official approaches runner Evelyne Hall of Chicago and asks her if she would consent to room with Tidye Pickett, a black sprinter. A number of white girls have already said no, the official says. "Sure, I'll room with her. Why not?" Hall replies.

On the second day of competition, Tolan beats Metcalfe in a controversial finish to win the 100-meters in 10.3 seconds, equaling the world record. Most of those at the finish line think Metcalfe hit the tape first, but the official photograph reveals Tolan to be the winner. The next day, newspapers herald the black sprinters' gold and silver accomplishments. The *Los Angeles Times* speaks of the great burden lifted from the athletes' "ebony shoulders."

Metcalfe, Tolan and Didrikson. The names speed around the world. Interest in the Olympics soars. Five young men from Kinsley, Kansas set out for Los Angeles, determined to see their former high school classmate, Pete Mehringer, compete in the wrestling competition. They arrive at the Games with only enough money for two of them to watch Mehringer wrestle in the finals. The cost of seats for most Olympic events runs high, when you consider that 50¢ buys a roast beef dinner. Track and field and boxing tickets cost $2 each, and seats for the wrestling events are $1 in the afternoon, $2 in the evening. "My friends drew straws to see who would get the tickets," remembers Mehringer. "I can still see their faces. I can still remember beating Eddie Scarf of Australia and I can still hear our national anthem, the way it was when they gave me the gold medal. Hard feeling

continued

Babe Didrikson rolled over the high-jump bar in a style officials ruled illegal. Movie stars Harold Lloyd and Douglas Fairbanks (seated center) *occupied press box. Inset: U.S. sprint stars Metcalfe (445) and Tolan (461) drew continual attention on Coliseum track.*

RECORDS FELL AND CONTROVERSY RAGED

Cycling road race bordered the Pacific in Santa Monica. Inset: Didrikson played golf with (from left) writers Grantland Rice, Paul Gallico, Westbrook Pegler, Braven Dyer.

to explain, winning the gold medal."

The great Finnish distance runner, Paavo Nurmi, will not be winning anything. Reports surface that he violated amateur rules by accepting under-the-table payments at several meets, and so Olympic officials bar him from competing in the Games. Nurmi takes the news stoically, calmly watching the Opening Ceremonies from the stands, then joining his teammates on the Finnish team bus.

Nonetheless, Nurmi continues to train during the Olympics, alone, gliding along a practice track one afternoon as Glenn Cunningham, America's premier miler, watches curiously, wondering what an Olympic race between the two of them might have been like. At the end of each lap, the Finn looks at his watch, monitoring his pace, and Cunningham marvels at how quickly Nurmi accelerates. "He moved effortlessly," remembers Cunningham. There are no rivals at Nurmi's shoulder, no encouraging crowd, just the soft crunching of his spikes into the cinder track, but he keeps running, into the darkness, as Cunningham sits watching.

Cunningham runs in the Games but does not win. On the final lap of the 1,500 meters, he founders on the home stretch, finally finishing fourth, as an Italian, Luigi Beccali, sprints home to victory. Cunningham has swollen, infected tonsils, but he refuses to alibi. "It was one of the greatest experiences of my life," he says later. "You can run in hundreds of races but there's something very different at the start of an Olympics. You can *feel* it. There is enormous tension in those last moments."

Everyone feels the tension, including race officials. They mistakenly make the finalists in the 3,000-meter steeplechase run an extra lap, and they incorrectly measure the staggered lanes for the 200-meters. The second error costs Metcalfe any chance he might have had of winning a gold medal. It appears that Metcalfe runs about three meters farther than the race's winner, Tolan, and afterwards Metcalfe shakes his head, muttering, "I've never run faster, never run faster. What happened?"

Finishing two yards ahead of Metcalfe, Tolan sets an Olympic record of 21.2, but he also has doubts about Metcalfe's lane. "I think so too, Ralph," Tolan says sympathetically, as Metcalfe rails one more time about the infamous lane. The scene cannot be forgotten, the loser seeking solace from his roommate and friend, the press scrambling after them, clamoring for attention, scribbling down words that sportswriters will convert into another *Amos 'n' Andy*-

type dialogue by the following morning. Metcalfe and Tolan commiserate softly. There are few private moments in an Olympics. There are none now. The two men walk away.

The women's 80-meter hurdles. Going for her second gold medal, Didrikson finds herself trailing most of the race, before pulling even with Hall in the final yards. The women hit the finish line seemingly together; indeed, Hall strikes the tape so hard that her neck bleeds. Officials declare Didrikson the winner, however, after a photograph shows Babe hitting the tape a split second before her teammate.

"It hurts me to hear 'silver medal,'" Hall says a half century later. "I won. Babe had good publicity, and a good publicity agent. The judges expected her to win. . . . If it had not been Babe Didrikson, if it had been someone from another country, the results would have been different. . . ."

In the following days, Babe meets Douglas Fairbanks and Mary Pickford, and plays golf with Grantland Rice and other famous writers. The legend grows a little more.

In the men's 400-meters, America's Bill Carr beats teammate Ben Eastman in a time of 46.2 seconds, another world record in an Olympics where records are being shattered with regularity. Writes Harry Carr in the *Los Angeles Times*: "It is doubtful whether these records will ever

continued

AT THE END A SENSE OF UNIVERSAL BROTHERHOOD PREVAILED

Jean Shiley won a gold in a controversial high-jump duel with Babe Didrikson. Inset: *Baron Nishi of Japan rode to victory in the equestrian Prix des Nations.*

Helene Madison, an American in the women's 100-meter freestyle event, almost misses her race after changing into her swimsuit at a friend's apartment. Casually strolling into the Olympic swim stadium, she hears the public-address announcer introducing her rivals. Without a warmup, she takes her position and swims the greatest race of her life. Unbelievable! A few minutes after leaving her friend's apartment, Madison finds herself a gold-medal winner. In the days to follow, a movie studio will sign her to a contract. "It was like make-believe," she says.

The women produce the Games' most bizarre stories. American divers Georgia Coleman, Katherine Rawls and Jane Fauntz are ordered back to the locker room by an indignant Hungarian official who insists that their "backless suits" are shamelessly provocative. The girls protest. But a U.S. coach agrees with the decision, somberly ordering them to change to regulation suits with a warning that "if any leeway is given to these girls, there's no telling where it will end." The American girls,

properly clad, sweep the diving event.

On August 14, the final day of Olympic competition, Baron Takeichi Nishi of Japan, on his horse Uranus, rides to victory in an equestrian glamour event, the Prix des Nations, on the infield of the Coliseum. A stoic man, Nishi suddenly begins weeping as he leaves the winner's platform with his gold medal. His teammates embrace him; the largely American crowd roars its approval; no other moment in these Games has been more visibly emotional. For a few idyllic moments the thousands of people in the Coliseum are in harmony; the world is at peace; there is a feeling of universal brotherhood. It is unreal, of course, but the world can use a dose of unreality. Then, a chorus sings *Aloha* and the Games come to an end. The Olympic flame is extinguished, and with it some of the harmony, the brotherhood, the illusion. Everything is all too real again.

In the aftermath of the Games, no one, not even Olympic gold medalists themselves, can escape the Depression. High jumper Shiley finds herself unemployed until a government program provides her with work. Hurdler Hall and distance runner Cunningham find the going difficult, too. The list of the struggling reads like a who's who of American sports. Even memories of those days under the sun in Los Angeles take on a harder edge. When former Olympians talk of them it is usually less of events than of three athletes—a

woman and two black men—pioneers all.

The three did not ask to be pioneers. The times thrust the role upon them. Metcalfe and Tolan competed under intense American scrutiny, all the while enduring the barbs, the stereotyping, the misspellings of their names. And there was Didrikson, the most potent sports symbol of her time, seemingly screaming with each throw of her javelin that women need not be weak and docile, that they could be winners and champions, stand up and speak out at press conferences, lead teams and each other, be something more than merely a husband's appendage.

Then there was Baron Nishi, perhaps the most arresting symbol of all, representing in the end the gulf between what these Games promise and what they can deliver. For when all the majesty ends, the Olympic Games are still games after all. Men, not sports events, deliver peace, and men do not make peace as well as they, say, ride horses, as Nishi discovered. Thirteen years later, while leading a unit of Japanese soldiers on Iwo Jima, near the close of World War II, Nishi suddenly found himself surrounded and badly outnumbered by U.S. Marines. According to survivors, Nishi, though gravely wounded, refused the entreaties of his own men to surrender and calmly shot himself to death. With him was a piece of Uranus' mane and an Olympic riding crop. Los Angeles '32 was very far away. ∎

ALBERTA

Wish you were here

© 1984, Government of Alberta

CALGARY

CALGARY '88

Summer Wishes, Winter Dreams Alberta is waiting to welcome you this summer. To the splendour of our Rockies, the energy of our dynamic cities and the tranquility of unspoiled lakes, forests and rivers.

We're waiting, too, for our own Olympic dream to come true. In 1988, Calgary will host the Winter Olympics. We hope you'll join us then - and now. For information, write: Travel Alberta, P.O. Box 2500, Dept. 132, Edmonton, Alberta Canada T5J 2Z4.

Travel Alberta
CANADA

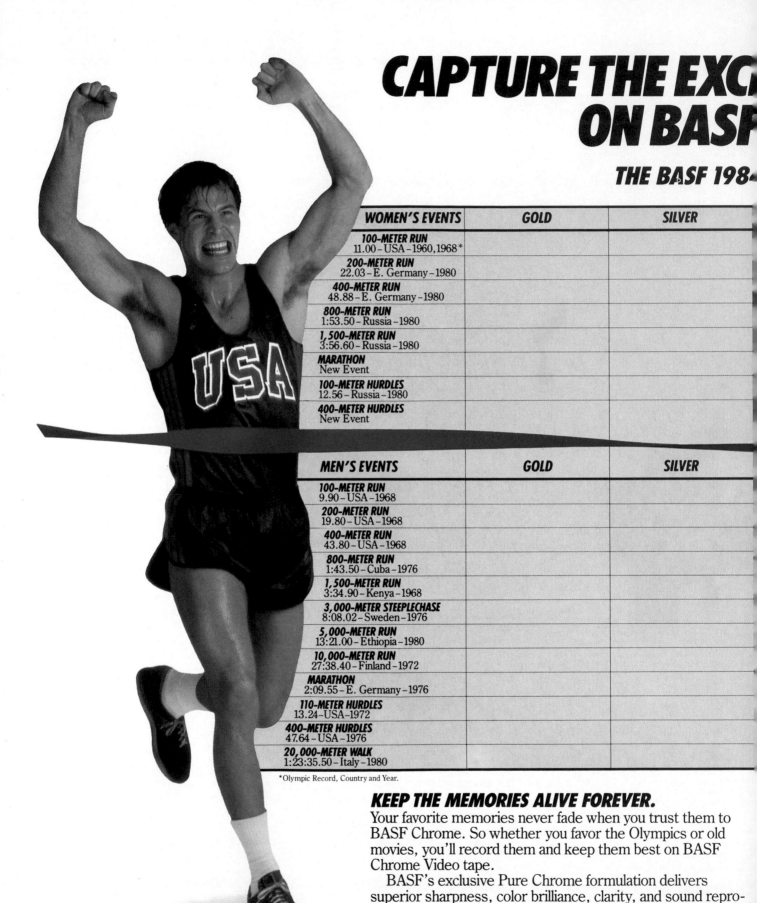

CAPTURE THE EXC
ON BASF

THE BASF 198

WOMEN'S EVENTS	GOLD	SILVER
100-METER RUN 11.00 – USA – 1960, 1968*		
200-METER RUN 22.03 – E. Germany – 1980		
400-METER RUN 48.88 – E. Germany – 1980		
800-METER RUN 1:53.50 – Russia – 1980		
1,500-METER RUN 3:56.60 – Russia – 1980		
MARATHON New Event		
100-METER HURDLES 12.56 – Russia – 1980		
400-METER HURDLES New Event		

MEN'S EVENTS	GOLD	SILVER
100-METER RUN 9.90 – USA – 1968		
200-METER RUN 19.80 – USA – 1968		
400-METER RUN 43.80 – USA – 1968		
800-METER RUN 1:43.50 – Cuba – 1976		
1,500-METER RUN 3:34.90 – Kenya – 1968		
3,000-METER STEEPLECHASE 8:08.02 – Sweden – 1976		
5,000-METER RUN 13:21.00 – Ethiopia – 1980		
10,000-METER RUN 27:38.40 – Finland – 1972		
MARATHON 2:09.55 – E. Germany – 1976		
110-METER HURDLES 13.24 – USA – 1972		
400-METER HURDLES 47.64 – USA – 1976		
20,000-METER WALK 1:23:35.50 – Italy – 1980		

*Olympic Record, Country and Year.

KEEP THE MEMORIES ALIVE FOREVER.

Your favorite memories never fade when you trust them to BASF Chrome. So whether you favor the Olympics or old movies, you'll record them and keep them best on BASF Chrome Video tape.

BASF's exclusive Pure Chrome formulation delivers superior sharpness, color brilliance, clarity, and sound reproduction—qualities that make BASF Chrome the winning choice for all your video recordings. So go with the proven

EMENT OF THE OLYMPIC GAMES
CHROME VIDEO TAPE.

LYMPIC TRACK AND FIELD SCORECARD.

BRONZE	WOMEN'S EVENTS	GOLD	SILVER	BRONZE
	400-METER RELAY 41.60 – E. Germany – 1980			
	1,600-METER RELAY 3:19.23 – E. Germany – 1976			
	RUNNING HIGH JUMP 6'5½" – Italy – 1980			
	LONG JUMP 23'2" – Russia – 1980			
	SHOT-PUT 73'6¼" – E. Germany – 1980			
	JAVELIN THROW 224'5" – Cuba – 1980			
	DISCUS THROW 229'6½" – E. Germany – 1980			
	HEPTATHLON New Event			

BRONZE	MEN'S EVENTS	GOLD	SILVER	BRONZE
	50,000-METER WALK 3:49:24.00 – E. Germany – 1980			
	400-METER RELAY 38.19 – USA – 1972			
	1,600-METER RELAY 2:56.10 – USA – 1968			
	POLE VAULT 18'1½" – E. Ger. – 1972/Pol. – 1976			
	RUNNING HIGH JUMP 7'8¾" – E. Germany – 1980			
	LONG JUMP 29'2½" – USA – 1968			
	TRIPLE JUMP 57'¾" – Russia – 1968			
	16-LB. SHOT-PUT 70'1½" – Russia – 1980			
	16-LB. HAMMER THROW 268' 4½" – Russia – 1980			
	JAVELIN THROW 310' 4" – Hungary – 1976			
	DISCUS THROW 221' 5" – USA – 1976			
	DECATHLON 8,618 pts. – USA – 1976			

winner—BASF. And no matter how often you replay or re-record, the quality never fades.

BASF congratulates all the athletes that make the 1984 Olympics a celebration worth remembering.

BASF
Chrome Audio & Video Tapes

L.A. TODAY

The Land Of Infinite Possibility

Amid the torch and other Olympic symbols is a city with dramatic personality

U.S. Team,
Your Best Friends Are Rooting For You!

WHEN HE arrived here some 50 years ago, he accosted W. C. Fields for an autograph— and skated off proudly, dubbed a knight, knowing he had a glorious future

ANGELENOS ON OUR WAY TO THE MOON

BY RAY BRADBURY

I GO TO EUROPE BUT RETURN TO America.

I go to France but come back to California.

I go to Paris but I live in Los Angeles.

"How can you *do* that?" certain of my friends protest. Isn't the Statue of Liberty made out of plastic these days? Isn't California the perfect state of non-being? Isn't Los Angeles where you put off to tomorrow what should have been done two months ago?

No. And again, no.

Allow me to zero in on L.A. and let California and the rest of the country survive while I digress.

I arrived here some 50 years ago at age 13, and had my first encounter with fame one summer afternoon in front of Paramount studios when I accosted W. C. Fields, who signed his name to a bit of paper, handed it back to me and cried: "There you are, you little son of a b———!"

Causing me to skate off proudly, dubbed

a knight, knowing I had a glorious future.

I was right, of course, because being a city that is not a city, a place with no core, an orange with no navel, L.A. is a conglomerate of small towns striving toward immensity and never making it, thank God. All of which means we have no kings, queens, or courts, no real pecking order, no hierarchies to prevent those of us who care to lean into creativity from running loose in the big yard. Oh, we have a minor royalty in the studios. But, fortunately, most actors, producers, directors and some few writers, do not read. Which means that the artists, novelists and anyone else crazy enough to work in the non-salaried world are free to do as they like, love and wish.

I have grown up here unnoticed. If I had grown up in New York, Paris or London, someone might have looked down, seen the flea, and squashed me. For, as we all know, those cities—those immense Duck Presses, where opinions on opinions on ideas are manufactured—are out to crush the creative spirit before it overrides the current fad, fashion or novelty notion held by a mindless minority of intellectuals in charge of policing the Duck Press.

Here in L.A. I simply don't have to cut my crust or tint my mind to any prevailing shape or hue. After all, our building toward landing on the moon was seeded and birthed 40 years ago in and around L.A.

Perhaps it is because we are somewhat frivolous and more relaxed that we have siphoned up the powers of the world. For that matter, one man, Walt Disney, madly in love with England and France, returned to our territory, from which he blueprinted Disneyland in California, Disney World and EPCOT in Florida—the imprint of which will change the history of the United States forever. Which means that in the years beyond 1984, the mayors of every major city and town in America will visit one of Disney's duchies, be stunned by the beauties of other countries funneled through Uncle Walt's eyeballs and into our imaginations, and go home to rebuild downtown Podunk and uptown Kansas City. A Los Angeles man with "Mouse Ears" will do all this to our towns, streets and lives.

I am reminded of an evening in Paris a few years ago when I looked from my hotel window the night before Bastille Day and saw what at a glance looked like thousands of Angelenos dancing in the streets.

"My God!" I cried to my wife, "I came to France to see Frenchmen, not Hollywood rock 'n' rollers jumping on the bricks!"

I plunged downstairs to see.

What I found was, of course, not 100,000 Hollywood hooligans but 100,000

continued

© 1980 L.A. Olympic Committee　　　　　　　　　TM

SUPPLIER OF ELECTRICAL APPLIANCES TO THE 1984 OLYMPIC GAMES.

Competition brings out the best.

Frenchmen *dressed* for a California climate that never arrived!

You see? We have conquered the world, and don't have enough sense to know it. Maybe it's just as well. With such knowledge comes arrogance. We are not arrogant yet, although I detect signs of it in this fling of mine. Perhaps late in the century, when the many small towns of L.A. connect up, and sign peace treaties with each other, and cross-pollinate theater groups, art mobs and political malfunctions, we will have found our navel, our pecking-order hierarchy and—at last—arrogance. Which will mean the death of creativity.

But that is not yet. For now, we Angelenos are dancing in the streets, dressed like *us*, on our way to the moon, Tokyo, Chungking. And not even an earthquake, or the London, Paris, New York intellectual establishments can stop us.

And when we have made landfall on Mars, and started toward Alpha Centauri, fired by blueprints mainly run up in L.A., we will glance back at all those doomers and doubters who never thought we could do it, and shout, in the words of dear Mr. Fields: "There you *are*, you little sons of b———s!"

HOLLYWOOD IS A STATE OF MIND

BY JOSH GREENFELD

A FRAMED PICTURE OF RONALD Reagan looks down at me. I am not in the post office. I am at my neighborhood haberdashery, standing at the cashier's counter with a couple of pairs of needed socks in hand. Above Ronald Reagan are Ted Knight and Louis Nye; below him is Walter Matthau. Ted Knight and Louis Nye have personally autographed their pictures but Reagan and Matthau haven't inscribed theirs.

"Was he really a customer here?" I ask the silver-haired cashier as she takes my money.

"Who?"

"The President."

She looks at the wall behind her and studies the picture as if asked to identify a mug shot.

"Of course," she nods. "He used to come in here often."

"What did he buy?"

"Socks," she pronounces, bagging my

EVERYTHING has its show business tie-in and show business ties into everything—his plumber is an ex-actor who will drop the plunger at a call from an agent, his electrician still likes to direct

purchase and handing me my change, "just like you."

You'll never find Lincoln or Washington—or even Harry Truman—on a Los Angeles haberdashery wall. After all, what movies did any of them make? What hit TV series have they appeared in recently? Never mind Mount Rushmore cameos or public television. I'm talking real credits.

Calvin Coolidge, a President in the silent-film era, once said, "The business of America is business." The business of Los Angeles is show. In Los Angeles everything has its show-business tie-in and show business ties into everything. L.A. is a company town and where the city ends and show business begins is impossible to discern. Hollywood, which is the local brand name for show business, is not so much a geographic fact as a state of mind—or mindless state—that is all-pervasive.

Let me explain: For example, if you spot a stylish gentleman behind the wheel of a Porsche, sporting a blazer with a foulard tie at his throat, chances are he teaches at UCLA. But a bearded kid in well-bleached jeans, casually slouching along a Westwood sidewalk, may well have been the second in command at MGM/UA in charge of worldwide production—as of late last week, anyway. At the same time you can also probably bet your diploma that the professor is trying to peddle his idea of a Renaissance sitcom to ABC-TV while the kid in the jeans is leading a seminar in Independent Movie Production Financing at USC on Saturdays.

The show-business influence is, as I say, everywhere. Junior high school students

read the trades, *Variety* and *The Hollywood Reporter*; studios build houses of worship; and celebrities run rampant in supermarkets. Especially, at the 10 items or less Express Checkout Lanes. Somehow it is the mark of celebrity to appear to be in great celerity even when one is shopping for celery.

But you'll rarely find a superstar in a supermarket. The fact of the matter is Frank Sinatra, Bob Hope, Marlon Brando, Robert Redford, Paul Newman, Dustin Hoffman, Al Pacino, Meryl Streep, Liza Minnelli all live out of town. In fact, the real status symbol in Los Angeles these days is not to live in Los Angeles at all. You can always spot the nouveau riche film director or the latest TV series star or gold-album singer. They're forever flying off to New York to look at co-op apartments or to Sante Fe to look at mud houses or to Washington to look at the White House. Anything to get away from L.A. and show business.

But I love wondering where and when and how each day will reveal its show-business connection. For example, I once had a washing-machine repairman whom I found it difficult to get through to on the phone. All I would get was his answering machine telling me to leave a message at the beep. Finally, one day when I did manage to reach him I asked for another number in case there was an emergency. "If you really have to get hold of me," he said, "call Universal and leave word with Lew Wasserman's office." Lew Wasserman happens to be chairman of the board of the world's biggest entertainment con-

continued

Ray Bradbury is known worldwide for his science fiction, including The Martian Chronicles, Fahrenheit 451.

Josh Greenfeld's books include A Child Called Noah *and the new novel,* The Return of Mr. Hollywood.

Marcia Seligson is the author of The Eternal Bliss Machine: America's Way of Wedding *and* Options.

Michael Fessier Jr., former columnist for New West, *writes features for the* Los Angeles Herald-Examiner.

Sara Davidson wrote the bestselling Loose Change *and the recent Double-day novel,* Friends of the Opposite Sex.

glomerate, MCA Inc., Universal's parent company.

On another occasion a carpenter, busily hanging doors for me, asked for the time. When I told him he abruptly stopped working and picked up his tools. "I've got to go," he announced. "I'm due over at Joey Bishop's house and I'm already late." He never told me what he was "due for," whether his appearance at Joey Bishop's was a professional one as a carpenter or a professional one, period. And he never did come back to finish hanging the doors for me, either.

Friends of mine have a Harrison Ford kitchen, every inch of it handcrafted by the *Star Wars* man himself for rock-bottom, earthbound prices. But that, of course, was before his success acting in outer space. Until then, Ford, like so many actors, supported himself by doing contracting and carpentry work in the kind of Malibu homes he only dreamed he could one day afford to acquire for his very own living space.

My present plumber is a former actor who will drop his plunger at the call of a casting agent. My electrician still likes to direct. A doctor was recommended to me recently as "the proctologist to the stars." And I admit having gone to "the chiro-practor of the stars," where Loretta Young and Milton Berle would make in-person, waiting-room appearances.

When I first came to live in Los Angeles I rented the house that Carroll O'Connor had before he became Archie Bunker. I now live next door to the house that Ronald Colman's secretary used to live in. I still don't know whether that's a step up or a step down.

But one day when I was house-hunting, the real estate agent looked gnawingly familiar. Suddenly I recognized him. "Didn't you once play Tarzan?" I asked. "Yes," replied Bruce Bennett. I turned to my seven-year-old son and excitedly informed him that when I was a child this man had been Tarzan.

"When you were a child," my son asked, blinking his eyes uncomprehendingly, "Tarzan was a realtor?"

Later, instead of waxing eloquent about the hardwood floors and kitchen tiles of a house he was showing, "the realtor" sidled over to me and mumbled, "I also was in *Mildred Pierce* and *The Treasure of the Sierra Madre.*"

Credits, credits, it always boils down to credits. But that's L.A. Or is it show business? In any case, there is no difference and viva that!

MOVING UP, SPREADING OUT, BEING FREE

BY MARCIA SELIGSON

MEET TRACI, MY HAIRDRESSER, the essential L.A. metaphor. She was born here 27 years ago, in the mid-Wilshire area, to parents who made a bundle in real estate, retired and moved to Palm Springs, from which they never emerge. Traci embodies practically everything I have to say about the Los Angeles lifestyle.

She is not pretty, really, but she's flashy enough to disguise the truth with her flaming orange hair that one week hangs rod-straight to her shoulders and the next is permed and spreads out sideways like a crinoline and the next is an H.R. Haldeman crew cut. She's consumed with clothes, shoes, purses and earrings, and although she goes shopping at least once a day she always looks slightly askew and silly, inevitably going three steps too far to the left in her commitment to being "original" and "outrageous."

continued

SHE embodies the L.A. lifestyle, an entrepreneur who always has a deal brewing— imports from Hong Kong, condos with nothing down

Photograph by Horst Wackerbarth

You needn't wait another four years to experience the Olympic spirit.

You'll feel it every time you fly Korean Air Lines. The spirit and total dedication that extends throughout our service—and throughout the host country of both the 1986 Asian games and the 1988 Olympics.

ONE OF THE BIGGEST EVENTS HERE WILL PROBABLY GO COMPLETELY UNNOTICED.

You'll never see what happens to the 66,000 pounds of ticket stubs, paper cups and such that are left behind after every event in the Coliseum.

All of it will simply be gone by the time you return for the next event. Just an hour and 15 minutes later.

The athletes sleeping in the Olympic Village won't hear a thing as our rubber-tired trash carts roll off to be quietly emptied into trucks waiting blocks away.

In fact, we've spent over a year making sure that no one notices any of the 6.5 million pounds of trash that will be discarded at the 1984 Olympic Games.

After any event. At any Olympic venue.

From the canoeing competition at Lake Casitas to the equestrian events at the Fairbanks Ranch 194 miles away.

We're Waste Management. And the L.A. Olympic Organizing Committee designated us to set up the elaborate system that is handling more trash in less than a month than most towns generate in a whole year.

Perhaps being the Official Solid Waste System Manager isn't the most glamorous job at the 1984 Olympics.

And we won't win any medals for it.

But the way we see it, keeping America beautiful before the eyes of the world is quite an honor.

Waste Management, Inc.
Helping the world dispose of its problems.

Traci is relentlessly cheerful, having adopted a pop-Buddhist stance of going with the flow and assuming the Universe is perfect no matter what. Except for those times when she is suicidally depressed. Fortunately, she never stays in either mood for longer than a few days: The highs always disintegrate when her lofty fantasies are not instantly fulfilled, and she dispels her "Black Pits," as she terms them, by either signing up for a new aerobics class, buying 11 new eyeshadows or launching into a vegetable-juice fast. Traci is always in motion.

When last I waited for her, Traci was fervently blow-drying away the client before me and sharing her wisdom. "You have your moon in Aquarius and Saturn conjuncts your sun," she gurgled, "so, *of course*, your positive energy space will be higher than his." The client nodded in agreement. Traci uses the word "create" incessantly, as in "I created a pair of red boots at Neiman-Marcus that are to kill." Or, "I'm creating love everywhere I go and now I need to create abundance." Which probably translates as Traci is making love regularly but can't make the payments on her red Porsche. Which is another story, L.A.'s red Porsches.

Traci's always got a deal brewing. Besides maneuvering hair into something it was never meant to be (her business card calls it PERSONAL CARE SUPPORT), she distributes natural herbal remedies, imports reptile address-book covers from Hong Kong which she peddles from her apartment, and takes weekend seminars in how to buy millions of bucks' worth of condominiums with nothing down. And that is primarily what I want to tell you about Los Angeles: Everybody is an entrepreneur, moving up, spreading out, being free. People don't just go to their daily jobs and then relax. Not here. Every poolman and chiropractor has a screenplay or a series cooking and "just about to happen." Computer programmers run weekend catering gigs or make macramé incense burners. Welcome to L.A. This is the land of Infinite Possibility.

We've known that for centuries, the movement westward no less than mythic in its message: West means liberation, the fruition of visions and goals, limitless opportunity for self-expression, daring and big success. Nothing to hold us back. The Gold Rush was short-lived and minuscule compared to the Dream Rush, which infuses us each day. It was, naturally, no accident that the movie business, in its infancy 70-odd years ago, deserted the cold and

THE mandate of our city is to honor the unconventional, exalt the new—we can create life the way we want it, if only for a moment

restrictive East and set up shop in Los Angeles, this seeding the spirit of monumental dreams that lies at the heart of this city. That same spirit rests beneath all the fads, trends, true innovation and key social movements that begin here and then sweep throughout America.

A few years ago a rich Beverly Hills woman named Alice Cohn changed her first name to Contessa and threw herself a coronation soirée at the toniest bistro in town. A few blocks away resides a psychic nutritionist, with a seven-month waiting list, who waves a box of granola over your head to ascertain if you're allergic to it. The opening of a neighborhood deli in Sherman Oaks is heralded by twin searchlights scanning the heavens as if announcing the Second Coming. A man I know is part of an eight-person marriage devoted to transcending petty human limitations and providing a Utopian model of Unconditional Love.

Is there a common denominator here? I think so. We will try *anything* that's different—fearlessly and without a touch of squeamishness. A new psychic surgeon just hit town? Sure, sign us up. We will experiment with our bodies and psyches (colonics, aura readings, Hellering, iridology) in ways that may not even have been *heard* of yet back East. We'll get "into" UFOs for a while, hang out at an ashram, invest our life savings in a new multilevel sales game, or dye our hair pink. This is not at all to say that eccentricity is absent from Cleveland. It is, however, a claim that the mandate of Los Angeles is to honor the unconventional, exalt the new, pat the head of the nutsy outrageous. Why not make yourself a Contessa in a city where we can create life precisely the way we want it, even if only for a fleeting moment?

One Wednesday morning toward the

end of January, while most of America suffered soul-shattering cold, my husband and I abandoned our careers, lowered the top of our blue Fiat convertible and zoomed out to Venice Beach. We spent the sun-soaked workday roller-skating the five-mile length of the boardwalk, jogging in the water's edge with our golden retriever, eating sprout salads at an outdoor café. I want you to know that we were neither guilt-ridden nor embarrassed for playing hooky, unafraid of being "caught." In fact, we felt utterly brilliant, lucky and blessed. We were simply doing what we came here from the East to do. Being free. Making it all Infinitely Possible.

A FAN'S NOTES

BY MICHAEL FESSIER JR

SOME YEARS AGO I WAS LED into the Santa Anita jock's room for an audience with Willie Shoemaker, the wealthiest, winningest jockey on the planet Earth. The timing was poor since he was receiving a between-races shampoo, and I was forced to conduct what to me was a most sober and significant discussion with a man partially hidden by a halo of soapsuds. The topic was the racetrack itself, Santa Anita, then, rumor had it, threatened with extinction. The land had become too valuable and might be more profitably used for a housing development or shopping mall. Shoemaker had been riding there since 1950, had won more millions than he could count for owners, fans and himself. What I wanted to know was what the track itself meant to him. Did he, as I did, have a strong sentimental attachment to a track that many call the most beautiful in the world? Did the infield flower gardens or the backdrop San Gabriel Mountains, or maybe the old wooden eagle that hung from the clubhouse ceiling have any special meaning for him? Would he, in short, care very much if the whole place were turned into a shopping mall?

"Not particularly," he said.

I believe he was living in Bel Air at the time and he said that without Santa Anita the dates would just go to Hollywood Park, which was closer to where he lived.

"No sentimental attachment at all?" I asked, unable to believe the king hadn't

continued

Photograph by Raul Vega

HE invested a racetrack with feelings other people invest in their cities— he had a racetrack in which to enjoy a comforting sense of geographic and social changelessness

some special feeling for a kingdom which had been so profitable for him.

Shoemaker had already grown weary of the conversation such as it was. His blue eyes remained impassive. "I'm really not sentimental about much of anything," he said.

Clearly, I would have to go elsewhere to find corroboration for my probably excessive devotion to a horsetrack.

Santa Anita then occupied a commodious 400 acres, a parking lot or two more than the entire principality of Monaco. Set in the blissfully named Greater Los Angeles province of Arcadia, 17 miles northeast of downtown L.A., Santa Anita was, like any racetrack, an increasingly curious anachronism. Beyond its high walls was the self-contained world which mixed elements of the urban and the rural with aspects of circus and rodeo added. All of it, finally, comprised a distinct society firmly rooted in English racing and breeding traditions hundreds of years old. It was only one of such enclaves in the area—there were also Hollywood Park, Del Mar and Caliente—but Santa Anita had an extra margin of class, it seemed to me.

For me, it had provided much fantastic theater over the years—two performances of which really stand out: in 1958, with Shoemaker up, Silky Sullivan, the great laggard, trailing by 40 lengths at six furlongs and still winning; in 1966, Johnny

Longden winning the last race of his career at age 59 on George Royal in that most leisurely and dramatic of classic races, the San Juan Capistrano Handicap on the grass.

But the races I had seen, the money won and lost, were still only part of the reason for my perennial love affair with Santa Anita. There was something else, something to do with the continuity that it supplied in Southern California.

We live in a region in which community definition has been blurred through the years by wave after wave of immigration. We have come to instinctively treasure certain enclaves rigidly defined from the surrounding confusion. Disneyland and Dodger Stadium did it for some, and for others a movie studio or aerospace complex or university campus. In its smallest and loneliest component, it is the private home. I had invested a racetrack with feelings that people in other parts of the country invest in their cities. I had no city as such. Instead I had a racetrack in which to enjoy a comforting sense of geographic and social changelessness.

Not that it could truly remain changeless. A year after my talk with Shoemaker—this was early in '72—a shopping mall did devour a portion of the Santa Anita grounds, a 72-acre slice that took out part of the old stable area and all of what was then the training track. But the track

itself did survive, I was grateful to see.

There were other changes as well. One of them is the absence of Joe Hernandez, who called every race every day from the time the track opened on Christmas Day, 1934, until his death on Jan. 27, 1972. As "the voice of Santa Anita" he had a special Spanish rhythm, a hoofbeat cadence in the very way he said Santa Anita. It was no reach at all to connect his Santa Anita to the match races wealthy Spanish landowners once staged not far from the present track. At last fall's Oak Tree meet, run at Santa Anita, a distinctly British-voiced South African was imported to do the racecalls and it was all right—Southern California becomes more indecipherably eclectic by the day—but his voice certainly didn't have the indigenous ring that Hernandez' voice had had.

It was Hernandez, fittingly enough, who had finally, somewhat grudgingly, seconded my own feelings for Santa Anita. After talking to Shoemaker that day I had gone up to see Hernandez in his announcer's booth, stuck like a wasp's nest high up in the girders of the grandstand roof.

It was certainly a heavenly view of things from up there. Tiny horses ambled toward the starting gate on the other side of the track and, as he had done so many times before, Hernandez flipped the switch and informed over 30,000 or so people:

continued

272

"It is now
early 60s,
tracker in
mustard sh
had come
consistent
thing of a
his feeling f
noying, self
ord. He kn
Santa Anita
in some wa
finger on.

Watching
heavy black
to me, "Sar
than you or
gate was so
sive action—
that it was
eyes off it. Y
broke conce
me. "It'll be
put together,

Four days
dent, Hernar
men by a he
noon halfwa)
have been h
and died late

But the gr
the foot of, ii
jestic San G

SOME
people c
that the
are no se
but she s
and sum.
her favor
time—w.
long gold
days and
nights

A lot of things could go haywire during the Olympic Games. Including your TV reception. Thanks to all the buildings and mountains in and around greater L.A.

So ABC's mobile camera truck is going to beam its signal out of the hills and valleys via a helicopter flying directly overhead.

Question is, with clouds and smog, if the helicopter loses the truck, will you lose the Olympics?

Absolutely not. Our Bendix radar, with its Beacon Trac feature, will enable the helicopter to follow the truck, no matter what comes between them. And you'll get to follow the games, no matter what direction they take.

ABC is going to great lengths to prevent problems. And we're going to do our best to stay on top of this one.

So sit back and enjoy the Olympics. They'll be brought to you in part by Allied. With as few interruptions as possible.

Official Sponsor
1984 Olympics

ALLIED

AS WE cruise along, the shrubbery bordering the freeway obscures our view of what lies beyond it— the unknown

art openings, and I wanted to attend them all. I loved the crowds, the pulsation, the electrifying sense that anyone who was important or outstanding in any field was close at hand.

But life was difficult in New York—and expensive. It was hard to engage in sports or exercise, and it took hours to reach the beach. I felt my body grow flaccid and pale. In the dead of winter I flew to California for a visit, and when the plane carried me back East my heart sank watching the scenery below turn from green to gray.

Ten years passed, and there came a night in November when I knew New York was finished for me. It was raining, bitter cold, and all the streets crossing Central Park were flooded. I was stranded on the East Side and my home was on the West Side. There were no taxis to be seen, so I got on a crowded bus, but in an hour the bus did not move an inch.

Desperate, a group of passengers banded together to walk across Central Park. In the blackness, frightened of muggers, we sloshed through lakes of rainwater, and the wind blew mercilessly and turned our umbrellas inside out. Cold tears ran down my cheeks.

When I finally reached my apartment, soaked through, I found the furnace for the building had broken and there was no heat or hot water. Huddled, shivering beside my oven, I vowed I would not spend another winter in the East.

I did not come back to Los Angeles right away, though. I went to Northern California, to Marin County, to pursue a fantasy. I rented a redwood cabin on a bluff over-looking the Pacific Ocean, with a corral so that I could keep a horse. I planted winter vegetables and attempted to make new friends.

Everyone I met was pretty, and every house, store and dental office had lots of hanging ferns and oak floors and stained-glass windows and platters of gourmet natural food. It was paradise, self-consciously so, and I felt terribly ill at ease.

A few days after I had moved into my redwood cabin, I heard a radio blasting in the woods. For 24 hours the radio was tuned to the same station, and the volume did not change. There were no houses in the woods, so I began to suspect that people might have wandered in there and met with trouble.

I walked to the edge of my deck and yelled (thinking if anyone was alive, he might respond): "Could you turn down the radio, please?"

Silence. Then a voice called to me from the woods: "Smoke a joint, and mellow out!"

I must tell you, I never did manage to mellow out. Some months later, I went to Los Angeles and decided to move there—on a trial basis. I liked the pace of the city and the fact that so many people were engaged in purposeful work. I found I was infinitely more comfortable in a city that was flawed. There was smog, and you had to spend hours in your car and the main topics of conversation were diet and the movie business. No one even pretended it was paradise.

To my amazement, I have now been "out here" 10 years. I have resolved, several times, to leave, usually after a brief trip East, but then a sweet torpor sets in. I think about frozen winters and fighting for taxis and no chance to ride a bike and all the heavy clothing I'd have to wear, and I stay.

Not everyone feels as I do about the weather; some complain that there are no seasons, but I see them. Summer is my favorite time, with long, golden days at the beach and balmy nights. Autumn means dry winds and clear, dramatic skies; winter brings poinsettias and birds of paradise; and in spring, the jacaranda trees burst with their lavender blossoms, so that whole avenues and boulevards are showered with purple flowers.

I have chosen body over mind, it seems. There is a price to pay, and I pay it. I miss the high cultural tone of the East, but if I were there, I would pine and wither like a hothouse flower suddenly transplanted. There is no way around it, I'm afraid.

The feel of sun on my skin makes me happy.

I NTIMATE ENCLAVES

BY MICHAEL LEAHY

I WAS ONLY 12, AND IT WAS ONLY a moment, like the sudden shifting of shadow to light, but it would forever change the way I viewed life in my little world. I sat in a new Buick, caught in a maddening freeway traffic jam with my best friend and his father, who glanced furtively at the empty city streets which lay underneath the freeway, thinking.

"That's where we should go," his son said, gesturing at the streets, 40 feet below us. The streets, eerily lit, ominously abandoned, with their clear passageway to our homes, lay before us like an open drag strip. "Why aren't we getting off the freeway?"

"We aren't getting off," said this man who had driven the same freeway route for 20 years, "because we're by East Los Angeles, and I've never seen it, and. . . ." I had never before heard that tone from an adult. It was fear. And, right then, I understood that the freeway had considerably less to do with speed than it had to do with its riders' craving for isolation.

continued

On Sundays now, during the football season, I often take my six-year-old nephew, Russell, to the Los Angeles Raiders games at the Coliseum, driving from Santa Monica to South Central Los Angeles, without leaving the security of the concrete ribbon. We park in a lot just across the street from the on-ramp to the freeway and when the game is over, I whisk Russell into his seat belt and soar up the on-ramp, 5 . . . 10 . . . 20 feet—two full stories above the uncertain streets heading toward downtown Los Angeles, too high to see any dilapidated tenements, hungry transients, angry gangs.

As we cruise along at 60 miles per hour the lush shrubbery bordering the freeway obscures our view of what lies beyond it, the unknown, the troubling, the very things which compelled us to plant the shrubs years ago. Behind the trees, south of the Crenshaw Boulevard exit, there are large black and Hispanic communities; to the northwest, Vietnamese enclaves and to the northeast, Korean. We pass Fairfax Avenue, which leads to a large Jewish community. Russell has never seen any of it. Nor have most of the people I know. The freeway permits you to see only what you want to see; on the ribbon you can forever sail over alien lands.

I heard a story the other day: A policeman, patrolling an Hispanic area in East Los Angeles, routinely asks motorists whom he stops, "Have you ever seen the sea?" Most say no. A few ask what the sea is like—how warm, what shade of blue, what size waves, what kind of bikinis the girls are wearing this year—as if the sea were a dream vacation spot, say, on the French Riviera. Actually, the ocean and the town of Santa Monica are just across the city from East Los Angeles, 15 miles

away, but at the end of those 15 miles is another galaxy, people with boats and surfboards, people with bigger homes, nicer cars, more money. "I don't feel relaxed there," one motorist said, shrugging.

So he stays in his own enclave. The enclaves are the great dividers in Los Angeles, and, over the years, they have wrestled each other for power and attention. During the 1932 Olympics, the city's political and social power resided in opulent Hancock Park, and other elite downtown communities whose power brokers elected the politicians, ran the city's newspapers, operated the private clubs, even brought the Olympics to town.

Today, power is fought over by a number of competing factions. The city's mayor and three of its councilmen are black. The Hispanic community, though it still has disproportionately few elected officials, stands to grow much larger in the city and Los Angeles County by the year 2000. The San Fernando Valley, once a sleepy rural community of small farms and massive orchards, is now a middle-class, conservative stronghold of over 1,000,000 people whose political inroads have often come at the expense of the city's corporate moguls and bluebloods.

To their credit, the Old Guard has faced up to all this. That has meant, among other things, dealing with the "arribistas," the upstarts, as one wealthy matron defined them: self-made entrepreneurs, aerospace executives, real estate magnates, computer wizards, and, of course, Hollywood's successful. For many years, the movers and shakers wanted nothing to do with Hollywood (one of the area's notable private schools would not even accept the daughters of Hollywood's famous), but time and the realization that worthy social and artis-

tic projects can no longer move ahead without Hollywood's money have a way of changing things. Still, meetings between the bluebloods and the arribistas have all the uncertainty of a cold-war summit conference. "I made friends over lunch with their leaders today. . . ." once said Dorothy Chandler of the publishing family and a well-known philanthropist, who had dreamed of erecting a music center in Los Angeles, and had approached the arribistas for financial support.

They are the modern-day 49ers, gatherers of the gold, fiercely independent entrepreneurs who came here in some cases to stake out a fortune, and then seized it. Evidence of their success can be seen everywhere, in businesses ranging from oil to apparel to real estate. The region's gross product is greater than that of either Australia or East Germany and exceeded by only thirteen nations in the world. As always, the foundation for the wealth is the land—choice land on beaches and in mountain resorts, fertile land, oil-rich land. The region produces about 10% of the nation's crude oil, and Atlantic Richfield, Occidental Petroleum and Union Oil all have established their corporate headquarters here. "People don't think of oil when they think of California," said a spokesman for Atlantic Richfield. "They think of those other industries. Well, those other industries tend to go through cyclical periods of good and bad. We don't."

Those "other industries" include, chiefly, aerospace and motion pictures. "The whole entertainment business is fickle," says a movie producer. "A big gamble." A casino, some call it. Yet, if losses are great sometimes, so, too, are gains and bonanzas. Data processing and computer indus-

continued

INDIVIDUAL EFFORT

The difference between a good company and a great company is individual effort.

We at Epson understand that.

It's why we value qualities like spirit. And determination. And drive.

We nurture those qualities in Epson people around the world; we reward, coax, encourage; we push our people to give their very best. Always.

In this way, we turn out some very fine computers and printers, liquid crystal displays, disk drives and other sophisticated electronic technology.

And something else.

We turn out some very fine people.

EPSON

Something extra.

HE DRIVES
the freeway,
passing places
he does not know—
and realizes
the freeway
has less to do
with speed
than its riders'
craving for
isolation

tries have soared here. Medical services have achieved spectacular growth, a trend likely to escalate as children of the baby boom grow older. The rapid successes of these industries and others—many of them speculative ventures—drive more entrepreneurs to the region every day, ready to gamble, fiercely believing in the efficacy of the golden dream.

"California or Bust!" It is still that kind of place for some. When I was in high school, I used to run through the orange grove of an elderly man named Charles, who, a few years before, had left Minnesota with his life savings. He had driven West, seen this orchard, and though he knew nothing about oranges, bought it. He had settled back then to watch it turn a handsome profit. It was harder than he imagined. Sometimes, spotting me, he would give me an orange, and tell me what had happened that day, what trees had ripened or over-ripened, what bugs threatened to infest his trees, what oranges had gotten cold overnight. "That orange feel hard to you?" Charles would ask me, and we would fumble with the orange, both of us absolute novices in all this. After a while, he would sigh and tell me about trout fishing.

A couple of years ago, I went to visit Charles. I arrived to find the orchard gone. A housing tract stood in its place. "Charles sold out for a tidy profit," said a gasoline-station attendant nearby. "He got what he came for."

Most of the orange groves are gone now. Land-use and development issues are now hotly debated topics, exacerbated by natives' feelings that some developers, attracted to the area's boom possibilities, do not possess a sufficient concern for the land. Said one resident at a city planning meeting: "We have to be concerned about the quality of life here."

That concern, within the arts, for instance, has burgeoned in recent years. The Los Angeles County Museum of Art has expanded its collection to include a center for German Expressionist art; the J. Paul Getty Museum in Malibu is known worldwide for its Greek and Roman antiquities; and the Norton Simon Museum in Pasadena has a first-rate collection of Renaissance and Impressionist art. The Los Angeles Philharmonic Orchestra, under the direction of first Zubin Mehta, and, recently, Carlo Maria Giulini, has emerged as a world-class symphony. Los Angeles is shedding its image as a city devoid of cultural and intellectual thought, a lotus land where Jacuzzis may be deep but humanity shallow.

One wonders how the myth has survived this long. For the land that created sitcoms like *Laverne & Shirley* is also the one that inspired the works of Nathanael West and Raymond Chandler. This is a land whose medical researchers have done internationally renowned work in the areas of cancer, heart disease, diabetes and liver infection, among others. This is a land

where astronomers regularly open the doors to the universe, where street-artists paint storefront murals, and promising young poets write verse that sings. This is a land with a billion-dollar redevelopment project drafted in unison by urban designers, city planners and politicians. It is a city fraught with problems, but inhabited by people with the acumen to solve them.

For all that, there are those who insist that this is no city at all, really, that it is merely many disparate communities spread around a nonexistent hub, a steel-gray backdrop of glittering skyscrapers and wide streets that become vacant at the end of each workday like a Nevada ghost town. It's true, we have no center, never claimed to, never wanted one. What we wanted was a refuge. The people who built this city envisioned its inhabitants living in the open air, away from the factories and office buildings in which they worked, imagined a land of intimate enclaves sheltered from the metropolis. And, good or bad, that is what they got. I think about that often these days when I drive the freeway, passing places I do not know.

That is part of the reason why I'm looking forward so much to the Olympics. Many of the events are being staged in areas in which I have never set foot, and so I am finally going to see East Los Angeles, Lake Casitas and El Dorado Park, where they will hold the archery competition. I will shake hands with people whom I've never met. I will see my city anew. ∎

No one
appreciates
the quest for the best
more.

Neiman-Marcus

Did You Hear The

One About **?**

Through the centuries the swirl of Olympic activity has provided oddities, amusements and springboards for assorted myths

By Dick Schaap

ID YOU HEAR THE ONE ABOUT the fencer who got caught rigging his electronic epée in 1976 so that the buzzer buzzed even when he didn't touch his opponent? Or the one about the runner from Suriname, the only athlete representing that country in 1960, who slept through the trials for his event? Or how about the American runner who covered much of the 1904 marathon course in an automobile, then jogged home to a champion's reception?

Those were some of the more amusing moments in Olympic history, unless, of course, you happened to be the fencer who had to go home to Kiev, the runner who had to go home to Suriname, or Thomas Hicks, the U.S. entrant who *really* won the 1904 marathon.

Humor has never been an *official* Olympic event, but the Games, in both their ancient and modern incarnations, have, as a pleasant side effect, induced laughter almost as often as they have induced agony and ecstasy, the emotional responses more commonly associated with athletic endeavor.

Some of the laughter has been provoked intentionally—by John Lardner, the essayist, for example. When he described the great Finnish gold medalist of the 1920s, Paavo Nurmi, a runner ahead of his time in more ways than one, Lardner wrote: "He has the lowest heartbeat and the highest asking price

LEGENDARY AND LATTER-DAY REAL Olympians include Ancient Greece's chariot-racing King Oenomaus, swimmer-turned-Tarzan Johnny Weissmuller, U.S. Army's wild-shooting pentathlon entry George S. Patton Jr., gold-medal-winning crew member and doctor-to-be Benjamin Spock, camera-clicking, tongue-wagging boxer Cassius Clay

MILO
of Croton,
wrestling hero
of the Games, B.C.,
toted his own statue
to Olympia
but was finally,
fatally
pinned by a pack
of wolves

of any athlete in the world." Some laughter has been provoked accidentally—by Jim Thorpe, the 1912 decathlon champion, for instance. When King Gustav V of Sweden told him, "Sir, you are the greatest athlete in the world," Thorpe replied: "Thanks, King."

The tradition of colorful Olympic characters, the raw stuff of humor, goes back to the Ancient Greeks, to Pelops, the man who, according to one legend, initiated the Olympic Games to celebrate his marriage to the daughter of King Oenomaus, Princess Hippodamia. The King was a protective father who insisted that each man who sought his daughter's hand whisk her away from her home in a chariot, then try to outrace her pursuing father. King Oenomaus caught the first 13 men who tried, and killed them. The next candidate, Pelops, bribed the royal charioteer to weaken the axle on the King's chariot. When Pelops took off with Hippodamia, and Oenomaus took off after them, the axle gave out, the chariot collapsed and—Long live the new King! Hippodamia had lost a father, but gained a husband.

If you believe that story, you'll appreciate the story of Milo of Croton, a man of strength, skill and endurance. Milo flourished in the sixth century B.C., a wrestler who, for a typical meal, feasted upon seven pounds of meat, seven pounds of bread and four or five quarts of wine. At Olympia, at one sitting, he ate an entire four-year-old bull. Six times an Olympic champion, Milo celebrated by carrying his own lifesized statue to its proper place in Olympia. He was, according to the sportscribes of his day, capable of holding a pomegranate in his fist so tightly no one

ABC-Television news correspondent Dick Schaap, winner of a 1983 Emmy Award, is also the author of more than 20 books, one of which is the new edition of An Illustrated History of The Olympics.

could pry open his hand, yet so gently not a single drop of juice dripped out. He could stand on a greased discus and brush away attackers without losing his footing. Milo's amazing career ended in a forest when, at one sitting, he was eaten up by a pack of wolves.

Milo was one of the first among many athletes who helped feed the Olympic myths. In 1896, the year the French Baron Pierre de Coubertin revived the Olympic Games, one of his countrymen, a runner, entered two strikingly dissimilar events. "Ze *cent* [100] meter and ze marathon," the versatile Frenchman told an American hurdler named Thomas Curtis, who recalled the conversation, but not the Frenchman's name, years later.

"How do you train for such different events?" Curtis asked.

The Frenchman smiled. "One day," he explained, "I run a leetle way, vairy quick. The next day, I run a long way, vairy slow."

Eight years later, in 1904, the most appealing figure of the Games in St. Louis was a tiny Cuban mailman named Felix Carvajal who, without any official Cuban team, staged his own fund-raising campaign to pay his way to the Olympics. He ran around a public square in Havana. Once a crowd gathered, Felix jumped on a wooden box and asked for contributions. He got enough to finance his passage to the United States and his participation in a dice game in New Orleans, his port of entry. Carvajal emerged from the dice game broke, but managed to work and beg his way up the Mississippi to the Olympic site. He soon became the friend of the American weightthrowers, who offered him food, lodging and advice. Felix accepted the food and lodging.

On a savagely hot and humid day, Carvajal awaited the start of the marathon wearing a long-sleeved

continued

shirt, long trousers and heavy street shoes. Martin Sheridan, an American weight-thrower, took a pair of scissors and clipped Felix's trousers at the knee. Then the race began, and Felix, in his cutoffs, kept up a surprisingly strong pace, cheerfully chatting with spectators in broken English. Once, he dashed off the course, into an apple orchard, and ate two green apples. The apples caused cramps, which forced the Cuban mailman to stop and rest. But Felix picked up the race and managed to finish a very creditable fourth.

In 1906, the first and only interim Olympics was held, in Athens, an event most notable for the straightforward description of the Opening Ceremonies provided by the manager of the U.S. team, Matt Halpin, who was clearly not a diplomat. "The Crown Prince Constantine handed out a line of guff to King George," Halpin cabled the *New York Evening Mail*, "after which George climbed down out of the swell imperial layout and contributed his spiel, which opened the Games."

The 1912 Olympics in Stockholm was memorable for the presence, on the American team, of several men who were considerably more famous fully half a century later. Only two of them were winners in Stockholm, and only one's fame endured purely because of his athletic ability.

He was, of course, Jim Thorpe, quite likely the most gifted all-around athlete the United States has ever produced. Another was Duke Kahanamoku, a Hawaiian swimmer who was still competing in the Olympics twenty years later (as an alternate on the water polo team). By then, Kahanamoku was the sheriff of Honolulu, a job he held for nearly three decades, a living symbol of Hawaii. He may not have invented the flowered shirt, but he certainly raised the wearing of it to an art form. In 1912, Kahana-

moku won the gold medal in the 100-meter freestyle.

A third who flourished after the 1912 Olympics was a young Army lieutenant, a West Pointer who had a chance to win the modern pentathlon championship. Had he finished first in the shooting competition he would have earned a gold medal. But George S. Patton Jr. could place no better than 21st among the shooters and slipped to fifth overall. Later, as Lt. General "Blood and Guts" Patton, commander of the U.S. Third Army in World War II, he helped achieve a more significant victory.

Another member of the 1912 team enjoyed more limited fame, even though he had one of the most visible jobs in the world. It is hard to imagine any job at which Pat McDonald, 6′ 4″ and 250 pounds, nicknamed "The Prince of Whales," a member of the Irish-American Athletic Club, winner of the gold medal in the shotput, would not be visible. Still, as a New York City policeman assigned to direct traffic in Times Square, McDonald was an unmistakable Manhattan monument.

McDonald was especially known for his gallantry—his willingness to stop traffic, walk to the curb and, arm in arm, escort a female pedestrian across the crowded intersection. McDonald invariably seemed to choose unattractive women.

"Why do you always pick the ugly ones?" Johnny Hayes, the 1908 Olympic marathon winner, once asked McDonald.

"For a simple reason," McDonald said. "Most of those women have never had a man escort them across the street. You should see the tips I get."

After a brief pause for World War I, the Olympics resumed in 1920 and continued to introduce athletes whose reputations would, eventually, extend far beyond the Games. That year an American named

continued

CUBAN mailman Felix Carvajal paid his way to the '04 Games and had his long pants snipped short by friendly U.S. Olympians so he could run a faster marathon

After the race is run,
the bar is cleared,
the weight is lifted,
the distance is measured,
the routine is judged
and the flag is unfurled,

we'll keep the Olympic
memories and achievements alive.

Los Angeles Times

For the Olympics. . .
a special kind of journalism.

HAWAIIAN swimmer Duke Kahanamoku competed in four Olympics from '12 to '32 and helped the Islands' shirt flower into world fashion

John B. Kelly won the single sculls championship and teamed with his cousin, Paul Costello, to win the double sculls, a rowing parlay that has never been matched. But Kelly, who once won 12 consecutive races, became far better known as the father of the late Princess Grace of Monaco. In 1924, hardly anyone except the most passionate rowing fan knew the name of the young man who rowed number seven on the gold-medal Yale University crew, but a quarter of a century later he was the most famous pediatrician in the world, Dr. Benjamin Spock. And one of his American teammates, a swimmer who completed his own brilliant Olympic career in 1928, kept on swimming for years, and swinging from vines, and pounding his chest, and getting rich: He was Johnny Weissmuller, who rose from king of the water to become Hollywood's Tarzan of the Apes. And, remarkably, Weissmuller's successor as an Olympic freestyle champion in 1932, Clarence "Buster" Crabbe, became the movie star who portrayed Flash Gordon.

The hero of London's 1948 Olympics, the 17-year-old decathlon champion, Bob Mathias, followed swimmers Eleanor Holm, Buster Crabbe and Johnny Weissmuller into show business. Mathias had flashed an early promise of wit in London when asked how he was going to celebrate his victory. "Start shaving, I guess," he said. But even in his most believable film role—when he portrayed "Bob Mathias, All-American"—he was no threat to Weissmuller. Mathias switched to politics and spent several terms in Congress polishing up his acting skills.

In 1952, the year Mathias won his second decathlon title, the man who dominated the Games also provided the most amusing lines—for observers and for himself. Emil Zatopek of Czechoslovakia won the 5,000- and 10,000-meter races, shattering the

Olympic records for both events. Then, fifteen miles into the marathon, breezing toward his third gold medal of 1952, Zatopek passed the favored British runner, Jim Peters. "Excuse me," Zatopek said. "I haven't run a marathon before, but don't you think we ought to go a bit faster?" When his first marathon ended and Zatopek owned a third Olympic record, he told reporters, "The marathon is a very boring race."

The 1952 Olympics started a run of boxers who later became world heavyweight professional champions. The first one was Floyd Patterson, who fought as a 17-year-old middleweight in Helsinki. "Patterson has faster paws than a subway pickpocket, and they cause more suffering," Red Smith suggested. Young Patterson did have his problems outside the ring. He had trouble understanding Finnish. "Every time I get my suit pressed," Floyd said, "it costs me 300 kilocycles."

One of the finalists in the heavyweight boxing division was disqualified, as a reporter noted, "for running for his life." The cautious fighter was a Swede named Ingemar Johansson (his silver medal was restored in 1982). With steadier nerves, he later became the second Olympian to win the world heavyweight championship, a tradition continued by Cassius Clay (the future Muhammad Ali), the Olympic light-heavyweight gold-medalist in 1960; by Joe Frazier, heavyweight winner in 1964; by George Foreman, heavyweight champ in 1968; and by Leon Spinks, light-heavyweight champ in 1976.

Clay was the hit of the Olympic Village in Rome in 1960. Armed with a small, inexpensive camera, he never stopped taking pictures, and he never stopped talking. After he won his event, he wore his gold medal around his neck for 48 straight hours. "First time in my life I ever slept on my back," Clay said.

continued

SEE WHAT MOVIES ARE MADE OF.

What makes the Universal Studios Tour the most unique experience in Southern California? It's the only place where you can actually see movies like the stars do—from behind the scenes!

Your day begins with a tram ride through our huge 420-acre movie backlot. You'll see 640 outdoor sets, buildings and facades, representing some of the most famous movie sets and locations ever created. Your journey includes an unforgettable encounter with some of Hollywood's greatest special effects, like the "Jaws"® attack, the parting of the Red Sea, a collapsing bridge and a chilling alpine avalanche. And just when you think you've seen it all, there's more action around the corner.

We'll take you to a sound stage where you'll learn the secrets of how movie makers create space battles and other spectacular feats.

In our fabulous Entertainment Center, you'll experience five live shows each depicting a different dimension of film making. You can discover your hidden talents when you star in our SCREEN TEST COMEDY THEATRE, witness the action-packed STUNT SHOW, be dazzled by real movie ANIMAL ACTORS, experience the awesome CONAN—A SWORD & SORCERY SPECTACULAR, and learn how WOODY WOODPECKER comes alive on the screen.

It's a full day of movie magic, live shows, shopping and dining. So, come be a part of the stuff dreams are made of at Universal Studios Tour.

UNIVERSAL STUDIOS TOUR® AN MCA COMPANY

Celebrating Our 20th Year

DISQUALIFIED
in the
'76 pentathlon
for phony touchés
with his epée,
he retreated
home to
a job as a
hackie

"Had to, or that medal would have cut my chest."

The Olympics of Clay was the Olympics, too, of Wim Essajas, the 800-meter runner from Suriname, who slept through his event, then wondered, "What are the folks back home going to say?" It was also the Olympics of "The Psych," a mental war among the shotputters, starring the 1952 and 1956 champion, Parry O'Brien, and his chief challenger, Bill Nieder. Of his rivals in general, O'Brien said, "All of them take senior-citizen psych, and I'm the senior citizen of the shot." Of his main rival in particular, O'Brien said, "Nieder is a cow-pasture performer. He can't win under pressure. In big meets, Nieder chokes up." O'Brien won the war of words, but Nieder won the gold medal. "You can't psych anybody," Nieder said with overwhelming logic, "when you're always two feet behind them."

In 1976, when Boris Onischenko was found to be wielding a doctored epée, the jokes were endless. Onischenko, a teacher in the U.S.S.R. and a former world champion in the pentathlon, was 38 years old when he rigged his electronic epée so that it would record touchés that never happened. When he was caught, and disqualified from the pentathlon, some people predicted he would never reach 39. Others said Soviet officials gave him a choice: He could go to Siberia, or he could marry Iuliana Semenova, the seven-foot star of the Soviet women's basketball team. In truth, Onischenko did neither. He was promptly shipped back to Kiev—where, at last report, he was working as a taxi driver. If you ever happen to get into Onischenko's cab, one suggestion: Check the meter carefully.

During the 1980 Games in Moscow, at least two visitors—Daley Thompson, the decathlon champi-

on, and his British countryman, Sebastian Coe, the 1,500-meter champion—had occasional good times on the town. One night, the two of them, and a sizable entourage, were invited to the Kosmos Hotel to have dinner with an American reporter. They were expected at 8:30 p.m. but by 9:30 they still had not arrived.

A few minutes before 10 p.m., Thompson, Coe and company were in trouble, storming the front door of the Kosmos, a clear violation of the rule that all visiting nonresidents of the hotel had to enter and leave through a back entrance, a rule that had little to do with logic. The British visitors were diverted to the back entrance, which, according to another rule, was to be locked for the night at 10 p.m. It was, by then, a few minutes after 10 o'clock.

Thompson took command. He put his arm around the shoulders of a Soviet security man and, with a great grin, announced loudly: "Can you believe it, mate? They want to keep me out! Me! They don't know who I am. Do you believe it?"

Soon the Soviet security man, whose name was Nikolai, was smiling, too. He told the British group they could enter the Kosmos. When would they have to leave? "Whenever you are ready to," Nikolai said, in perfect English. "You have to meet people halfway. Call me Nicholas."

Thompson promptly invited Nicholas to dinner. Nicholas declined, but guided the visitors through the security maze to the dining room. As Nicholas turned back to his post, someone called out, "See you later."

The Soviet security man met him halfway once more. "See you later," Nicholas said. "See you later, alligator." ■

The Best Athlete Ever

For this first Olympics since his name was returned to the record books, a tribute to the skills of Jim Thorpe— and a revealing look at the forces that shaped them

By
Jack
Newcombe

I T MAY HAVE BEEN IRONI-cally appropriate that Jim Thorpe's singular Olympic achievement was without official sanction for nearly 70 years. The one athlete in the history of the Games to win the all-around competitions in both the pentathlon and decathlon, he saw his medals taken away and his name removed from the records only months after earning them. But the action by the International Olympic Committee only hardened the attention, decade after decade, on what he had accomplished in the Games of 1912. The crusades on his behalf were cyclical and the volunteers came from all over: Thorpe family and friends, civic groups and private do-gooders, a U.S. President, members of Congress and state legislators, all rallied to get Thorpe's name and records restored, his forfeited awards returned. And with each new drive another generation became aware of the man's athletic marvels. To be banished and exalted was Thorpe's quaint destiny.

The public was generally aware of the reason for his disqualification by the International Olympic Committee: It was revealed early in 1913 that Thorpe had played professional minor-league baseball before competing in the Olympic Games at Stockholm. But the violation seemed no more than an erasable misdeed as, over the years, the distinction between amateur and professional blurred. Also, in a larger

sense, why was his behavior considered so unique? The comfortable old American inclination to hero-worship has led so often to disenchantment, with idols left crumbled in the debris of accepted codes of conduct.

Thorpe stood out as both a historical victim and performer in sports. The combination fattened the legend. He was, according to an Associated Press poll, "the greatest athlete of the half century" and he was also the tragic figure whose life was scarred by the world beyond the arena. He was a two-time All-America halfback at the Carlisle Indian School in eastern Pennsylvania. He scored 25 touchdowns one season. His four field goals were responsible for Carlisle's upset of Harvard in 1911. He was a player-pioneer in professional football and the game's first significant gate attraction. In baseball, his record shows he was a part-time player for six seasons in the National League. In other sports, ranging from basketball to billiards, he astounded a number of spectators though his feats remained largely unrecorded. There was no counting the "eye-witnesses" who saw him leap from a standing start over a billiard table to celebrate a winning shot.

But Thorpe's very real accomplishments and the legendary parts that flowed with them tend to obscure an important role he played in U.S. sports. He was the brightest of a flowering of American Indian athletic

talent that emerged for a brief time early in the century, a forerunner of the emergence of other minorities—blacks in boxing, baseball, basketball and football and Hispanics in boxing and baseball. Thorpe was very much a product of the white man's educational system and exploitation of Indians. And he was one of the few who managed to beat whites convincingly on their own scoreboards.

Thorpe's background as a Sac and Fox mixed blood, which was to influence all he was to become as an adult and athlete, was not markedly different from that of others of his Indian generation. His first home was a rough cabin close to the North Canadian River, which served as the southern boundary of the Sac and Fox reserve in Oklahoma Territory. His father, Hiram, who produced at least 19 children by five wives, was the son of an itinerant Irish blacksmith who married into the tribe before its forced removal from Kansas in 1869 by the government. Hiram collected his tribal payments, raised and traded horses and was an aggressive presence in what were known as the Seven Deadly Saloons of Keokuk Falls. His recorded conflicts with the law included whiskey-running on the reservation, a federal offense. His third marriage, to Charlotte Vieux, a large woman of French-Potawatomi heritage, resulted in the birth of a son, George, followed closely by the birth of twin daughters, Mary and Margaret, both of whom

Before and after his gold-medal performances in the 1912 Olympic Games, Jim Thorpe was an All-America halfback at the Carlisle Indian School. In his last football season there he scored 25 touchdowns.

died within a few years. On May 27, 1887, twin sons, James and Charles, were born.

The recital of birth, illness and death in the expanding Thorpe household was a reason that six-year-old Jim and Charles were sent to the Sac and Fox mission boarding school some 20 miles north of their home. The twins found themselves in a strange environment where the Indian pupils were forbidden to use their tribal names or speak their own language. Charles placidly made the transition. Jim was constantly restless and sometimes rebellious—his behavior pattern at the government boarding schools he attended over a period of 19 years. One teacher found him "uninterested in anything except the outdoor life," although she said he was very good at exterminating class-

At Stockholm, Thorpe competed in the individual broad jump event, then leaped again in the pentathlon and decathlon. His best effort was 23′ 2½″.

room flies by snapping a piece of rubber.

In the winter of '97, Charles died of pneumonia at the mission school, yet another child death for the Thorpes. The loss of his twin brother and playmate only increased Jim's determined battles with authority. When he ran away from the school several times, his father threatened to send him so far he "won't be able to find his way home." In 1898, he was taken 300 miles north to the Haskell Institute in Lawrence, Kansas, operated by the Indian Education Department.

The 11-year-old truant was issued a uniform and introduced to a school curricu-

Jack Newcombe is the author of the acclaimed Jim Thorpe biography, The Best of the Athletic Boys, and of the new novel, In Search of Billy Cole.

lum that emphasized military discipline and manual training. As one of approximately 600 Indian boarding pupils at Haskell, Jim became acquainted with athletic competitions in which he later excelled—running, baseball and football. Haskell played an ambitious football schedule against Midwest colleges and celebrated its own hero, a French-Oneida all-around athlete and football star named Chauncy Archiquette, whom young Thorpe much admired.

Thorpe's confinement at Haskell ended the way it had at the Sac and Fox Mission School: He ran away and headed home, walking and grabbing train and wagon rides all the way from eastern Kansas. He wasn't home long before his escape took him out of Indian Territory to the Texas border, where he supported himself for several months as a ranch hand.

Hiram Thorpe's feelings toward his itinerant son were suggested in a letter, probably written for him, to the Sac and Fox Agency in December 1903: "I have a boy that I Wish you would Make rangements to Send of to School Some Ware. Carlyle or Hampton . . . he is 14 years old and I Cannot do anything with him. So please at your Earlest Convence atend to this for he is getting worse very day—and I want him to go and make somthing of him Self for he cannot do it hear—"

Thorpe was approaching 17, not 14, when he arrived two months later at Carlisle. He became one of about a dozen Sac and Fox in the Indian enrollment of 599 boys and 470 girls from tribes throughout the country. The normal stay was five

years; many, including good athletes, were there much longer. Carlisle was the pride of the Bureau of Indian Affairs education program. The school, which emphasized the basics and manual trades, thrived under the idealistic leadership of Richard Henry Pratt, who strongly believed in "immersing the Indians in our civilization. . . ." The process met with general success but there were young Indians, such as Jim Thorpe, who were not so readily baptized.

Pratt's zeal to "civilize" his pupils—and to promote his school—stimulated an expanding sports program. Football and track coach Glenn S. (Pop) Warner, who attended and coached at Cornell, had arrived at Carlisle in 1899. His first Indian football team beat Penn, gave Harvard a monumental struggle, and dramatized his inventive ideas—reverses, multiple laterals, fake punts and passes—which were to influence how the game was played for decades.

Thorpe's football career at Carlisle began in the intramural, or, as they were known there, "shops league" scrimmages—Tailors vs. Printers or Harness Makers vs. Blacksmiths. He entered class track meets and later played varsity baseball. The school's best all-around athlete was a little Tuscarora Indian named Frank Mt. Pleasant, who ran the 100-yard dash in close to 10 seconds, broad-jumped over 23 feet (he finished sixth in the 1908 Olympics), and was one of the first really effective passers in football.

In the spring of 1907, Thorpe, nearing 20 and a short distance away from competing on Mt. Pleasant's level, achieved his first notoriety at Carlisle. His Sac and Fox classmate, Sadie Ingalls, in her obligatory monthly letter "home" to the Indian Agent, commented: "I am sorry to say James Thorpe is in the guard house for running away from his country home. . . ." Thorpe had been on an "outing" term— the Carlisle program to acquaint students with the "civilized" world by placing them in white households as laborers or domestics—when he walked off a vegetable farm in New Jersey.

Thorpe was released from the guardhouse in time to compete in the school's annual Arbor Day track and field meet, leading his class to a victory over the upper grades. Thorpe won the 120-yard hurdles, finished second in the 220-yard dash, and beat all rivals in the high jump with a leap of 5′ 3″. His speed and jumping ability encouraged Pop Warner to enter him in varsity competition and in dual meets against

continued

Penn State and Bucknell. Thorpe earned enough points for his first varsity "C."

The deaths of his father and mother by 1904 had left him in a position similar to many of his schoolmates. He was a government ward; a Shawnee businessman and the Indian Agent were his guardians. Travel with the varsity or the small burst of attention he received may have been the reason Thorpe now wrote the Sac and Fox Agent in Stroud, Oklahoma and requested money. His appeal was a modest one; he wanted $50 to purchase a suit, a Panama hat, a watch, a pair of shoes. Orphan children of the Sac and Fox were entitled to annuity payments and Thorpe had been given a $1/15$ share in his family's tribal allotment holdings, mostly leased land for grazing and crops. "Dear Sir: I would like you to do me a favor," he wrote, ". . . to send me Fifty dollars from my lease money being this is my first letter to you I hope that you will fill out my request." Nevertheless, the Sac and Fox Agent turned down the simple request.

In August 1907, Sadie Ingalls updated her regular reports on the Sac and Fox at Carlisle. She wrote that the school's old hospital was to become "the residence of the athletic boys and I think James will enter the football squad."

Thorpe was one of 60 who competed for positions on what Pop Warner thought was his strongest Carlisle team. Thorpe had yet to fill out physically, and his narrow, sloping shoulders made him appear slighter than he was. Football was new to him, but, like many Indians, he was a keen observer of techniques demonstrated by those older and more skilled. His personal tutor was Albert Exendine, a Cherokee-Delaware mixed blood from Oklahoma, who had been selected as an end on Walter Camp's All-America list. Exendine had finished his Carlisle schooling and was taking special courses at a local commercial college, Conway Hall, but Warner saw this as no reason to keep him out of the lineup. Later head coach of several college teams, including the Oklahoma Aggies (now Oklahoma State University), Exendine said that novice Thorpe was "quick at doing things the way you showed him. He wasn't afraid and I kept at him about being mean when he had the ball. . . ."

Substitute running back Thorpe played briefly in Carlisle's early one-sided victories at Indian Field. He did much of the ball-carrying as a scrub backfield beat Bucknell, 15–0. Among the impressed supporters was a student, Sarah Mansur, who sent a reassuring message to friends on the

*C*arlisle's adaptable football team changed into the school basketball uniforms at the end of the season. Thorpe (second row, left) also entered a number of indoor track meets during the winter.

reservation in Oklahoma: "We, the Sac and Fox children are doing our best to make less trouble for the employees around here. . . . We are very proud of our only football boy from home, James Thorpe."

In the school's big game against the University of Pennsylvania—the band and some students who had enough savings made the annual train trip to Philadelphia—Thorpe was in for a few plays. Carlisle's passing led to an impressive 26–6 victory before a crowd of 22,500. Then, Harvard was beaten for the first time, 23–15, as Mt. Pleasant returned a kick for a touchdown and set up two other scores with long passes. "The speed of the Aborigines on a dry field and the forward pass lowered Harvard's banner," one writer commented.

The Warner system, which set daring standards on the football field, had a pragmatic base. The athletic dorm, where Thorpe qualified for residence, was made possible by profits from the athletic association, which included coach and director Warner, the school superintendent, a treasurer and all student winners of a varsity "C." Game receipts—as much as $17,000 for the Indians' visit to the University of Chicago—boosted a fund that soon was conservatively invested in railroad bonds.

For a few years at least, Warner let his best athletes share in the football fund's success. During the 1907 and '08 seasons, cash payments and nonreturnable loans amounting to $9,233 went to players. Re-

serve back Thorpe was not a top beneficiary, but he received $500 during that period. All varsity letter-winners were awarded a $25 suit and a $25 overcoat. The chosen few, selected by Warner, were also given a pleasing line of credit at Mose Blumenthal's haberdashery in downtown Carlisle.

Thorpe's arrival as a football player and track performer of great potential coincided with the enrollment of Gus Welch, a student from the Chippewa tribe. Welch, three years younger than Thorpe, became his running mate in football and track, a roommate in the athletic dorm, and a lifelong friend. In 1907, while living in Wisconsin, Welch had used bounty money from a wolf kill to travel to Minneapolis to see the Carlisle football team defeat the University of Minnesota. He asked for a tryout, although he had never held a football before, and apparently impressed Warner enough so that at age 17 Welch entered Carlisle and soon became one of the most prominent and influential of the athletic boys.

In the 1908 Penn Relays, Thorpe publicly demonstrated his abilities in the high jump (his winning height was 6 feet) and the hurdle races, in which he worked hard to improve his crude form. But he was then overshadowed by Warner's best track performers—Mt. Pleasant, in the broad jump, and Louis Tewanima, in distance races.

Tewanima became a favorite example at the school of the success of the assimilation process. He was one of a small group of Hopi Indians from the Southwest who had been rounded up as prisoners, placed in a government school near the Painted Desert and then sent to Carlisle. Their long hair cut short, their language and customs denied them, they were squeezed into an alien place of dormitory and classroom. One thing the Hopi boys could do to satisfy a native yearning was to run swiftly at long distances. Coach Warner noticed them hanging around the running track—"a wild-looking bunch with furtive eyes." Tewanima's Carlisle medical report hardly suggested he would become the school's most famous runner: " . . . round shoulders, prominent clavicle . . . has emaciated look." But in 1908 he finished ninth in the Olympic marathon and, in 1912, second in the Olympic 10,000 meters.

Thorpe's football education was sharply advanced in the 1908 season when Warner gave him the kicking responsibility. By the Penn game, his reputation as a placekicker and punter evoked this comment in a Philadelphia newspaper: "The Indian field

continued

general does not even wait for 3rd down (the last down) to try a field goal. Thorpe drops back, the little quarterback [Mike Balenti] kneels on the ground, and bing! the cunning toe of Thorpe sends it spinning between the goalposts. . . ." Against Penn, Thorpe ran 60 yards for a touchdown that enabled Carlisle to tie the game, 6–6. In a losing effort at Harvard, Thorpe's eight punts covered 342 yards. The Indians were defeated twice in a 13-game season that ended on December 2 at Nebraska, where the unprepared Cornhuskers were bewildered, according to a game report, by the "Aborigines' use of cross-bucks, fake kicks and passes."

Thorpe's emergence as a star in track and football was delayed by a decision he made the following spring. He joined the

Tossing the discus was not one of Thorpe's strong points, but he was first in the event in both the Olympic pentathlon and decathlon competitions.

seasonal exodus of Carlisle athletes for the professional and semipro baseball leagues. Thorpe and teammate Jesse Young Deer went to Rocky Mount in the new East Carolina League where they were offered about $25 a week. Thorpe played the infield, pitched (9 wins, 10 losses), hit lightly and ran the bases hard. After the season he went home to Oklahoma. He apparently had no intention of returning to Carlisle, because he requested that all funds held for him at the school be sent to him at the Sac and Fox Agency. In Carlisle school records he was listed as "a deserter." The following year, 1910, he went back to the flourishing little tobacco towns of North Carolina for another season of minor-league baseball.

But Thorpe was one dropout Warner did not let easily slip away. Warner encour-

aged him by letter to return to Carlisle, play football and prepare for the 1912 Olympic Games. Albert Exendine encountered Thorpe in Anadarko, Oklahoma and told him he should go back to school, no matter what the official attitude was toward "deserters." In early September, Thorpe was back in the football dorm at Carlisle, and in a letter to the Sac and Fox Agency, wrote: "I have decided to stay for two years longer . . . our prospects for a good [season] is great. . . ."

Gus Welch, 5′ 9″ and 155 pounds, was the new Carlisle quarterback and a strong complement to Thorpe. He was fast—an excellent middle-distance runner—and an imaginative play-caller. Welch had a touch of hero-worship for Thorpe, who, in turn, admired his young friend's wit and leadership ability—Welch was voted class president in 1912. Thorpe and Welch roomed together, drank together (much to official dismay) and were key parts in a Warner backfield that included veteran Possum Powell, a Cherokee who had played baseball with Thorpe in Carolina, and Alex Arcasa, a trim Colville athlete from the Northwest. In the Harvard game, these running backs—and Thorpe's place-kicking—produced an epic, 18–15 victory. Welch made the decision to let Thorpe try a field goal from the Harvard 48-yard line late in the game. Thorpe had wanted to punt, but his placement was beautifully true, one of the four he converted that day.

In the winter, Olympic training for Thorpe and Welch centered in the school gym until Carlisle's resurfaced cinder track was dry enough for use. Tewanima ran his

distances on town sidewalks and roads. Warner entered them in as many eastern indoor meets as possible, with Thorpe concentrating on events in the pentathlon. He was up to 6′ 5″ in the high jump and a shotput mark of 47′ 9″.

When it came time in June for Carlisle's Olympic competitors to board the ocean liner *S.S. Finland* in New York for Stockholm, Thorpe and Tewanima joined trainer-chaperone Pop Warner. Welch, a qualified runner in the 400- and 800 meters, was left home in America with a serious throat ailment.

Thorpe later said that the ocean voyage—living aboard the passenger liner—was the greatest part of his Olympic adventure. There were conflicting stories of Thorpe's activities at sea: He was either seen running and exercising diligently with other members of the U.S. team or observed eating and sleeping his way across the Atlantic. Whatever the case, he landed in Stockholm ready to take on the world. At 25, he was at a physical peak: 5′ 11″ and 180 pounds, with a chest measurement of 39.7″ and a 32″ waist. In his own phlegmatic, competitive way he was not about to fail in the pentathlon and decathlon challenges given him.

His pentathlon victory was assured when he finished first in four of five events. In the decathlon, contested over three days, he won the hurdles, the high jump, the shotput and the discus. His times and distances in the pentathlon and the decathlon events measure exceedingly well with the best of that era. They also invite comparison with the performances of Bob Mathias in the 1952 Games, Milt Campbell in '56 and later decathlon champions. Thorpe's time for the 1,500 meters, 4:40.1, was better than that of Mathias, Campbell or Rafer Johnson. His pentathlon broad jump, 23′ 2¹⁄₂″, was farther than Mathias reached in the '52 decathlon. In the high jump, Thorpe cleared 6′ 1¹⁄₂″, about an inch away from the leaps of Mathias and Campbell.

One may marvel most at the fact that he also competed in the individual high jump (he finished fourth) and the broad jump (seventh) or at the way he ran the 200 meters and 110-meter hurdles. His pentathlon 200-meter time was 22.9. America's 200-meter gold medalist, Ralph Craig, ran his race in 21.7. Twenty years later, in the '32 Games, Eddie Tolan's Olympic best was 21.2. Thorpe's 110-meter hurdle mark, 15.6, was only a half-second away from the gold-medal effort by Frederick Kelly of the

continued

298

U.S. Perhaps nothing better demonstrates that as an all-around athlete Thorpe was far ahead of his time than his decathlon point total—8,412—which stood as a record for 20 years.

To the predominantly Scandinavian crowds in Stockholm, Thorpe was admired as the "horse" of the Olympics. To King Gustav V of Sweden, who presented Thorpe with victory wreaths, two gold medals and the decathlon challenge cup offered by Czar Nicholas of Russia, he was "the greatest athlete in the world." The Philadelphia *Inquirer* offered a more chauvinistic assessment: "The real hero of the whole Olympiad is Jim Thorpe, the Indian—the real American. . . . Jim at present hails from Carlisle, but his home is out West, where a generation or so ago his ancestors were killing buffaloes and American soldiers with equal facility."

Thorpe's rounds of celebrations led him through post-Olympic track meets and parties in Europe, an automobile caravan on New York's Fifth Avenue, a civic salute in Philadelphia.

For both Thorpe and teammate Tewanima, there was great relief in being honored on home grounds at Carlisle. In the day-long celebration on August 16, 1912, paid for by local donations, they were hauled through the sun-bright streets in an open carriage. At the Dickinson College athletic field, the two Olympians sat uncomfortably listening to long speeches before offering their own terse thank-yous. Somewhere between the ceremony's finish and the beginning of the school dance that evening, Thorpe disappeared and had to be hauled out of a local saloon by one of Pop Warner's deputies. The dance lasted until 1:45 a.m., with Thorpe demonstrating his endurance on the dance floor. Later, Jim gave his friend, Gus Welch, who had missed competing at Stockholm, an Olympic hat and one of his running shoes. Louis Tewanima happily distributed some of the medals he had won during the year to girl students, who wore them as buckles on their shoes. Then the Hopi Olympian headed West to return to his Indian life, and was eventually honored as a priest of his tribal clan.

Thorpe, meanwhile, was persuaded into another football season by Warner, who reminded him that it would raise his value as a pro ballplayer. In a letter to brother Frank in Oklahoma, Jim wrote: "Well, Bud, I'm right back in the game again, playing football . . . I have the chance to make a bunch of dough after leaving school. . . ."

During this long, 14-game season,

*R*eservation Indians were photographed upon arrival at the Carlisle Indian School. When enrolled they were given haircuts and uniforms and required to speak only in English.

Thorpe's finest performance was his last for Carlisle. He scored three times in a rout of Brown in a snowstorm at Providence. A local paper carried the result: "The Real Score. Thorpe 32, Brown 0." The touchdowns brought his individual point total to 198 for the year, one of the highest ever recorded in college football.

The game ended an era of athletic supremacy at Carlisle. In 1914, a congressional investigation into the disciplinary practices and use of funds (particularly those of the athletic department) resulted in the dismissal of the superintendent and Pop Warner. Three years later, the school was closed by the government.

A newspaper exposé of Thorpe's seasons as a professional minor-league baseball player brought a swift resolution, dated Jan. 27, 1913, by the Amateur Athletic Union of the U.S. and sent to the International Olympic Committee. It read, in part: "The Amateur Athletic Union regrets that it permitted Mr. Thorpe to compete in amateur contests during the past several years and will do everything in its power to secure the return of the prizes and the re-adjustment of points won by him and will eliminate the records from the books."

Thorpe's trophies and medals were shipped back to Stockholm aboard the *S.S. New York* and the medals distributed to the second-place finishers. When the official report of the Vth Olympiad was published later in the year, Thorpe's disqualification was in the record.

If Thorpe felt bitterness toward those who acted to disqualify him—and toward all who were aware that he, like other college athletes, had accepted pay for play—he kept it within. He went about the business of signing a major-league baseball contract with the New York Giants in February; he made preparations for a wedding at Carlisle with his school sweetheart, Iva Miller. Like most great athletes who reach an abrupt turn in their careers, he did not sense that the banquet years were already slipping behind him. When his mediocre baseball career stretched into long periods of impatient bench-sitting, he was still able to play football in Canton, Ohio, where the pro game was haphazardly taking shape. For a time he was a strong gate attraction in the Canton area and was paid $250 a game. When local support declined, he gathered former Carlisle football players and hit the road with a team called the Oorang All-Indians. The payoff wasn't much, but it was, in a way, a return to the game he once dominated and enjoyed.

Thorpe's life through three marriages and many changes of address was, of course, the inglorious odyssey of many famous athletes. The absence of his medals, his highest athletic honors, made the loss of his great strength and talents seem even more tragic. A coon-hunting companion who lived near Thorpe in Yale, Oklahoma, said that Jim carried his burdens, whatever they were, with dignity. "I never knew him in those few winters when he seemed unhappy. If he got drunk and hung over, he would sober up until he came out pleasant. If he didn't know you or took a dislike, he wouldn't offer you liquid in your throat to put out a fire in your belly. But if you were his friend there wasn't anything he wouldn't do for you. He was an Indian."

On Oct. 13, 1982, Thorpe's name was returned to the record books. On Jan. 18, 1983, after nearly 70 years of campaigns on his behalf, and nearly 30 years after his death on March 28, 1953, six of Thorpe's children were present at a ceremony in Los Angeles. In it, International Olympic Committee president Juan Antonio Samaranch returned the pair of gold medals. The event brought joy to family members and a widespread feeling that justice had finally triumphed, no matter how long the wait. The medals were back where they belonged, and Thorpe's name returned to the official record. In a final irony, he and the second-place finishers in the pentathlon and decathlon are listed as being in a tie. Thorpe, of course, won big, lost a lot, and never finished even. ■

Ghost Town.
Where the Wild West comes alive with stagecoach rides, can can girls and shoot outs.

Roaring 20's.
Barnstorming returns with the Parachute Jump and the Double Loop Corkscrew.

Camp Snoopy.^{SM}
Rides and fun specially designed by **Snoopy** for all his friends.

Fiesta Village.
Relive early California to the tune of the Mariachi and the taste of authentic Mexican food.

SNOOPY: © 1958
United Feature Syndicate, Inc.

Your trip to Los Angeles wouldn't be complete without a visit to Knott's Berry Farm.

That's because Knott's has the only authentic Wild West Ghost Town in Southern California...and there's a lot more. We've also recreated the exciting streets of a Roaring 20's city, plus all the rides and fun of a real Mexican Fiesta. Even **Snoopy** has his very own mountain camp at Knott's Berry Farm.

Altogether Knott's has over 165 wild rides and shows waiting for you and the whole family. By the way, there's great shopping and dining, too.

So while you're visiting Southern California, stop by...we're just 10 short minutes from Disneyland.

While you're with us, you can even have your picture snapped with **Snoopy**...our very own gold medal winner here at Knott's.

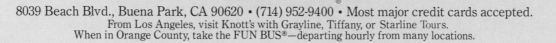

8039 Beach Blvd., Buena Park, CA 90620 • (714) 952-9400 • Most major credit cards accepted.
From Los Angeles, visit Knott's with Grayline, Tiffany, or Starline Tours.
When in Orange County, take the FUN BUS®—departing hourly from many locations.

JCPenney

Salutes The 1984 Games

Sports plate, $30   German lidded tankard, $55   Signature plate, $17

Ceramic bell, $7 Collector spoons, $5 each Fork and spoon set, $9 Sam the Eagle figurines, $8 each
Official glassware: on-the-rocks or hiball, 3.50 Short mug, $4 Tall mug, $10

Available in larger JCPenney stores.

©1984 The JCPenney Company, Inc.

USA adidas®

Running short or singlet, 11.99 Sport short, $14 Shirt, $15 Warm-up pant, $26 T-shirt, 8.99 Roll bag, 14.99
Not shown: Tank top, 12.99 Long-sleeve T-shirt, 13.99 Boy's T-shirt, 6.99 Cotton, poly/cotton or nylon.
Men's USA sport socks in patriotic red, white and blue. Cotton/polyester blend in crew or over-the-calf lengths,
2.99 each.

Olympic Treasure On Public View

A Los Angeles museum houses one of the world's distinguished collections

A gracious old city mansion inhabited by vivid athletic memories

R ICH IN MEMORY, abundant in detail, striking to the eye, the mementos displayed here present a highly unique documentary of Olympics past. Included, on the preceding pages, are a vase awarded to 1924 pole-vault champion Lee Barnes; a ceremonial sabre; the discus Lillian Copeland threw to a record in the 1932 Games; the shoes and scarf worn by hurdler Evelyne Hall in '32; a replica of the 1952 Helsinki Olympic Stadium; Temple of Zeus model where ancient Olympians were honored; and Olympic medals and miniatures. The souvenirs are on view at one of the world's outstanding sports museums, the First Interstate Bank Athletic Foundation in central Los Angeles. More than just a repository of Olympic memories, the museum offers items representing heroes and events in some 30 sports.

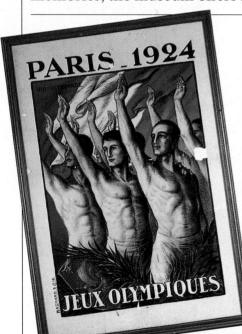

PARIS · 1924

VIII OLYMPIADE

JEUX OLYMPIQUES

Among the Olympic posters on display at the Foundation is one from the '24 Games in Paris in which Paavo Nurmi ran his marvelous distance races.

An autograph-seeker at the 1936 Games in Berlin had this pair of wooden shoes signed by more than 100 of the competing athletes.

Gold-medal winner Lillian Copeland of the U.S. threw this discus to a record at the '32 Games.

This torch was part of the relay that brought the Olympic flame to the Opening Ceremony at the '68 Games in Mexico.

The uniform worn by officials at the '32 Olympics in Los Angeles included a velvet jacket.

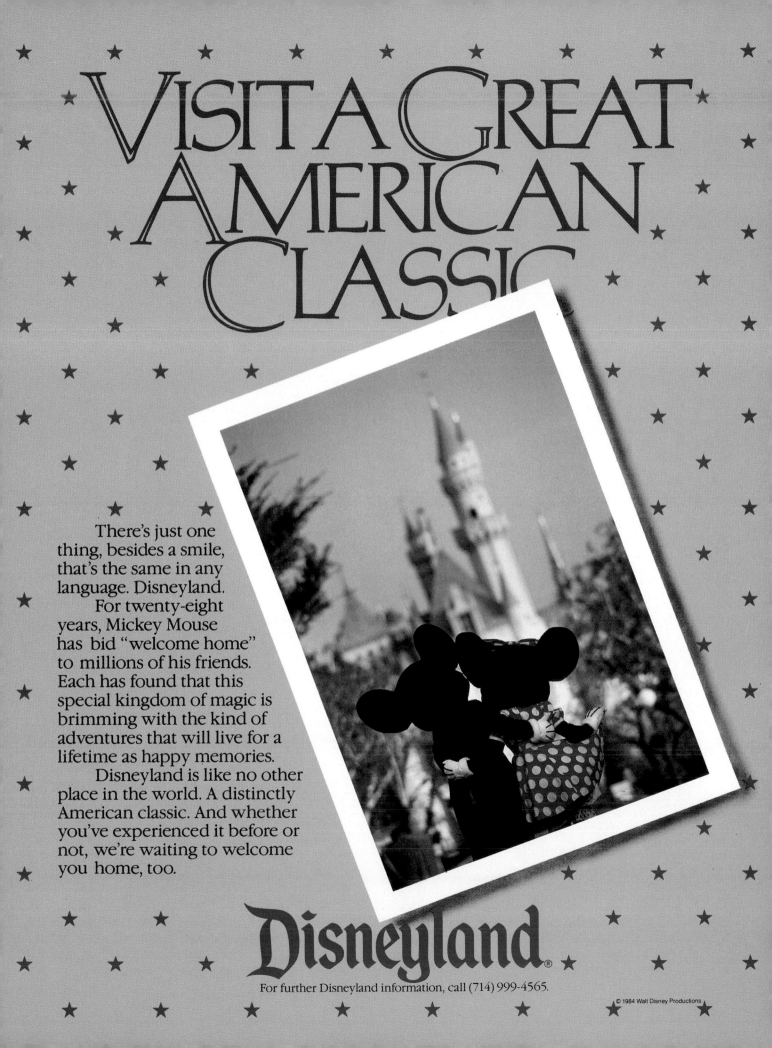

VISIT A GREAT AMERICAN CLASSIC

There's just one thing, besides a smile, that's the same in any language. Disneyland.

For twenty-eight years, Mickey Mouse has bid "welcome home" to millions of his friends. Each has found that this special kingdom of magic is brimming with the kind of adventures that will live for a lifetime as happy memories.

Disneyland is like no other place in the world. A distinctly American classic. And whether you've experienced it before or not, we're waiting to welcome you home, too.

Disneyland.

For further Disneyland information, call (714) 999-4565.

MEDALS, models, memorabilia—more than 50,000 items of sports nostalgia

Display cases are filled with Olympic gems that date back to the first modern Olympic Games held in Athens, 1896.

Runners brought the Olympic flame from Olympia to Berlin with this torch in 1936—the first time it was carried from Greece to the host city.

The Royal Dutch coat of arms, circled by Olympians, was souvenir plate design for the '28 Olympiad.

Prince Tsuneyoshi Takeda of Japan, an IOC member, donated torch (below) that was included in ceremonies for the '64 Games in Tokyo.

Bob Mathias wore these U.S. colors when he won the decathlon for the second time in '52.

A runner carries the flame on its journey from Greece in a poster offered by the Japanese in '64.

SEE WHAT THE WORLD IS COMING TO.

Business leaders are abandoning the congestion and sprawl of yesterday's cities in favor of fresh air and intelligent planning.

The communities developed by The Irvine Company provide these benefits in an exceptional 68,000-acre Orange County location. This has become the nucleus of a new business and financial hub for the entire Pacific basin.

And with good reason:

These communities offer the world's foremost living and working environment. They're centrally located between Los Angeles and San Diego. And they're served by convenient freeways and a major airport.

You'll also find the west's largest selection of commercial and industrial property. Carefully planned for local and regional shopping centers, financial centers and industrial parks. Including the largest master planned industrial complex in the country.

The year-round Mediterranean climate is friendly to business and residents alike.

Housing is plentiful and designed to meet a variety of needs and lifestyles.

And the quality of life is enhanced by excellent schools, a major university, ample shopping, medical centers, fine restaurants, spacious parks, beaches and recreational facilities.

Twenty-six years of effort by the Master Planner and Master Builder have made these new business and residential communities most successful.

See for yourself what the world is coming to.

There is no time like the present to experience the future.

For information, call Bob Osbrink, The Irvine Company, (714) 720-2910.

THE IRVINE COMPANY

AWARDS to be cherished by both Olympic victors and also-rans

*1896 Bronze
Winner unknown*

*1908 Commemorative
Athlete unknown*

*1924 Gold
Fidel LaBarba, U.S.
Boxing, flyweight*

*1952 Commemorative
Juno Irwin, U.S.
Diving*

The gold medal (below) was won by Murray Rose of Australia for the 400-meter freestyle in 1960 at Rome. All competitors receive Olympic commemorative medals such as those shown elsewhere on the page.

*1900 Gold
F.C.V. Lane, Australia
200-meter freestyle*

*1904 Gold
James Lightbody, U.S.
1,500-meter run*

*1928 Commemorative
Frank Wykoff, U.S.
Track and field*

*1964 Commemorative
Prince Takeda, Japan
Member IOC*

*1932 Gold
Dallas Bixler, U.S.
Horizontal bar*

Embark on an odyssey that will change your life forever.

Fantastikó! That's what you'll say when you first set eyes on LeisureVillage Ocean Hills, a fantastic new adventure in living in North County San Diego. With architecture inspired by Mediterranean sea villages and Aegean hill towns, it's Leisure Village, European-style.

Che bella! How beautiful! In The Ocean Hills Country Club,™ in fully-equipped studios, you'll discover talents you never knew you had. Ceramics. Lapidary. Woodworking.

And there's The Nautilus Studio. The Photography Lab. The Chamber Music Studio.

You'll swim. Play tennis, play golf.

Dance. Enjoy parties, concerts and shows.

All with the most interesting new friends.

Magnifique! That's how you'll feel in your magnificent new villa home. With its soaring ceilings, private courtyard, garden views. And best of all, you'll feel secure, thanks to a

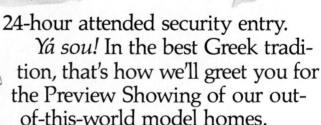

24-hour attended security entry.

Yá sou! In the best Greek tradition, that's how we'll greet you for the Preview Showing of our out-of-this-world model homes.

The journey starts here. And now. Don't miss the boat. Come live the dream.

✿ LEISURE VILLAGE
Ocean Hills™

THE foundation that has celebrated performers for the past 48 years

Museum gardens and lawns, decorated with sports sculpture, invite visitors to stroll.

Bill Schroeder, originator and managing director of the Foundation, stands beside the six-foot World Trophy honoring top amateur athletes back to 1896.

Waldi the dachshund was the mascot of the '72 Olympics. Mischa the bear took over in '80. It's Sam the eagle this year.

Beneath a swirl of flags, a discus thrower looks out over Antwerp in a poster from the '20 Games in Belgium.

VIIth OLYMPIAD ANTWERP (BELGIUM) AUGUST-SEPTEMBER 1920

Clockwise from top: the bronzed shoes worn by medal winners Lillian Copeland in '32, Rafer Johnson in '60, and Craig Dixon in '48.

After a day of watching great amateurs, why not come home to great professionals.

Olympic updates on the hour all day long,
with extended daily coverage every morning at 6, 7 and 8 A.M.

We still treat news as if it matters.

The Day the Camels Went Crazy...

and Other Adventures

The most famous Olympic arena in America, L.A.'s Coliseum has a rich and varied history

By Scott Ostler

The Reverend Billy Graham once preached to 134,254 people in the Los Angeles Memorial Coliseum, a respectable turnout. But at one of the Coliseum's most successful events, the paid attendance was two.

It took place in 1971 when a local man named Charles Elkins rented the Coliseum for a private luncheon with his girl friend. A table was set in the middle of the empty football field and the couple dined in magnificent privacy. Following a bottle of Cristal champagne (vintage 1964), a pound of caviar, a rack of lamb (medium rare), carrots, green beans, potatoes, lingonberries, cucumbers (for her) and béarnaise sauce (for him), Elkins summoned the waiter and bid him open and pour a 1959 Haut-Brion.

"I raised my glass," Elkins recalls, "and said, 'I have a question for you.'"

The raised glass was the cue for a Coliseum employee to activate the scoreboard, which popped the electronic question: DARLING EVA, WILL YOU MARRY ME?

"I was very nervous," Elkins says. "I had no idea if she would say yes or no. I could just picture a TV announcer running up with a microphone, saying, 'She turned you down, eh?' "

But after an appropriately dramatic delay, Eva said yes. They were married and have remained so ever since.

As the TV announcer might say: Ah! Where but the Coliseum, that noble edifice built upon a gravel pit, its very construction a tribute to the dreams and ambitions of a plucky little coastal town?

The ancient Colosseum in Rome, great grandfather to the L.A. Coliseum, and built in the first century A.D., had a long run of live entertainment, ranging from duels between gladiators and exotic beasts to mock naval battles. The Los Angeles Memorial Coliseum is only 61 years old but already boasts a history that would make its ancient predecessor proud.

The Xth Olympiad was celebrated here and the first Super Bowl. Big time pro football and major league baseball were introduced to the Pacific Coast here. Soon-to-be President John F. Kennedy delivered his nomination acceptance speech on this field, and Generals Doolittle and Patton were honored under the stadium lights.

Also, Duke Snider threw out his arm trying, unsuccessfully, to heave a baseball out of the Coliseum. A worker here almost became a non-intentional self-sacrifice to the gods of the Olympic torch. An actress filmed a TV special in which she danced in step with the scoreboard. Through it all, the Coliseum has maintained its concrete dignity, even when under siege from water bugs, gate crashers, scalpers, vandals, crooked promoters and berserk circus camels.

Dismissed by its earliest critics as "sheer civic folly," the Coliseum has been all that and more. It has been a landmark, a legacy, a friend, and it can be a teacher. It has offered the citizens of L.A. many lessons. For example:

GRAVEL PITS ARE RECYCLABLE: When the Coliseum was nearing completion in 1923, workers were attacked by a gang of stablehands, upset because the structure was going up where their horseracing track had been. Civic leaders had declared Exposition Park, where the Coliseum is located, to be suffering from a "declining morality." A 76,000-seat outdoor stadium with Roman-inspired architecture, it was

CA 15

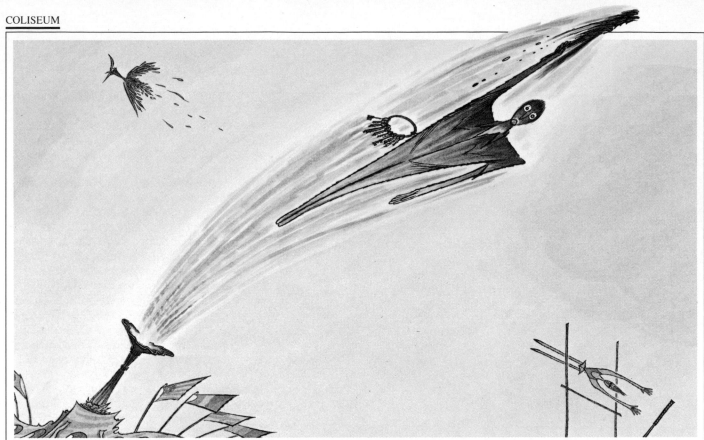

TOM THE TORCHLIGHTER RISKED A ROCKETING RIDE TO LONG BEACH WHEN HE STRUCK AN ILL-TIMED MATCH IN THE LINE OF COLISEUM DUTY.

decided, was just the thing to spruce up the decaying area. A huge gravel pit, which had been the center of the racetrack, was further scooped out. The new Coliseum was built into and around the removal.

The city of Los Angeles had its magnificent arena and was well into the big time. Ahead were days of glory and more lessons to be learned, such as:

NEVER TRUST A MAMA WATCHDOG: In the winter of '75, on the eve of a full slate of football, a drunken vandal sneaked into the Coliseum. He beat into rubble some of the scoreboard control systems, causing thousands of dollars worth of damage.

An inquiry disclosed that the Coliseum security consisted of one night watchman and two watchdogs, Mandy and Solax. "One (Solax) died two weeks before the incident and the other (Mandy) had pups and sleeps a lot," a Coliseum spokesman explained, failing to provide an alibi for the night watchman.

Neither watchdogs nor wildlife have really fared well here.

A large German shepherd watchdog ran out of the Coliseum office one day, skidded on the polished terrazzo floor of the peristyle, crashed and broke his neck. His name was Lucky.

Tickets for a Coliseum circus some 30 years ago were selling poorly, so the promoter, an ex-newsman, let a lion "escape" into the empty stands. Then he notified the press and the police, in that order, that a lion was loose in the Coliseum. "The lion was toothless and half dazed," recalls Bill Nicholas, Coliseum general manager from 1946 to 1973. "At least 40 policemen poured in here with guns drawn. The poor old lion just looked at 'em and finally walked back into its cage. But it worked. The promoter got his publicity and the ticket sales picked up."

The lion-on-the-loose incident had been preceded some years earlier by an unscheduled circus act at the Coliseum that drew considerable negative box-office publicity. Several camels ran amok and 30 spectators were bitten before the animals could be controlled.

DIAMONDS ARE NOT FOREVER: Until the summer of 1958, the Coliseum, minor indignities aside, was generally considered one of the most impressive sports arenas in the world. But that summer it became a national joke. That was the year major league baseball, or an unreasonable facsimile, came to the Coliseum. It was the first of four seasons of the infamous "Chinese

Wall," which was baseball's most bizarre and controversial ball-park feature.

When Walter O'Malley moved his Brooklyn Dodgers to Los Angeles, he had to choose between playing in a nice, compact ball park (Wrigley Field) that couldn't seat many fans, or a huge arena (the Coliseum) that could seat a lot of fans but didn't offer reasonable proportions for a ball field. Since O'Malley's chief motive for moving the team West was money, he decided against Wrigley Field.

In its day, the Coliseum has comfortably hosted ski jumping, motocross competition, midget auto racing, ice shows, boxing matches, basketball games and even a golf driving contest. But it was decidedly wrong for baseball.

There were other problems. The Coliseum's football tenants didn't want their field messed up by a pitcher's mound and dirt basepaths. They demanded that the baseball diamond be installed at the east (peristyle) end. This would mean that during day games the sun would shine directly into the batter's eyes. No problem. A firm in Arcadia proposed floating a balloon, 50 feet in circumference, high over the Coliseum. Moved by wires, the huge balloon would throw a shadow to shield the batter's eyes from the sun. "It may sound *continued*"

Los Angeles Times *columnist Scott Ostler has been named California Sportswriter of the Year for the last three years.*

King Harbor:
the warmest welcome
in California

crazy, but it'll work," said a spokesman for the firm.

O'Malley and the Coliseum Commission agreed with the first half of that statement. They installed the field at the west end and placated the football tenants with the world's oldest placater—money. In this case, a break on their rent.

The diamond was perfect except for just three flaws—leftfield, centerfield and rightfield. Leftfield was too short, 251 feet down the line, about 75 feet short by any sane major league standards, and it remained short into left-center and beyond.

In hopes of preventing a rash of embarrassingly cheap home runs, the Dodgers erected a wire screen, 140 feet long and 42 feet high, suspended between a tower on the leftfield foul line and another tower at left-center. It was a giant spiderweb designed to capture line drives ascending with tremendous velocity toward the deep rows of customers. It stopped many of the well-hit line drives, but it provided no defense against lazy fly balls that plopped into the stands for 252-foot homers.

Baseball purists, pitchers and lefthanded hitters screamed. The purists and lefthanded hitters also screamed when, to compensate for the cramped leftfield, the Dodgers made centerfield and rightfield the approximate size of Yellowstone National Park (420 feet to right-center). The purists, pitchers and lefty hitters never did accept the Chinese Wall, but the fans did.

"No single attraction in the Coliseum's 36-year history has captured the fancy of the citizenry as has the leftfield fence," commented sportswriter Melvin Durslag.

The Dodgers estimated that 250,000 of their 1,800,000 paying fans that first season came expressly to see the Wall.

There were 193 home runs hit at the Coliseum in 1958, tops in the major leagues. Of those, eight went to rightfield, two to center and 183 to left.

The Dodgers departed their misshapen playing field in '62—after setting an all-time, single-game attendance record of 93,103 in 1959 at an exhibition game—and settled into their own new compact stadium. The Chinese Wall came down, the Coliseum's dignity was restored, and the other tenants were left to their seasonal squabbles.

The Coliseum has been the home of the USC Trojans, UCLA Bruins, pro football Buccaneers, Dons, Rams, Chargers (one season), Raiders and Express, and of the soccer Wolves, Toros and Aztecs. The college football tenants, who for long had the gridiron much to themselves, battled to

prevent the invasion of the pros. Of course, both the college and pro football teams fought fiercely against the invasion of the Dodgers. When the ex-Oakland Raiders moved in for the 1982 season, the Bruins moved out in a huff and the Trojans threatened to do the same. Even the Rams, who had left for Orange County several years before, protested the Raiders' arrival. But with the Raiders came something L.A. pro football fans had been waiting for since 1951—a championship team.

NEVER GIVE A SUCKER AN EVEN BREAK: In 1958, two men purchased the rights to all beer sales in the Coliseum, paying a total of $2,300. This would have been one of the sweetest business bargains of the century, except:

—Each of the two men, in separate deals, bought "exclusive" rights to the beer sales.

—It wasn't until 1971 that the Coliseum Commission rescinded the ban on alcoholic beverages in the Coliseum.

When it comes to making a buck at the Coliseum, there are all kinds of angles, many of them crooked.

Take the scalpers. Please. They come in all shapes and sizes. A lawyer was arrested for scalping, as were a Coliseum program manager and a USC trainer. They were dabblers, amateurs. The real pros often hire neighborhood kids to do the actual scalping, letting the kids keep a small percentage.

L.A. scalpers basically are a resourceful lot. One Coliseum scalper during the brief Dodgers' era had business cards printed for his "ticket agency." The phone number given on the card was that of a public telephone booth next to a main stadium ticket window.

A distant relative of the scalper, in the pest classification, is the sleazy promoter. Perhaps the most famous was the carpet-bagging hustler and quick-exit artist who promoted a daredevil show in the Coliseum and then, personally, pulled off the best stunt of the day. As the show was starting, he made the rounds of the ticket booths with a pillowcase in hand. "We're out of cash at the other booths," he explained at each booth, scooping up the money. He split town with everyone's share of the gate.

The statute of limitations had expired on his crime, committed in the 1940s, so the man returned 25 years later, and was allowed to promote a Wild West show in the Coliseum. He tried to sneak out again, leaving behind an office full of suckers

continued

who had provided him with free advertising on credit. But Coliseum assistant general manager Ken Good headed him off and, ignoring a feigned heart attack by the man's assistant, led the man to face his creditors.

"Hey," the man said to Good, admiringly, "you're the only guy who never let me get away with anything."

A more direct box-office assault was made by two gunmen who robbed the box office in 1954 after a Pro Bowl game and led police on a crosstown car chase. One of the robbers, an alumnus of Folsom and Walla Walla prisons, surrendered the loot and with it his streetcar token.

"I don't suppose I'll be needing it," he said. "I ain't goin' anywhere."

For those who like to keep a watch on crime statistics, the record for most arrests at an event is 80. Tied for the lead are the 1954 Coliseum Relays (80 juveniles arrested, 200 deadly weapons seized) and a 1973 Watts Festival concert (22 adults, 58 juveniles arrested). By 1974 the citizens were mad as hell and decided they were not going to take it anymore. An anti-crime rally was planned and authorities expected a crowd of 50,000. Attendance was 350.

MURPHY'S LAW MUST BE OBEYED: The Olympic torch, which burns proudly high atop the peristyle arches on special occasions, is lit by an electronic ignition system. But in the old days it was lit by hand. One worker climbed an iron ladder inside the torch, carrying an eight-foot-long stick, with kerosene-soaked rags on the tip. He lit the rags and then rapped on the pipes, a signal for a man below to open the gas valves feeding the three coffee-can-sized jets.

One day, however, a worker named Tom forgot to remove a heavy set of keys from his belt, and the keys sounded loudly against the rungs as he climbed the ladder. The man below heard the clanging and opened the gas valves. By the time Tom struck a match to ignite his torchlighter, there was enough gas in the torch to blow him to Long Beach.

Tom was hurt, but not seriously. Not as seriously as he was hurt a few years later at a Coliseum track meet when, in the line of duty, he was hit by a wildly thrown discus and suffered a broken back.

The Coliseum first-aid room treats some 100 people during an average event, for everything from hangovers to heart attacks. "Until the last couple of years, I don't think we had a single event where we didn't have one or two deaths," said Tillie Annis, who worked in the Coliseum first-aid room for 40 years. (There was at least one Coliseum

A TOOTHLESS, LOOSE LION PAID OFF FOR THE CIRCUS, BUT TOO MANY DRIPPING CANDLES COST A RELIGIOUS RALLY.

childbirth, during a Fourth of July fireworks pageant in the early fifties.)

Murphy's law has had its steady application to the Coliseum. Skydivers featured in a football halftime show in the '70s overshot the mark and ended up dangling themselves from trees in adjacent Exposition Park. Duke Snider, strong-armed Dodger outfielder, hurt his arm attempting to throw a baseball out of the Coliseum; he reached Row 60, 19 rows short of the top, and was fined $275 by the Dodgers. Worshipers at an annual "St. Mary's Hour" once dripped so much candle wax that the Coliseum billed the archdiocese an extra $1,700 for the cleanup.

During the 1960s, bomb threats were the rage and the Coliseum was a favorite target of prank phone callers. During the '68 USC-Notre Dame game an apparent bomb was found near the field and officials were ready to order an evacuation. Then a TV crewman claimed the "bomb"—a microphone pack.

A group of USC students planted a smoke bomb under the UCLA cheerleaders' platform in 1957. By mistake, they used a bomb that might actually have detonated. Fortunately, two kids playing under the platform found the bomb and yanked the wires. An investigation of the incident was headed by a USC activities advisor by the name of Dud Johnson.

YOU CAN CONFUSE ALL OF THE PEOPLE SOME OF THE TIME: The scoreboard. Fans have booed it, critics have roasted it, Mitzi Gaynor has had a love affair with it. Occasionally, it has even given us the score.

The twin scoreboards you see now are the fourth generation, installed in 1983 at a cost of $8 million and are the

largest color video boards in the world.

The second version of the Coliseum electrogram scoreboard was a technological marvel in 1937, but an outdated antique 30 years later.

In July of 1972, the Coliseum Commission proudly unveiled the third version, its $1.6 million, state-of-the-art, TV-screen scoreboard, boasting instant-replay capability, among its other attributes. However:

—The Rams banned the instant replays. They did allow animated commercials, though.

—Water seeped into the circuits, causing damage. "For $1.6 million, you didn't expect it to be waterproof, did you?" wrote sportswriter Rich Roberts.

—The very first time it was used for a game, the scoreboard went on the fritz. The computer technician responsible for keeping the board accurately informative was home with the flu.

—For weeks the board malfunctioned. It gave the wrong data, burst into crazy images and went blank. When a touchdown was scored, up came 103 MINUTES TO PLAY. But no score. The fans booed.

Most of the bugs were ironed out by 1977. Still, human error could not be totally avoided. During one football game, the scoreboard operator became incapacitated and his teenage daughter took over. She flashed such information as FIFTH DOWN, 100 YARDS TO GO and FIRST DOWN AND 60.

Mitzi Gaynor filmed a TV show in 1973 at the Coliseum. Through the miracle of special effects, she sang and danced with the scoreboard, which flashed her the message: I LOVE YOU.

More appropriate might have been: NOT TONIGHT, I'VE GOT A SHORT CIRCUIT. ∎

★ ENTERTAINMENT FOOD SPIRITS ★
★ 200 CALIFORNIA ARTISTS OF LAGUNA BEACH INVITE YOU TO THE 18TH ANNUAL ★
SAWDUST
FESTIVAL
★ AN INNOVATIVE ARTIST VILLAGE BUILT FROM THE ★
GROUND UP EVERY SUMMER IN PICTURESQUE LAGUNA BEACH

JULY 7 thru AUG. 26   MAP   7 DAYS A WEEK

SUNDAY *thru* THURSDAY
10:00 A.M. to 10:00 P.M.

FRIDAY *and* SATURDAY
10:00 A.M. to 11:00 P.M.

◉ LOS ANGELES

✪ LAGUNA BEACH

PACIFIC OCEAN

◉ SAN DIEGO

ART DEMONSTRATIONS DAILY.....
COMPLIMENTARY
COLOR POSTER
WITH EVERY PAID ADMISSION
Adults 1.50 KIDS UNDER 12
FREE WITH ADULT

They Lost It In The MOVIES

BY JEFF SILVERMAN

In its treatment of Olympic heroes and Olympic themes, Hollywood has trivialized true drama and heart

BY 1932, AMERICA HAD long since gone film crazy, and Hollywood sat in the center of the hysteria. Though the nation remained deep in the Depression, Americans went to the movies in record numbers—to find adventure, to fall in love, to laugh and cry and forget their troubles. But they also went for information.

AN ORIGINAL M·G·M TARZAN HIT
GREATEST OF ALL!

TARZAN
THE APE MAN

M-G-M'S ALL-TIME GREAT

from M-G-M

THRILLS AND EXCITEMENT BEYOND YOUR WILDEST DREAMS!

TARZAN AWAKENED HER AT DAWN TO SAY..."I LOVE YOU!"

WITH
JOHNNY WEISSMULLER
NEIL HAMILTON
C. AUBREY SMITH
MAUREEN O'SULLIVAN
BASED UPON THE CHARACTERS CREATED BY EDGAR RICE BURROUGHS
ADAPTATION BY CYRIL HUME · DIALOGUE BY IVOR NOVELLO
DIRECTED BY W. S. VAN DYKE · A METRO-GOLDWYN-MAYER PICTURE

The movies then, like television today, brought the news from the printed page into the neighborhood. At the local theater, the newsreel infused the events of the day with a new life, immediacy and presence; if newspapers could *tell* you something, the camera could preserve it and then *show* you. And the camera could go anywhere. Suddenly we were no longer at

THE MOST FAMOUS *Hollywood and Olympic hero connection began with the Tarzan movies of the '30s and swimmer Johnny Weissmuller.*

a distance—we were where the action was.

So when the Olympic Games first came to Los Angeles, the newsreel cameras were there to capture all the important action. But strange things can happen when a camera gets too close to Hollywood. An urge sets in to create rather than simply record. And it took such Hollywood creativity to get Klopstokia involved with the '32 Games.

Klopstokia?

Yup, *Klopstokia*. In case you've forgotten, Klopstokia was a country whose imports, exports and inhabitants could all be described as "goats and nuts." But in this plot the human variety of nuts did possess astonishing athletic ability. So when a private benefactor announced his intention to endow the winningest nation in the '32 Games with a huge cash grant, Klopstokia—a country in desperate need of financial transfusion—went for the gold. And in a sweep of medals, the country's president, W. C. Fields, produced a stunning double: After *hoisting* a 1,000-pound weight to win the weightlifting honors, he then managed to *fling* it far enough to win the shot-put event as well.

Only in the movies, you say? Of course. The picture, made just after the L.A. Summer Games, was called *Million Dollar Legs*. Klopstokia was a wacky little state bordered solely by imagination, and if *Legs'* depiction of the Olympics, which included footage of actual competition, fell far short of reality, it demonstrated that the Games themselves made an entertaining backdrop for a movie.

Since then, the surprise has not been how many pictures with Olympic themes have been produced or how generally undistinguished they have been—the Oscar-

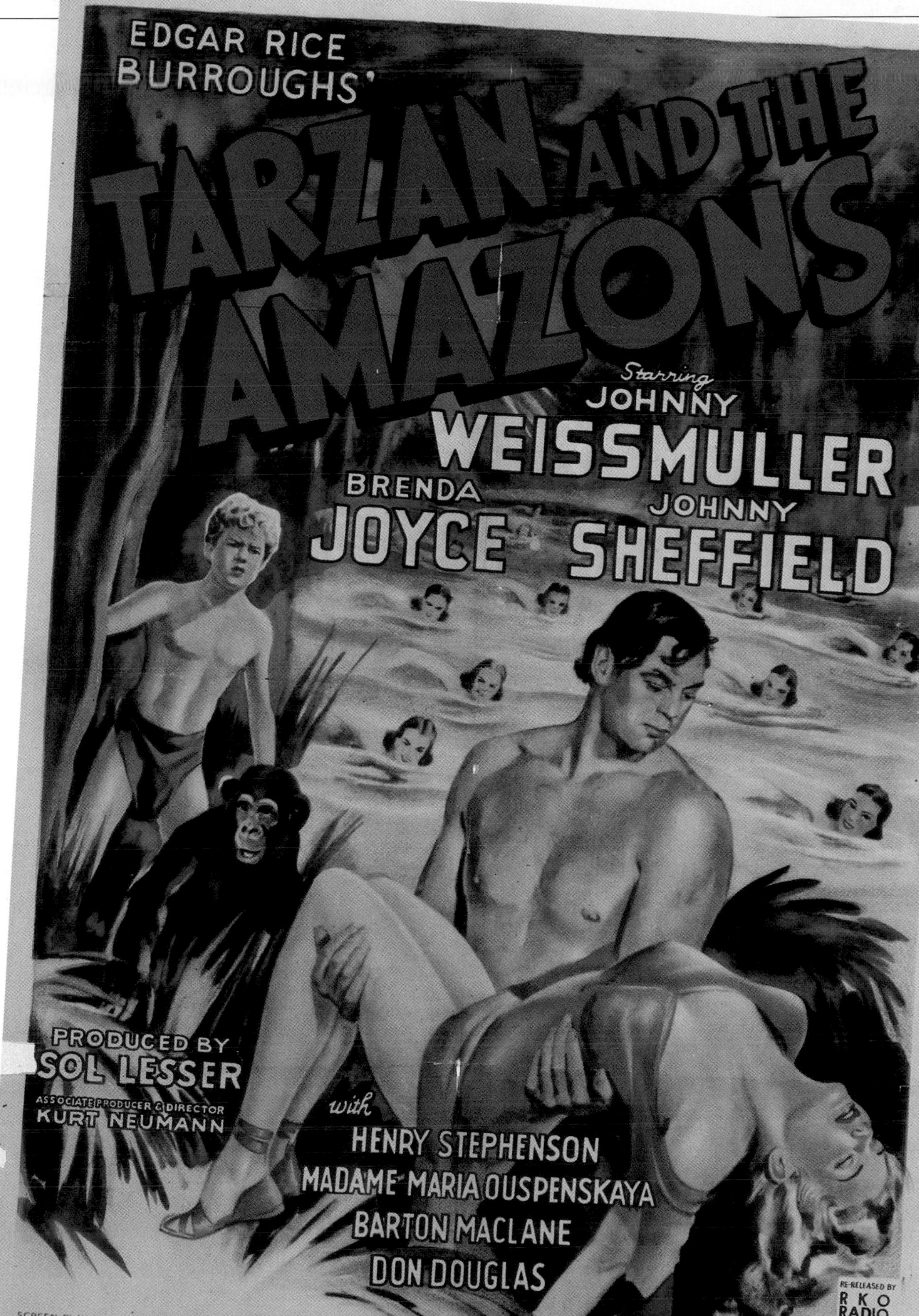

Posters courtesy Ronald V. Borst, Hollywood Movie Posters

winning British production of *Chariots of Fire* being a notable exception—it's been how few times the movies have reached into the Games and from them pulled a decent story. Generally, Hollywood has been unenthusiastic about sports films on the grounds that even if you conceive a good plot with mass appeal, it's difficult to find actors who can resemble authentic athletes. But Hollywood has been enthusiastic about signing up Olympic heroes—the Buster Crabbes and Johnny Weissmullers of the past; the Rafer Johnsons and Bruce Jenners more recently—and trying to turn them into stars of the screen.

The record book on the relationship between Hollywood and the Games is long and colorful, but qualitatively, it's no better than a bad B movie. If the "Olympics According to Hollywood" were to be taken seriously, we'd believe, for example, that the reward awaiting Spiridon Loues, the Greek shepherd who finished first in the marathon in 1896, was neither the winner's medal nor the honor he brought to his Hellenic homeland, but rather the hand of actress Jayne Mansfield, tendered as in-

Jeff Silverman, former Hollywood columnist for the Los Angeles Herald-Examiner, *is now writing for television.*

centive before the race. No kidding. It's right there in the plot of the 1962 comedy *It Happened in Athens*, made by 20th Century-Fox. We'd believe, too, that the Berlin Games of 1936 were filled with foreign agents who stole robot airplanes and threatened Olympians to cover their intrigue. That piece of news comes from *Charlie Chan at the Olympics*.

Then there's *Wee Geordie* competing in his kilt and winning the hammer throw at Melbourne in '56. And Cary Grant, in *Walk, Don't Run*, stripping to his skivvies to heel-and-toe it with the competition in the Tokyo Olympics in '64. And director Michael Winner's 1970 effort, *The Games*, in which we are told that "the Olympics is nothing but war in track shoes," and that all Americans run under the influence of drugs and party whenever they're not running. Even *Chariots of Fire*, the Academy Award-winning Best Picture of 1981, ignored truth for the sake of drama. One example of many from the film: Eric Liddell, the Scottish sprinter who ran for God's pleasure, knew six months before the Paris Games of '24 that the heats of the 100-meter dash had been scheduled for a Sunday. Since his conscience would not permit him to compete on the Sabbath, he trained instead for the 200- and 400-meter races. His

unswerving beliefs were only in conflict on film. A small point? Perhaps. Yet without it, there would have been no movie.

But that's Hollywood.

The Olympians who have moved on to careers in pictures say that Hollywood has treated them not much better than it has treated the Games. They talk about never really being taken seriously, about frustration and rejection, and frivolous roles that capitalized on the immediacy of their names. As the late Buster Crabbe, winner of the 400-meter freestyle at Los Angeles in '32, once put it: "My whole life was changed by one-tenth of a second—the time by which I beat the Frenchman. If I had finished second or third, Paramount wouldn't have given me another look. But they immediately discovered latent histrionic abilities in me."

"It's very simple," says filmmaker Bud Greenspan. "It's exploitation. The athletes can't act. So they're made quick use of while they're hot." An award-winning documentarian, Greenspan is directing the film of the L.A. Games. Latent histrionic abilities, he points out, work both ways—for the athletes as well as the industry that exploits them. "It's really like the cat chasing its tail," he explains. "What comes first? Do you take two or three years off

and try to channel the discipline that made you a great athlete into learning how to act? Or do you take advantage of the promotion and publicity that got you there? Everybody opts for the latter—make some money, and then maybe work on your acting."

"Hollywood," concurs David Wolper, producer of such TV blockbusters as *Roots*

and *The Thorn Birds* and the 1972 Olympic film, "is where they come because this is where the quickest fortune can be made out of their fame."

If that is the case today it was also true when the industry was young and opportunity seemed to be everywhere. Following the 1928 Olympics, Douglas Fairbanks, the

silent-screen star, a rabid sports fan and active athlete who trained regularly on his own running track, met a young shotputter and well-known football star from the University of Washington named Herman Brix. After winning the silver medal in the shotput at the '28 Games in Amsterdam, Brix moved to Los Angeles to compete for the Los Angeles Athletic Club. "A friend-

A BULL NECK AND *broad back helped weightlifter Harold Sakata, a '48 silver medalist, play Oddjob in* Goldfinger.

ship of sorts developed with Fairbanks," recalls Brix, now a real-estate executive in Beverly Hills, "and I used to train at his quarters on the old lot. He kind of wanted me to get into pictures. He encouraged me."

By 1932 MGM had acquired the rights to *Tarzan The Ape Man*. A mainstay of the silent-film era, Tarzan now—in the era of the talkies—would be using real words, so to speak, for the first time. The search for a "talking" king of the jungle was on. Joel McCrea was turned down (not famous enough), so was Clark Gable (good face, but, alas, no body). Fairbanks suggested Brix. At 6′ 3″ and just over 200 pounds, Brix certainly looked the part. Director W. S. Van Dyke saw him and agreed. But when Brix unexpectedly broke a shoulder, Van Dyke had to search elsewhere.

Van Dyke brought in gold-medal swimmer Johnny Weissmuller, who had dominated Olympic freestyle events in '24 at Paris and in '28 at Amsterdam, for a screen test and asked him to strip. "Then," Weissmuller remembered, "they asked me could I climb a tree and I said yes, and they asked me could I pick up a girl and walk away with her and I said yes . . . and that's all there was to the test. I had the part!"

continued

The film's success produced imitations, and where was it easier to find potential movie ape men than among athletes in the 1932 Games. Before the Opening Ceremonies, Paramount bused in swimmer Buster Crabbe and 18 fellow Olympians for a screen test. "They took us to wardrobe," Crabbe recalled, "and gave us G-strings,

While still a law student at USC, Crabbe had appeared in several films as an extra, but it was his performance in *King of the Jungle* in '33 that brought him screen fame. With the vital Olympic boost, he had himself a career that included a Tarzan serial, a Buck Rogers serial, several episodes of Flash Gordon and Billy the Kid and more

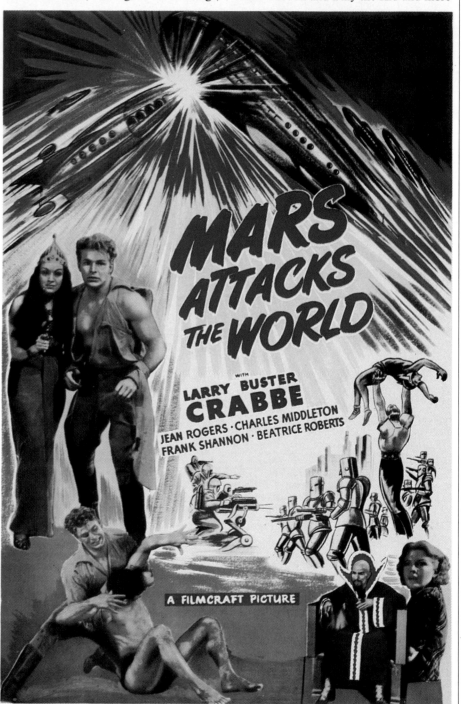

then took some pictures. Then they had us all throw a spear and pick up a *papier-mâché* rock. 'Make it look heavy,' they told us. A few days after the Olympics they called me back." Crabbe had, of course, won a gold in the 400-meter freestyle.

AN OLYMPIC WIN *boosted Buster Crabbe into an acting career as "King of the Serials."*

than 100 feature films, mostly westerns.

"They called me the 'King of the Serials,'" said Crabbe in the mid-'70s. "I always wished I could have been in one really good film. But once they decide you're a guy who can fall off a horse and take a breakaway table over your head, there's really nothing you can do about it. . . . But people still remember me because I was part of their bringing-up. This gives me a good feeling."

Ex-Olympian Herman Brix fought the stereotype and figured out a way to lick it. Having missed a Tarzan role in 1932 because of the shoulder injury, he got a chance to play Tarzan in 1935 when the "ape man's" creator, Edgar Rice Burroughs, co-produced his own movie, *The New Adventures of Tarzan*.

Brix went on to *Tarzan and the Green Goddess* in 1938 and regular serial roles, then dropped out of films and enrolled in an acting workshop. While studying, he continued to audition for movie roles, but, he recalls, "I'd always get the brush-off. They said the public only sees Herman Brix as a strong muscleman, a Tarzan." He changed his name to Bruce Bennett.

He remembers going to the Warner Brothers casting director for a screen test after being "discovered" as Bennett in a stage production. He was given a part to learn and when he reported back in a few days, he says, "The casting director had spread open on his desk a copy of a magazine, in which were pictured all the former Tarzans—including Herman Brix. 'Is this you?' the director said. And I said it was. And he says, 'You're Brix. Then goodby, we can't use you.'"

Brix-Bennett later had an interview at Columbia Pictures. "I didn't let them know who I was," he says. "I didn't tell them about my past." Brix-Bennett eventually went on to co-starring roles with Joan Crawford in *Mildred Pierce*, and Humphrey Bogart in *Dark Passage* and *The Treasure of the Sierra Madre*. "I was always very careful about not stressing my athletic past," he says. "I was doing some good roles, and my athletics might have made some people question whether I should or shouldn't keep getting these roles. If you were an athlete, the thinking was, you couldn't possibly have the capacity, the sympathy, the understanding, the charisma—whatever—to be a competent dramatic actor. It was very touch-and-go in those days."

Swimming star Eleanor Holm had less lofty ambitions when Hollywood courted

CA 27

her after the '32 Games. "I was a pretty good-looking dame in those days," she reminisces. "But I never really wanted to be an actress. Not that it was forced on me—oh, no—but when I saw the money they were paying, I said, 'O.K., O.K.' They treated me like a queen. They sent me to all the best teachers.... It's a shame that somebody with real interest hadn't been in my spot. They could have come along real great. But I never thought of myself as an actress. I was a swimmer."

Indeed, when Warner Brothers told her she couldn't take time out to compete in the '36 Games, she bought back her contract, qualified for the Olympic team and proceeded to make headlines with her performance aboard the *S.S. Manhattan*, the ship carrying the American athletes to Europe. Holm never competed in Berlin because, U.S. Olympic officials charged, she had trained too willingly at shipboard parties. When they warned her to stop, Holm refused, and the Committee bounced her from the team. A petition signed by the majority of her fellow Olympians failed to bring about her reinstatement.

The scandal made her a star. "All I can tell you," she says now at age 71, "is I was a good-looking backstroke swimmer. If I had won, I still would have been just a good-

ELEANOR HOLM *and Glenn Morris, unfriendly co-stars and Olympians, became jungle teammates in* Tarzan's Revenge.

looking backstroke swimmer. All of a sudden I was a glamour girl, and I'll tell you why: I wasn't drinking booze. It was champagne! Understand," she says, "I would still rather have won the gold medal. But I would never have made the money I did had I just won."

She shared top billing with Weissmuller

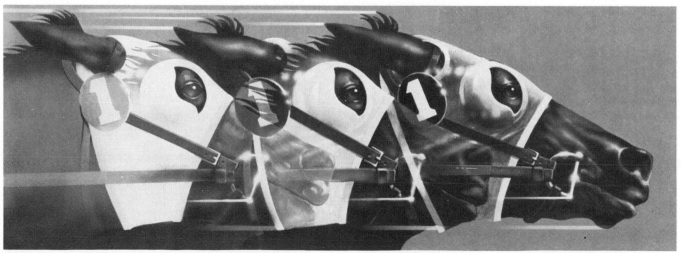

in *Aquacade*, produced by Billy Rose, whom she would later marry. In 1937 she returned to Hollywood for her one starring role in a feature film, *Tarzan's Revenge.* Her leading "ape man" was Glenn Morris, the decathlon victor at the Berlin Games, and, according to Holm, one of the few members of the '36 team who had refused to sign the reinstatement petition. The Morris-Holm picture might have been called "Eleanor's Revenge."

"We used to frame him all the time," she says.

Holm's fans on the camera crew even snipped the vines so integral to any Tarzan escapade. She says, "When he'd go Ahhhhhhhh and swing, he'd fall on his butt." The *onscreen* chemistry between the two was described by one critic this way: "In the love scenes, Eleanor looks like she's ready to spit in Tarzan's eye." There's more. While the film was being made, the producers dragged Morris to a party, showing him off as the new Tarzan in town. Big mistake. Lupe Velez, who was then *Mrs.* Weissmuller, happened to be in attendance. She ran right up to Morris, kicked him in the shins, and screamed, "You are not him! There is only one Tarzan, and that is my Johnny!" Small wonder *Revenge* remains the only film in which two Olympic gold medalists ever starred together.

Call it exploitation by Hollywood or call it a desperate attempt by an Olympic hero to cash in on faded glory, but the Jim Thorpe movie experience is a sad example of the linkage between the screen and sports stars. In the early '30s, two decades after his decathlon triumph in '12, Jim Thorpe was cast as an Indian in B-grade horse operas. He also picked up small change as an uncredited movie extra whenever possible. In May 1938, MGM began filming *Too Hot To Handle* with Myrna Loy and Clark Gable. The script called for a scene involving a fire on a gambling barge anchored well offshore. The studio needed several hundred extras to plunge from the barge into the water, and more than 600 candidates showed up at Hermosa Beach to be tested. They were required to swim 600 yards fully clothed, in 60° water. Of the more than 100 who couldn't complete the course, one, the victim of a severe leg cramp, was Thorpe. He had to be rescued by lifeguards.

His other principal dealings with the movies concerned the making of *Jim Thorpe—All American*, a 1951 film unusual in the honesty it displayed in treating the decline of the former athletic great. In 1931, Thorpe had sold the rights to his story to MGM for $1,500. By the time Warner Brothers acquired those rights 20 years later, Thorpe, broke and undergoing treatment for lip cancer in the charity ward of a Philadelphia hospital, was asking for more money. He was eventually paid a small amount as a consultant to the production, but Thorpe was rarely in evidence on the set, more by the studio's insistence than his own choice. As stories of Thorpe's circumstances began to emerge, Warner's preferred that he just go away. He had become an embarrassment to the studio's tight-fisted policies.

"My own personal contact with him during the filming," recalls Burt Lancaster, who played the title role, "involved drop-kicking. He came out of the stands and tried to teach me. It was sort of touching. I remember his wife had opened a bar during the filming and the producers went crazy and bought her out."

Thorpe was, of course, more than just an Olympic champion; he had been a football star, a major league baseball player—and later a fallen hero. But as an Olympic decathlon champion he provided Hollywood with an athletic role model that has been used with no significant benefits to

continued

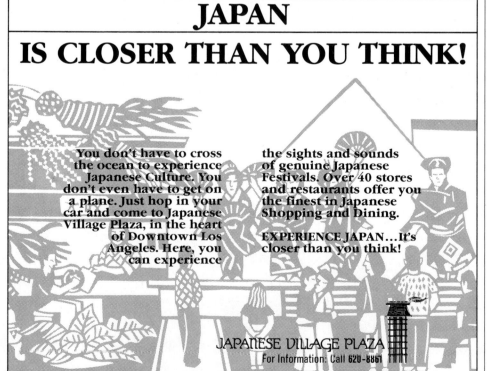
the movie-going public, to the heroes turned actors or to the art of filmmaking. With Thorpe as the first, the decathlon winners—the all-around Olympic champions—became popular film commodities.

Rafer Johnson, who won a decathlon silver at Melbourne in '56 and a gold in Rome in '60, says, "Of all Olympic events, the one that ends up getting the most publicity and certainly the most media coverage is the decathlon. A decathlon athlete has 10 *different* events. Doing something else is just an extension of that—the 11th or 12th event. . . . There is something in their personality that would lead them into trying different things perhaps more readily than someone else might."

But if acting is a sort of 11th event, it has yet to be mastered quite the way these Olympians were able to master the first 10. Bob Mathias, decathlon hero of the 1948 Games in London and the 1952 Games in Helsinki, stretched a film career through four pictures, including the lead in *The Bob Mathias Story*, and one short-lived TV series. After back-to-back films in Greece in the early '60s, including *It Happened in Athens*, and the long period of inactivity that followed, Mathias left the business and eventually turned to politics. "I had sat on my rear for about nine months after thinking I had made it as a great big star—you know, one job after another," he recalls, "and at that point I said, 'Well, I'm not an actor, really.' "

While Johnson, like Bruce Jenner after him, remains more closely linked with television sports commentary than with the big screen, his film career lasted substantially longer than Mathias'. And though he still yearns for that one good role—"I think we're always looking for another fling," he concedes—it's the one that got away from him that best shows how amateur sports rules have changed in the last two decades. The movie was *Spartacus*, shot just prior to the 1960 Games in Rome. Kirk Douglas tested Johnson for the featured role of the black gladiator, and was sufficiently impressed to offer him the part. But even though Johnson had appeared briefly in two movies, "the AAU objected and wouldn't give me permission to take it," he says, "because they said it would make me a pro."

After the Games, Johnson signed a contract with 20th Century-Fox. Over the next decade and a half, he appeared in more than a dozen films including *None But the Brave*, *The Games*, a pair of Tarzan epics (as the heavy, not as Tarzan) and also in the TV mini-series *Roots*. His most powerful feelings about films are reserved for the system that Hollywood perpetuates, a system that doesn't necessarily honor good performances with expanded opportunities. "Brilliance in any endeavor should lead to something better," he says. But it can be "just the opposite of that in the movie business." This is a disturbing thought to those, like Johnson, who once worked and succeeded at becoming best in the world at something, an accomplishment more permanent than stardom. The 1948 weightlifting silver medalist Harold Sakata, who played James Bond's menacing foe, Oddjob, in *Goldfinger*, once said, "Being in a movie made me a famous person, but the proudest moment of my life took place in London."

Bruce Jenner recently has also had to come to grips with the fickle nature of the film business. Though Jenner has successfully parlayed his 1976 decathlon heroics into a mini-industry of television commentary, commercial endorsements and a personal line of clothing, a film career remains a hurdle. He has starred in one feature, *Can't Stop the Music*; one TV-movie, *Grambling's White Tiger*; and seven episodes of the series *CHiPs*. He goes up for parts regularly. "I can usually get in the door," he says. "Landing the job is something else. They love to see you because they know the name. They say, 'Gee, sure, let's take a look at Bruce.' But they don't take you seriously." Producer David Wolper supports Jenner's view. "You always know the Olympics are the reason these guys get in the door," Wolper says. "And I think certain producers who are sports nuts like to use athletes. It's fun to have them around, to talk to them, to chew the rag about the events they were in. I happen to be one of those producers. If I can use an athlete, it's fun for me."

"What you've got to do," continues Jenner, "is get your foot in the door and then keep it in there and continue to work and continue to be very humble, be able to stand an awful lot of rejection. You've got to learn to do it like everyone else. You've got to do your homework, pay your dues, start at the bottom and work your way up. There's no easy way."

Nor has there been an easy way to teach actors how to portray athletes realistically on film, which contributes to Bud Greenspan's view that one reason "sports movies don't work is because they haven't been done well." Dennis Weaver agrees. "Almost anytime an athlete really looks at an actor making a film about something like

continued

THE MONSTER THAT ROCKED A LOST CIVILIZATION!

Stalking out of a time of unbridled passion and terror it comes...the half-man, half-beast that made a civilization bow down before it—and feed its gargantuan lusts!

THE MINOTAUR
THE WILD BEAST OF CRETE

starring

BOB MATHIAS · ROSANNA SCHIAFFINO · ALBERTO LUPO · RICK BATTAGLIA

Screenplay by S. CONTINENZA · G.P. CALLEGARI · DANIEL MAINWARING · Directed by SILVIO AMADIO · Produced by AGLIANI-MORDINI-ILLIRIA FILM

TECHNICOLOR* · TOTALSCOPE · RELEASED THRU UNITED UA ARTISTS

the Olympics, you know it's fantasy," says Weaver. A star of such TV series as *Gunsmoke*, *McCloud* and *Emerald Point N.A.S.*, Weaver finished sixth in the decathlon at the 1948 Olympic Trials. "You look and say, 'That guy can't run,' or 'that guy can't throw.' It's obvious that they're not Olympic quality."

More and more, though, these days actors get the look of their performance right. Susan Clark won an Emmy for her inspired recreation of Babe Didrikson in the 1975 television biography *Babe*. She says, "It was a question for me of getting into what I thought I could interpret of Babe's spirit. There's no way I could pretend even to myself that I could physically *do* what she could do, but I could find the

THE LIFE STORY OF Bob Mathias was turned into a film, but the decathlon champion ended his Hollywood acting career after four forgettable movies.

physical outlet of her spirit well enough to at least *act* it." Three months of training four hours a day with a UCLA track coach helped her understanding of that spirit.

A former coach added much to the spirit of *Chariots of Fire*. Tom McNab—triple-jumper, novelist, sports historian and coach of the British track team for both the '72 Munich Games and '76 Montreal Games—was hired as an adviser, first to work on the film's Oscar-winning script, then with the actors themselves. "We trained them for three months," he says. "It's a complex training I put them through, and not just in athletics. It's a training of the mind, too. The important thing for the actor is to know the nature of the athletes. You can't teach a man of 31 to be a fast runner, but you can teach him how to look and behave like a fast runner."

Looking the part is one of the small things that can turn a good movie into a memorable one. It adds a texture of reality to the illusion that film naturally creates. Because *Chariots of Fire* seemed so true, the dramatic license it took with the quests of Harold Abrahams and Eric Liddell hardly mattered in the end. By exploring what drove Abrahams and Liddell to compete with the intensity they exhibited, and then providing a background that seemed as real as a television special of today's events, the story flourishes.

The ancient Greeks used to honor their Olympic heroes and preserve their accomplishments in the hymns and odes of their lyric poets. Those poems did more than just offer praise, they tried to reveal an essential truth about the nature of man. Film now is one of the mediums serving the role that the ancient Greeks expected of poetry. It is an art form for the masses that, at its best, helps define and explain ourselves and our culture by the images it projects on the screen. And the best films continue to dig, to explore the same questions of human success and frailty the ancient poets sought to explore.

Films like *Chariots of Fire* succeed because they tap into the human spirit and tackle the age-old questions and from them create a work of art. That the particular spirit the award-winning movie tapped into belonged to a group of remarkable athletes with hope in their hearts and wings on their heels only shows us how much we—and the movies—have been missing through the years. The Games are rich with such stories of determination and courage. To overlook them is a shame. To shortchange them is to shortchange our own possibilities. ■

Saks Fifth Avenue welcomes the world and salutes the Summer Games

FINALS WILL BE HELD ON FRIDAY 8:15 P.M.

How the simple exchange of information will be turned into an electrifying Olympic event.

Events at 23 separate locations, stretched over 4,500 square miles. Participants from 153 countries, speaking over 50 languages, housed at three Olympic villages. Obviously, the movement of information may be the most intricate and demanding event at the 1984 Los Angeles Olympics.

To meet these extraordinary demands, AT&T has created a highly advanced electronic messaging system. It's an unprecedented combination of computer software and lightwave technologies. Yet it incorporates the same features of reliability and ease of use that the American public has come to expect of its phone system.

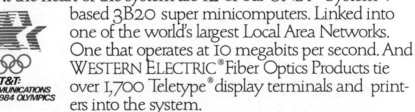

With this unique system, the 50,000 members of the Olympic family will have instant access to all event results and schedules within a minute. Each of them will even have an electronic mailbox, so they can send messages to one another. And the electronic messaging system will give journalists connections from 60 Olympic sites to news bureaus all over the world.

At the heart of the system are 12 of our UNIX™ System V-based 3B20 super minicomputers. Linked into one of the world's largest Local Area Networks. One that operates at 10 megabits per second. And WESTERN ELECTRIC® Fiber Optics Products tie over 1,700 Teletype® display terminals and printers into the system.

AT&T: TELECOMMUNICATIONS SPONSOR 1984 OLYMPICS

From data pool to swimming pool, we will always be up for the competition.

AT&T. Applying the technologies of microelectronics, lightwave and software to make the dream of the Information Age a reality.

©1984 AT&T Technologies, Inc.

OLYMPIC RECORDS

In those events where numbers can be compared from Games to Games, here are the all-time best

Mac Wilkins of the U.S. used a shot to strengthen the arm that set a discus mark in 1976

Because of differences in courses and conditions, no Olympic records are kept in canoeing, equestrian, modern pentathlon, rowing or yachting.

TRACK AND FIELD

MEN

Event	Name	Country	Year	Result
100 meters	James Hines	USA	1968	9.95
200 meters	Tommie Smith	USA	1968	19.83
400 meters	Lee Evans	USA	1968	43.86
800 meters	Alberto Juantorena	Cuba	1976	1:43.50
1,500 meters	Kipchoge Keino	Kenya	1968	3:34.91
3,000-meter steeplechase	Anders Garderud	Sweden	1976	8:08.02
5,000 meters	*Brendan Foster	G.B.	1976	13:20.34
10,000 meters	Lasse Viren	Finland	1972	27:38.35
Marathon	Waldemar Cierpinski	E. Ger.	1976	2:09.55
110-meter hurdles	Rodney Milburn	USA	1972	13.24
400-meter hurdles	Edwin Moses	USA	1976	47.64
20-km walk	Maurizio Damilano	Italy	1980	1:23:35.5
50-km walk	Hartwig Gauder	E. Ger.	1980	3:49:24.0
4x100-meter relay		USA	1972	38.19
4x400-meter relay		USA	1968	2:56.16
High Jump	Gerd Wessig	E. Ger.	1980	7' 8¾" 2.36 meters
Pole Vault	Wladyslaw Kozakiewicz	Poland	1980	18' 11½" 5.78 meters
Long Jump	Bob Beamon	USA	1968	29' 2½" 8.90 meters
Triple Jump	Viktor Saneyev	USSR	1968	57' 0¾" 17.39 meters
Shotput	Vladimir Kiselyov	USSR	1980	70' 0½" 21.35 meters
Discus Throw	*Mac Wilkins	USA	1976	224' 0" 68.28 meters
Hammer Throw	Yuri Sedykh	USSR	1980	268' 4½" 81.80 meters
Javelin Throw	Miklos Nemeth	Hungary	1976	310' 4" 94.58 meters
Decathlon	Bruce Jenner	USA	1976	8,618 points

WOMEN

Event	Name	Country	Year	Result
100 meters	*Annegret Richter	W. Ger.	1976	11.01
200 meters	Baerbel Woeckel-Eckert	E. Ger.	1980	22.03
400 meters	Marita Koch	E. Ger.	1980	48.88
800 meters	Nadezhda Olizarenko	USSR	1980	1:53.43
1,500 meters	Tatyana Kazankina	USSR	1980	3:56.56
100-meter hurdles	Vera Komisova	USSR	1980	12.56
4x100-meter relay		E. Ger.	1980	41.60
4x400-meter relay		E. Ger.	1976	3:19.23

The Reward Must Be Worthy
Of The Dream.

Jostens

Official Supplier Of 1984 Olympic Games Medals

High Jump	Sara Simeoni	Italy	1980	6' 5½" 1.97 meters
Long Jump	Tatyana Kolpakova	USSR	1980	23' 2" 7.06 meters
Shotput	Ilona Slupianek	E. Ger.	1980	73' 6¼" 22.41 meters
Discus Throw	Evelin Jahl- Schlaak	E. Ger.	1980	229' 6½" 69.96 meters
Javelin Throw	Maria Colon	Cuba	1980	224' 5" 68.40 meters

'These Olympic records, were set in the preliminaries and semifinals.

ARCHERY

MEN	points			
FITA Double Rounds	2,571	1976	Darrell Pace	USA
90 meters	592	1976	Darrell Pace	USA
70 meters	634	1976	Darrell Pace	USA
50 meters	644	1976	Darrell Pace	USA

30 meters	701	1976	Darrell Pace	USA
WOMEN				
FITA Double Rounds	2,499	1976	Luann Ryon	USA
70 meters	589	1976	Valentina Kovpan	USSR
60 meters	626	1976	Valentina Kovpan	USSR
50 meters	618	1976	Luann Ryon	USA
30 meters	690	1980	Ketwane Lossaberidze	USSR

SHOOTING

Free Pistol	581	1980	Aleksandr Melentev	USSR
Rifle—Prone	599	1972	Ho Jun Li	N. Korea
		1976	Karlheinz Smieszek	W. Ger.
		1980	Karoly Varga	Hungary
		1980	Hellfried Heilfort	E. Ger.
Rifle—Three Positions	1,173	1980	Viktor Vlasov	USSR
Rapid-Fire Pistol	597	1976	Norbert Klaar	E. Ger.

Come to Canada.

Trap Shooting	199	1972	Angelo Scalzone	Italy	
Skeet Shooting	198	1968	Yevgeny Petrov	USSR	
		1968	Romano Garagnani	Italy	
		1968	Konrad Wirnhier	W. Ger.	
		1976	Josef Panacek	Czech.	
		1976	Eric Swinkels	Netherlands	
Running Game	589	1980	Igor Sokolov	USSR	
Target		1980	Thomas Pfeffer	E. Ger.	

SWIMMING

MEN

Event	Athlete	Country	Year	Time
100-meter freestyle	James Montgomery	USA	1976	49.99
200-meter freestyle	Sergei Kopliakov	USSR	1980	1:49.81
400-meter freestyle	Vladimir Salnikov	USSR	1980	3:51.31
1,500-meter freestyle	Vladimir Salnikov	USSR	1980	14:58.27
100-meter backstroke	John Naber	USA	1976	55.49
200-meter backstroke	John Naber	USA	1976	1:59.19
100-meter breaststroke	John Hencken	USA	1976	1:03.11
200-meter breaststroke	David Wilkie	G.B.	1976	2:15.11
100-meter butterfly	Mark Spitz	USA	1972	54.27
200-meter butterfly	Mike Bruner	USA	1976	1:59.23
200-meter individual medley	Gunnar Larsson	Sweden	1972	2:07.17
400-meter individual medley	Aleksandr Sidorenko	USSR	1980	4:22.89
4x100-meter freestyle relay		USA	1972	3:26.42
4x200-meter freestyle relay		USA	1976	7:23.22
4x100-meter medley relay		USA	1976	3:42.22

WOMEN

Event	Athlete	Country	Year	Time
100-meter freestyle	Barbara Krause	E. Ger.	1980	54.79
200-meter freestyle	Barbara Krause	E. Ger.	1980	1:58.33
400-meter freestyle	Ines Diers	E. Ger.	1980	4:08.76
800-meter freestyle	Michelle Ford	Australia	1980	8:28.90

continued

Alberto Juantorena of Cuba who ran his record 800 meters eight years ago

100-meter backstroke	Rica Reinisch	E. Ger.	1980	1:00.86
200-meter backstroke	Rica Reinisch	E. Ger.	1980	2:11.77
100-meter breaststroke	Ute Geweniger	E. Ger.	1980	1:10.11
200-meter breaststroke	Lina Kachyushite	USSR	1980	2:29.54
100-meter butterfly	Kornelia Ender	E. Ger.	1976	1:00.13
200-meter butterfly	Ines Geissler	E. Ger.	1980	2:10.44
200-meter individual medley	Shane Gould	Australia	1972	2:23.07
400-meter individual medley	Petra Schneider	E. Ger.	1980	4:36.29
4x100-meter freestyle relay		E. Ger.	1980	3:42.71
4x100-meter medley relay		E. Ger.	1980	4:06.67

WEIGHTLIFTING

52 kg/114.4 lbs kg/lbs

Snatch	110/242	Bong-Choi Ho	1980	N. Korea
Clean & Jerk	137.5/302.5	Aleksandr Voronin	1976	USSR
Total	245/539	Kanybek Osmanoliev	1980	USSR

56 kg/123.2 lbs maximum

Snatch	125/275	Daniel Nunez	1980	Cuba
Clean & Jerk	157.5/346.5	Yurik Sarkisian	1980	USSR
Total	275/605	Daniel Nunez	1980	Cuba

60 kg/132 lbs maximum

Snatch	130/286	Viktor Mazin	1980	USSR
Clean & Jerk	160/352	Nikolai Kolesnikov	1976	USSR
Total	290/638	Viktor Mazin	1980	USSR

67.5 kg/148.5 lbs maximum

Snatch	147.5/324.5	Yanko Rusev	1980	Bulgaria
Clean & Jerk	195/429	Yanko Rusev	1980	Bulgaria
Total	342.5/753	Yanko Rusev	1980	Bulgaria

75 kg/165 lbs maximum

Snatch	160/352	Assen Zlatev	1980	Bulgaria
Clean & Jerk	200/440	Aleksandr Pervy	1980	Bulgaria
Total	360/792	Assen Zlatev	1980	Bulgaria

82.5 kg/181.5 lbs maximum

Snatch	177.5/390.5	Yurik Vardanian	1980	USSR
Clean & Jerk	222.5/489.5	Yurik Vardanian	1980	USSR
Total	400/880	Yurik Vardanian	1980	USSR

90 kg/198 lbs maximum

Snatch	170/374	David Rigert	1976	USSR
Clean & Jerk	212.5/467.5	David Rigert	1976	USSR
Total	382.5/841.5	David Rigert	1976	USSR

100 kg/220 lbs maximum

Snatch	180/396	Ota Zaremba	1980	Czech.
Clean & Jerk	217.5/478.5	Michael Hennig	1980	E. Ger.
Total	395/869	Ota Zaremba	1980	Czech.

110 kg/242 lbs maximum

Snatch	185/407	Valentin Christov	1980	Bulgaria
Clean & Jerk	240/528	Leonid Taranenko	1980	USSR
Total	422.5/929.5	Leonid Taranenko	1980	USSR

Over 110 kg/242 lbs

Snatch	195/429	Sultan Rakhmanov	1980	USSR
Clean & Jerk	255/561	Vasily Alexeyev	1976	USSR
Total	440/968	Vasily Alexeyev	1976	USSR

This month, the world will come to America.
And ABC Sports will bring the Olympics to the world.

For over 10,000 athletes, it will be the fulfillment of a dream. For ABC Sports, it will be the effort of a lifetime—the greatest undertaking in the history of television. ABC Sports' exclusive coverage—virtually all of it live—will number 136 hours in the United States alone, more than the last three televised Summer Games combined. And, as host coordinating broadcaster, we'll bring the competition, the spectacle and the glory to more than 2½ billion people around the world. This summer, the Olympics are coming to America. And the world will be watching—thanks to ABC.

ABC SPORTS
The Olympic Tradition Continues...

CULTURAL EVENTS

Los Angeles 1984 Olympic Games

OLYMPIC ARTS FESTIVAL

JULY 31
Tuesday

8 p.m.   American Tap – Japan America Theater

AUGUST 1
Wednesday

8 p.m.   American Tap – Japan America Theater

AUGUST 2
Thursday

8 p.m.   American Tap – Japan America Theater
                  Olympic Jazz Festival – John Anson Ford Theater

AUGUST 3
Friday

8 p.m.   American Tap – Japan America Theater
                  Olympic Jazz Festival – John Anson Ford Theater

310

Augmenting the athletic competition is a distinguished schedule of exhibits and performances in the arts

FROM THE collection of official Olympic fine art posters, examples on these pages display the artists' use of expressionistic painting, drawing and photography to celebrate the spirit of the 1984 Games

Some things just don't need changing.

The Olympics sure have changed since '32. About the only thing that hasn't is the official drinking water. Arrowhead. Still comes from the same, delicious mountain springs. Still so naturally pure it needs no chemicals or chlorine. Maybe that's why, 52 years later, Arrowhead was named the official water again.

311 **Official water of the Olympic Games. 1932, 1984.**

AUGUST 4
Saturday

8 p.m.   Twyla Tharp Dance – Pasadena Civic Auditorium
             Telemann
             Lay Me Down
             Nine Sinatra Songs
             Bad Smells

AUGUST 5
Sunday

2 p.m.   Olympic Jazz Festival – John Anson Ford Theater
8 p.m.   Twyla Tharp Dance – Pasadena Civic Auditorium
             Telemann
             Lay Me Down
             Nine Sinatra Songs
             Bad Smells

AUGUST 7
Tuesday

8 p.m.   Dance Theatre of Harlem – Pasadena Civic Auditorium
             Four Temperaments
             Fall River Legend
             Stars and Stripes

AUGUST 8
Wednesday

8 p.m.   Dance Theatre of Harlem – Pasadena Civic Auditorium
             Serenade
             Streetcar Named Desire
             Firebird

AUGUST 9
Thursday

8 p.m.   Dance Theatre of Harlem – Pasadena Civic Auditorium
             Concerto Barocco
             Le Corsaire
             Agon
             Troy Game

AUGUST 10
Friday

2 p.m.   Dance Theatre of Harlem – Pasadena Civic Auditorium
             Concerto Barocco
             Le Corsaire
             Agon
             Troy Game
8 p.m.   Dance Theatre of Harlem – Pasadena Civic Auditorium
             Serenade
             Streetcar Named Desire
             Firebird

AUGUST 11
Saturday

2 p.m.   Dance Theatre of Harlem – Pasadena Civic Auditorium
             Serenade
             Streetcar Named Desire
             Firebird
8 p.m.   Dance Theatre of Harlem – Pasadena Civic Auditorium
             Four Temperaments
             Fall River Legend
             Stars and Stripes

continued

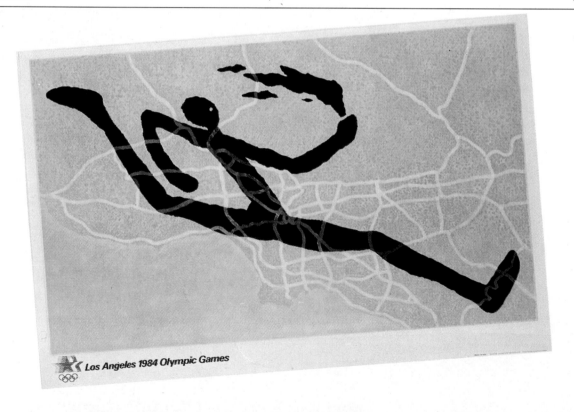

Los Angeles 1984 Olympic Games

Martin Puryear

Official U.S. Athletic Federation Photographic Posters

Washington Street Publishers, through the sale of our photographic fine art posters, is proud to support the training of our American athletes as they prepare for the 1984 Summer Games.

As the official publishers of The Athletic Federation poster art, we are pleased to announce that our posters are available through art galleries, sporting good stores and other retail outlets nationwide.

To receive our complete catalog, please send $1.00 in check or money order to:
Washington Street Distributors
National Sales Office
632 E. Colorado Street
Glendale, Calif. 91205

Master Card & Visa honored for poster sales only. Add $1.50 for postage & handling.

008 FREE STYLE 24"x 36" — $12.00	200 CYCLING 22"x 34" — $15.00	202 SWIMMING 21"x 36" — $10.00

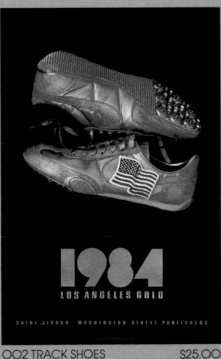

009 U.S. BOXING 21"x 36" — $12.00	002 TRACK SHOES 24"x 36" — $25.00	004 LOS ANGELES 24"x 36" — $15.00

We are what others pretend to be.

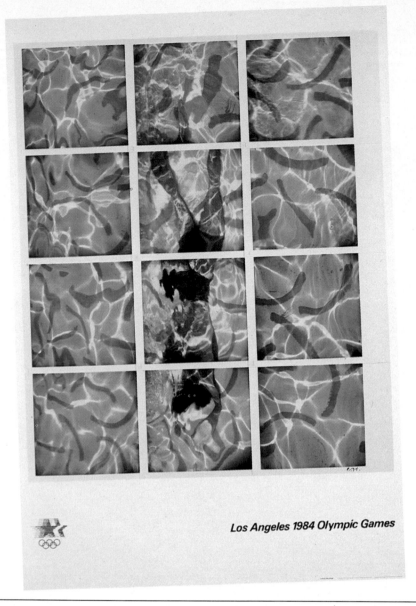

Los Angeles 1984 Olympic Games

EXHIBITIONS

LOS ANGELES AND THE PALM TREE: IMAGE OF A CITY
Arco Center for Visual Art
How the 35,000 palm trees planted for the 1932 Olympics affected the city's skyline and its image in art, advertisements and movies.
Through September 22. Monday-Friday, 9:30 a.m.-5:30 p.m.
Saturday, 11 a.m.-5 p.m.

IN CONTEXT
The Temporary Contemporary
Museum of Contemporary Art
Major environmental and monumental works by American artists.
Through August 12. Wednesday-Friday, 11 a.m.-8 p.m.
Saturday-Monday, 11 a.m.-6 p.m.

LOS ANGELES . . . LEGACIES OF THE 1932 OLYMPIC GAMES
City Hall, third-floor Rotunda and Bridge Gallery; Central Library, first and second floors

Official documents, plans, photographs, programs and other memorabilia from the 1932 Olympics.
Through August 31. City Hall: Monday-Friday, 8 a.m.-5 p.m.
Library: Monday, Wednesday, Friday-
Saturday, 10 a.m.-5:30 p.m.
Tuesday, Thursday, Noon-8 p.m.

RETROSPECTIVE OF THE 1932 OLYMPIC GAMES
Los Angeles County Museum of Natural History
Memorabilia and photographs from the 1932 Olympics.
Through September 30. Tuesday-Sunday, 10 a.m.-5 p.m.

CALIFORNIA SCULPTURE SHOW
Fisher Gallery, University of Southern California
Twelve large sculptures by California artists are exhibited in Los Angeles for the first time.
Through August 7. Tuesday-Saturday, Noon-5 p.m.

MASKS IN MOTION
Craft and Folk Art Museum

continued

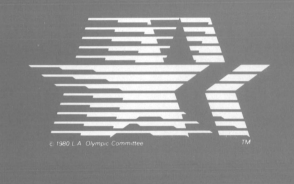
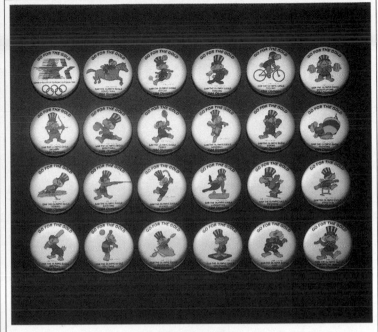

Masks from around the world.
Through August 12. Tuesday-Sunday, 11 a.m.-5 p.m.

KAHURANGI: SMALL TREASURES OF NEW ZEALAND
Pacific Asia Museum

More than 70 objects of bone, ivory, jade, ceramics and textiles by 16 contemporary artists and a selection of antique Maori artifacts.
Through October 21. Wednesday-Sunday, Noon-5 p.m.

OLYMPIC ROWING: INTEGRITY AND TRADITION
University Art Museum, University of California, Santa Barbara

Old and new rowing equipment, including racing shells and oars, racing shirts, photo murals and a video presentation.
Through August 5. Tuesday-Saturday, 10 a.m.-4 p.m.
Sunday, 1 p.m.-5 p.m.

ART OF THE STATES: WORKS FROM A SANTA BARBARA COLLECTION
Santa Barbara Museum of Art

Contemporary American painting and sculpture.
Through August 26. Monday-Wednesday, 11 a.m.-5 p.m.
Thursday, 11 a.m.-9 p.m.
Friday-Sunday, Noon-5 p.m.

A DAY IN THE COUNTRY: IMPRESSIONISM AND THE FRENCH LANDSCAPE
Los Angeles County Museum of Art

One hundred and twenty-five masterpieces—many on international loan—by Monet, Pissaro, Cézanne and others divided into nine different landscape themes.
Through September 16. Daily, 9 a.m.-6 p.m.

AUSTRALIA: NINE CONTEMPORARY ARTISTS
Los Angeles Institute of Contemporary Art (LAICA) and various locations throughout the city

New art from Australia.
Through August 14. Tuesday-Friday, Noon-6 p.m.
Saturday, Noon-5 p.m.

TWO EXHIBITIONS: NEW YORK, SAN FRANCISCO
Newport Harbor Art Museum, Newport Beach

Action/Precision: The Direction in New York, 1955-60; an in-depth study of artists from the New York School, and The Figurative Mode: Bay Area Painting, 1955-65 includes the work of San Francisco artists.
Through September 9. Tuesday-Sunday, 11 a.m.-5 p.m.

continued

Los Angeles 1984 Olympic Games

Carlos Almaraz

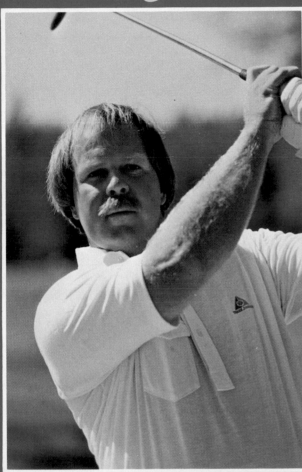

Capture it all

Ever since the 1956 Winter
Games, *Sports Illustrated* has
brought you all the drama
and beauty of Olympic
competition.

For the 1984 Olympic
Games of Los Angeles, we're
providing the most extensive
coverage ever. Our Special
Preview issue (over 500
pages) in July is the biggest
issue in our 30-year history.
And *Sports Illustrated*'s
fast-closing weekly issues
throughout the Games will
feature complete coverage
that is colorful and timely.

This year's Olympic Games
will be the greatest sports
spectacle of our time. Capture
it all while the moments are
fresh, and the stories are
news. In *Sports Illustrated*.

Sports Illustrated
America's Sports Newsweekly

Photography by Tony Duffy for <u>Sports Illustrated</u>.

Los Angeles 1984 Olympic Games

THE MOSAIC IMAGE: THE FIRST 20 YEARS OF THE MUSEUM OF CULTURAL HISTORY
Frederick S. Wight Art Gallery, UCLA

Three hundred of the most important pieces from the museum's shows over the past 20 years, including Northwest Indian masks, Nigerian cast bronze objects and pre-Columbian Peruvian ceramics.
   Through August 19. Tuesday-Sunday, Noon-5 p.m.

BUGAKU: TREASURES FROM THE KASUGA SHRINE
George J. Doizaki Gallery, Japanese American Cultural and Community Center

The first American showing of treasures from the Shinto shrine in Japan's ancient capital of Nara.
   Through August 26. Tuesday-Sunday, 11 a.m.-5 p.m.

AUTOMOBILE AND CULTURE
The Temporary Contemporary
Museum of Contemporary Art

The changing image of the car is shown through more than 200 paintings, sculptures, drawings, posters and photographs.
   Through August 12. Saturday-Monday, 11 a.m.-6 p.m.
         Wednesday-Friday, 11 a.m.-8 p.m.

THE WORKS OF CARLOS ALMARAZ
Los Angeles Municipal Art Gallery, Barnsdall Park

Selected pastels and drawings which capture the energy of Los Angeles.
   Through August 26. Tuesday-Sunday, 12:30 p.m.-5 p.m.

ART IN CLAY: 1950s-1980s IN SOUTHERN CALIFORNIA
Los Angeles Municipal Art Gallery, Barnsdall Park

Three decades of ceramic art as shown by 61 artists.
   Through August 26. Tuesday-Sunday, 12:30 p.m.-5 p.m.

OLYMPIC PHILATELIC EXHIBITION
Pasadena Center Conference Building

Stamps commemorating the Olympic Games, from 1896 to the present.
   Through August 12. Monday-Sunday, 10 a.m.-6 p.m.

THE BLACK OLYMPIANS: 1904-1984
California Museum of Afro-American History and Culture

A multimedia presentation looking at black participation in the Olympic Games.
   Through January 15, 1985. Monday-Sunday, 10 a.m.-5 p.m.

WE'RE INSURING THE OLYMPICS BECAUSE
OUR BUSINESS IS ENSURING PEOPLE'S DREAMS.